IMAGES
of America

FROSTBURG

FROSTBURG

How they began it I cannot say,
But they started a path and it ran away
Till it climbed the hill at the mountains' feet;
And it grew from a path to a little street,
Where ever and ever so long ago,
In the dawn's and the twilight's gentle glow,
The miners crept, with their head-lamps burning,
To the mine-mouths far in the mountains turning,
Looking for all the world like eyes
Moving along 'twixt the fields and skies.

How you get up to it, on my word,
It's likely you fly like a morning bird;
For ever the trolley winds the hill
Through a gap all grand and a gorge all still;
By a farm all golden with garnered grain,
And a blue ridge yonder, a bird's refrain,
A crystal torrent, a mud stained funnel,
Where the water pours out of the great mine-tunnel,
Emptying its saffron and sulphur-stained stream
In the cups of the valleys of mist and dream.

Still on the trolley, and still we rise
Till it's just reach out and you'll touch the skies;
Then all of a sudden it's right straight up,
And we've climbed clear over the rim of the cup,
And there—by the Great Task-Master's will,
We have come to a city upon a hill!
And the broad, live streets of a clean fine town,
Where the blue skies bend so gently down;
And there, in his mighty and masterful way,
Great Savage stands guard at the gates of day!

O, if you listen perhaps you'll hear
The voice of the valleys of rest ring clear
With magic music of green hill-side
And the drift of the river's rippling tide,
Where far, like a river of silver, runs
Potomac's flood to the seas and suns
Of Old Virginian plains and meadows,
Where gray ghosts dance in the aerie shadows,
And rose-red lips of youth and gleam
Bring back old days of life's lost dream!

Anyway, here is a town to love,
So near to the dear, green peaks above—
So dear to the hearts of the twilight glow
That dream and dream of the long-ago
When here was a cabin and there a cot
And the teeming Town of To-Day was not;
But the miners marched in a single file
Over the paths of the mountain mile—
Their lights, like shimmering fire-flies, glancing,
And the fairy folks on the hill-side dancing.

—*Bentztown Bard in Baltimore Sun.*

Folger McKenzie, a writer for the *Baltimore Sunpapers* known as *The Bentztown Bar*, penned this poem in honor of Frostburg's Centennial in 1912. The poem was first published in the Autumn Picnic Souvenir Program of September 1911, was later printed on the title page to the Centennial Celebration Souvenir book. It has been reprinted in several other booklets and town histories.

IMAGES
of America

FROSTBURG

Tom Robertson

ARCADIA
PUBLISHING

ISBN 978-0-7385-1422-2

Published by Arcadia Publishing
Charleston, South Carolina

Printed in the United States of America

Library of Congress Catalog Card Number: 2001099796

For all general information contact Arcadia Publishing at:
Telephone 843-853-2070
Fax 843-853-0044
E-mail sales@arcadiapublishing.com
For customer service and orders:
Toll-Free 1-888-313-2665

Visit us on the Internet at www.arcadiapublishing.com

Contents

Acknowledgments		6
Introduction		7
1.	The National Road	9
2.	Alma Mater	19
3.	When Coal Was King	31
4.	Going “Up Street”	49
5.	From the Town’s Attic	81
6.	Eckhart Mines	105
7.	Celebration Time	115

ACKNOWLEDGMENTS

While mine is the only name on the cover of this book, the development of this collection has certainly not been a solo effort! Acknowledgments and thanks must go to the following.

A very special thank you must go to Betty VanNewkirk, at whose urging I undertook this venture, and who has become a mentor, a role model, and most importantly, a dear friend. Betty is a wellspring of information on this town that she and her husband, Bill, adopted, a town that has adopted her as one of its own.

Thank you to all of my friends and colleagues at the Frostburg Museum. Without your knowledge, help, and friendship this book would not have been possible. All proceeds from this volume will go directly to the Frostburg Museum Association so they can continue their labor of love in preserving the town's past.

To Paul Berry whose help was invaluable and whose friendship is special.

To Mary Jo Price with the special collections at Frostburg State University for her help and interest (and, of course, as a fellow lover of the National Pastime).

Thanks to Matt, Robin, Phyllis, and all of my colleagues at the Allegany College of Maryland Library.

To my wife and partner, Kim, and my very special children, Matthew, Marigene, and Hillary—Daddy will turn off the computer now, girls!

To my parents, Marilyn and Joseph Robertson, who actually got to go to Beall High.

And most importantly, to Harry A. Fuller Sr., who first showed me Frostburg and helped me to know and understand the meaning of roots . . . this is for you Pepa!

Introduction

There is often a very organic relationship between a town and its residents. People shape the town and the town, in turn, shapes the people. Just as people grow, change, and mature, so too do the towns in which they live. And nowhere is there a better example of the relationship between a town and its people than Frostburg.

Family names familiar at the turn of the 20th century can still be found in great numbers in businesses, telephone directories, and school honor lists at the turn of the 21st century. The creation and expansion of Frostburg State University brought many new faces, some just in passing, and others to stay, but each playing a part in the story of the community. Economic opportunity in the 19th century called many immigrants from across the ocean to settle in the area, who added their own distinct cultures to a growing mix of customs, religions, and ideas. Downturns in those same economic conditions in the 20th century forced many to leave, but now some have returned to raise new families or to retire to their hometown.

Just as a life runs from formative years through growth and change to quiet maturity, so does the story of Frostburg. Forming out of the arrival of the National Road in the early 1800s, Frostburg enjoyed a boom time in the late 19th century when "coal was king," and now relaxes, watching the younger generations develop as a college town with each period adding a new and exciting chapter to the life of the town.

While the weather is sometimes challenging, Frostburg was not named for our often "frosty" winters, where it was noted by a 19th-century visitor that, "winter comes early and lingers late." Carved out of the Revolutionary War Military lots, the Frostburg area became a major stop on the original National Road. Frostburg grew as the significance of the National Road grew. The town was given the name Frostburg for Meshach Frost, who owned and developed property along the National Road and became the town's postmaster in 1821.

While coal had been known in the area for years, it was not until the mid-1800s with better transportation that the rich veins were tapped. The coal explosion of the late 19th and early 20th centuries brought a boom and a wave of prosperity that Frostburg rode to significant heights. The miners of the area broke many of the stereotypes associated with coal miners of other areas. These men were the "best-dressed miners" who owned their own homes, kept livestock, and grew crops. The early miners were predominately English, Scots, Welsh, and German, each bringing with them their own unique and rich cultural heritage. By the late 19th century, Italian and eastern European immigrants added their ethnicity and background to the region.

Frostburg also boosted a rich cultural and social scene. Theaters and opera houses provided much entertainment during the late 19th and early 20th centuries. Many festivals and celebrations took advantage of the parks and open spaces in the area. Frostburg has even boasted that, at one time, the town had more bars and churches per capita than any major city on the East Coast. While that may have been more than a slight exaggeration, Frostburg became an ethnically diverse but close-knit community.

The coal miners of the area also appreciated the value of education. It was through their diligent efforts of persuasion and fund-raising that State Normal School #2 (now Frostburg State University) was established in Frostburg in 1898, and not in another Western Maryland town as many politicians wished.

Little did those miners know how important their efforts to establish the school in Frostburg would be for the town. As the coal boom withered and died, Frostburg's role as a college town began to blossom. In 1934, the school became a four-year teacher's college, evolving into Frostburg State College and in 1987, Frostburg State University.

Today Frostburg State University helps define the community. The university and the town are linked in many ways and both benefit from each other. The rich, ethnic flavors of the town's past often carry on, mixing with the diversity of the college population.

The boom years of Frostburg are now a century old. Declining economic opportunities in the late 20th century caused many young people to leave the area in search of work, but the rich heritage and the quality of life in Frostburg keep the community strong and vibrant.

This collection of photographs shows the various stages of Frostburg's biography. Starting with the arrival of the National Road, which put the town on the map, we weave through the growth of the college town from the creation of the Normal School to Frostburg State University. We see the miners working in the dark, damp mines beneath the town, who, by their sweat and sacrifice, brought economic prosperity and notoriety to the area. They left a work ethic that is still seen in many of Frostburg's residents today. These photographs, the majority of which come from the collection of the Frostburg Museum, show how the residents worked and played. And most importantly, how they grew as people and as a community. This is their story. This is Frostburg.

One

The National Road

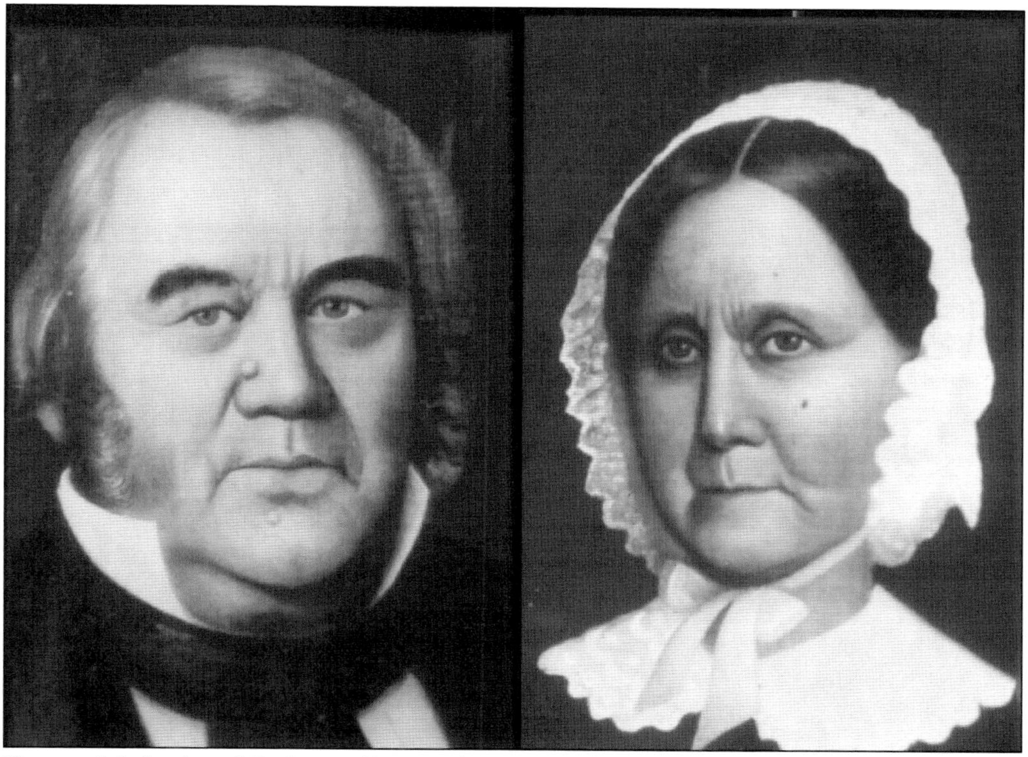

Here are Meshach and Catherine Frost as they appeared in the early 19th century. Meshach was a prominent businessman who later became the postmaster of the town, and from him Frostburg got its name. The graves of the couple are located in the courtyard of St. Michael Catholic Church on Main Street.

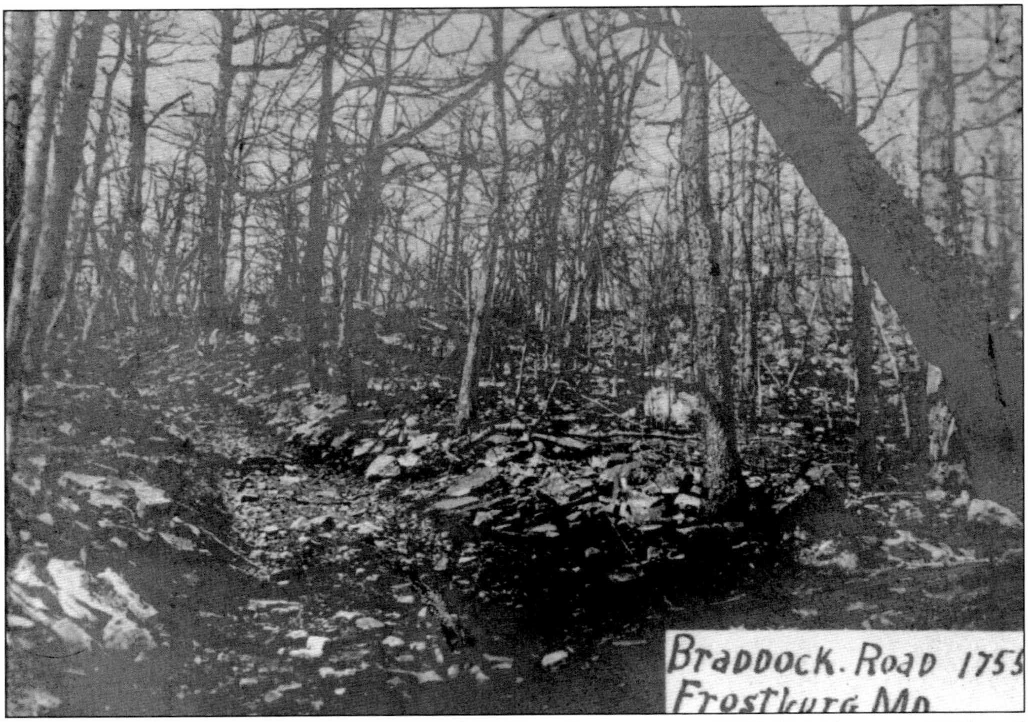

During his ill-fated advance on the French at Fort Duquesne in 1755, British general Edward Braddock's men established what became known as Braddock's Road. The road, which was little more than a rough-cut wagon path, passed just to the south of present day Frostburg, through what is now the campus of Frostburg State University, and over Savage Mountain near the present roadbed of Interstate 68.

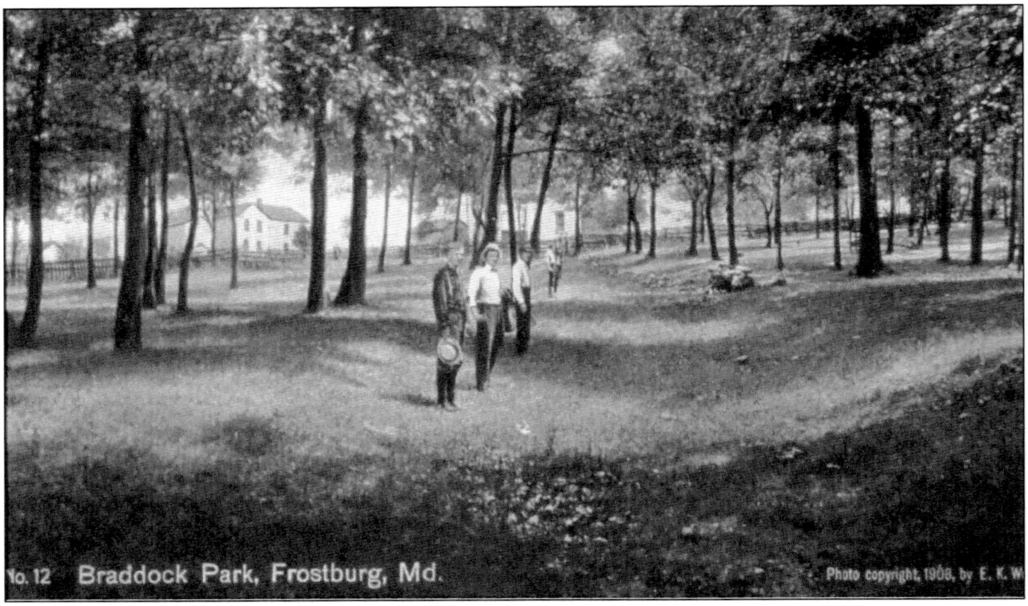

The above depiction is of the remains of Braddock's Road as it appeared in 1908, as an indentation running through Braddock Park. The park was a choice location for picnickers and family reunions for several generations.

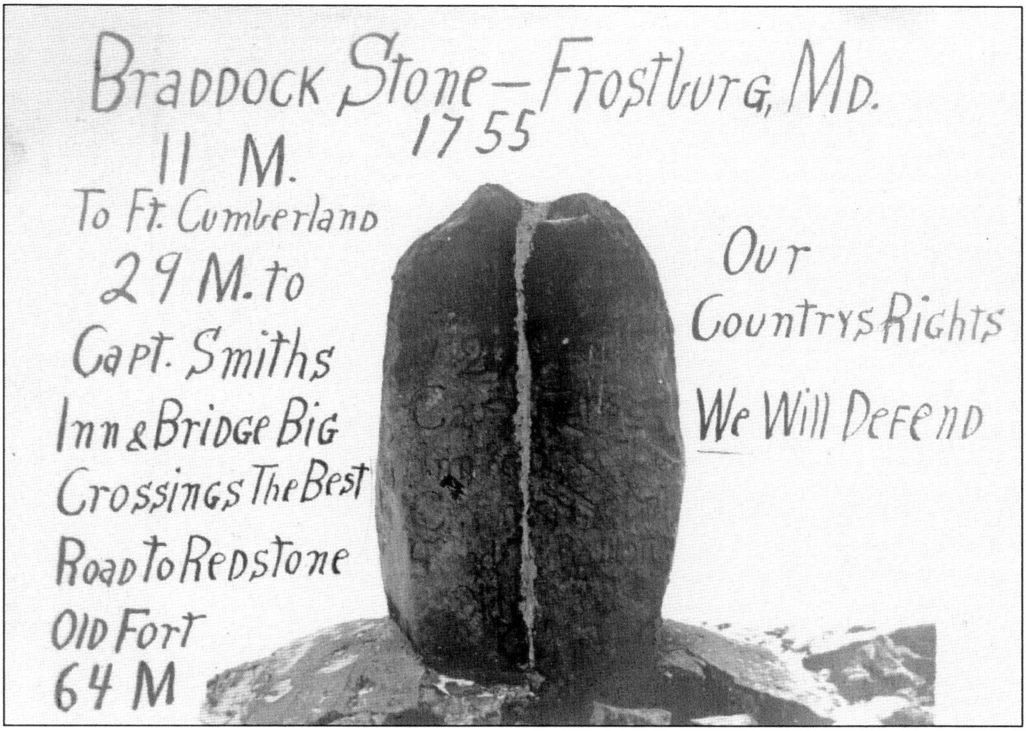

Surrounded in myth and legend, it was once believed that the Braddock Stone was inscribed by a member of Braddock's Army. But the Captain Smith's Inn and the Bridge at Big Crossing were built after 1755, so it seems that the stone is no more than an advertisement for accommodations for travelers along the Braddock Road before the building of the National Road.

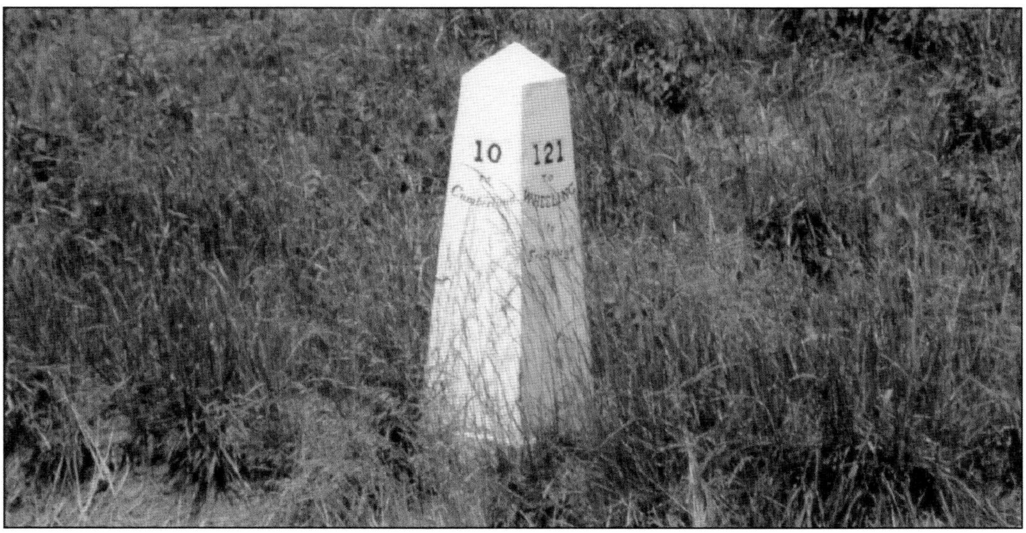

Mileage markers were placed along the National Road, giving the distance between Cumberland and Wheeling, as well as the nearest town. This marker, just to the east of Frostburg, shows the 121 miles to Wheeling and the 12 miles to Cumberland, with Frostburg just a mile away to the west. This marker was moved from its original position on the National Road to its present location following the completion of the "new" Route 40.

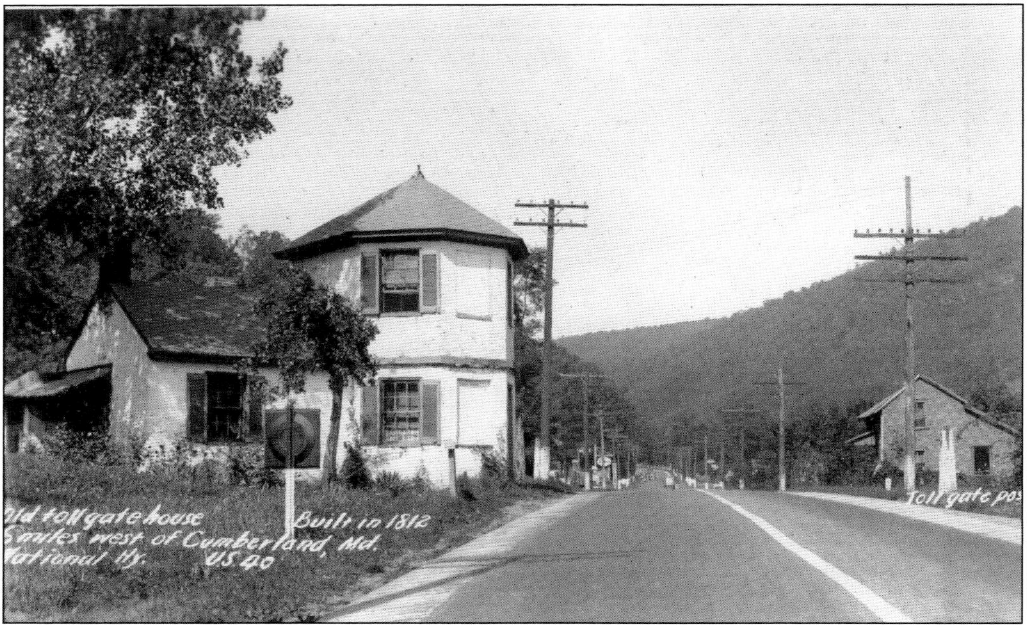

By 1834, it was necessary to charge tolls to those moving along the road. To collect the tolls, toll-takers were selected and houses were built for them. The first tollhouse on the road is located five miles east of Frostburg, in LaVale. Still standing, the tollhouse served as the residence for many families after the road was no longer a toll road.

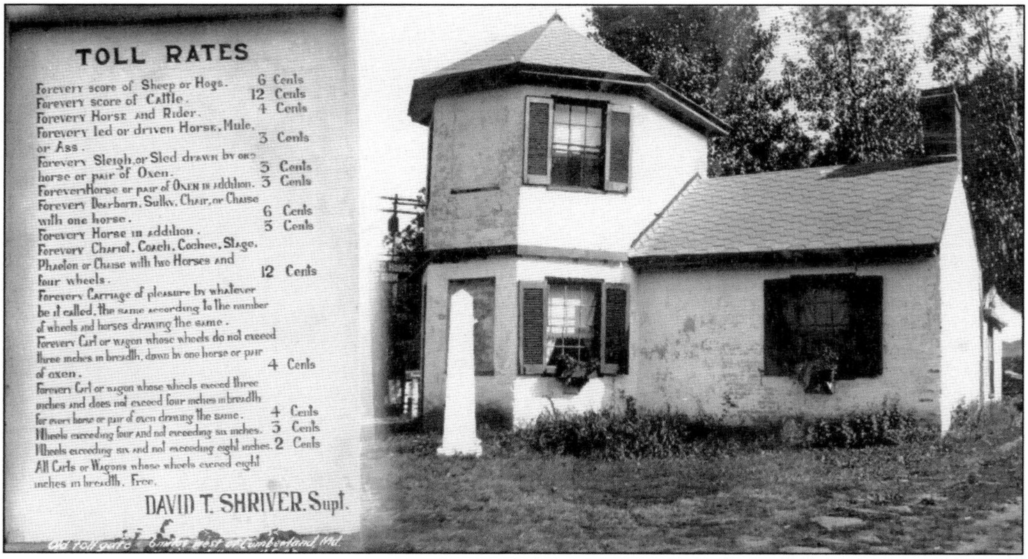

Still listed on the sides of the tollhouse in LaVale are the toll rates for those using the turnpike. Wagons, freight, and livestock all were scheduled for toll. Those exempt from the toll included those going to church on Sundays and those on their way to a gristmill! A pole or "pike" was placed over the road and, upon paying the prescribed toll, the toll-takers would turn the pike, allowing the traveler's journey to continue.

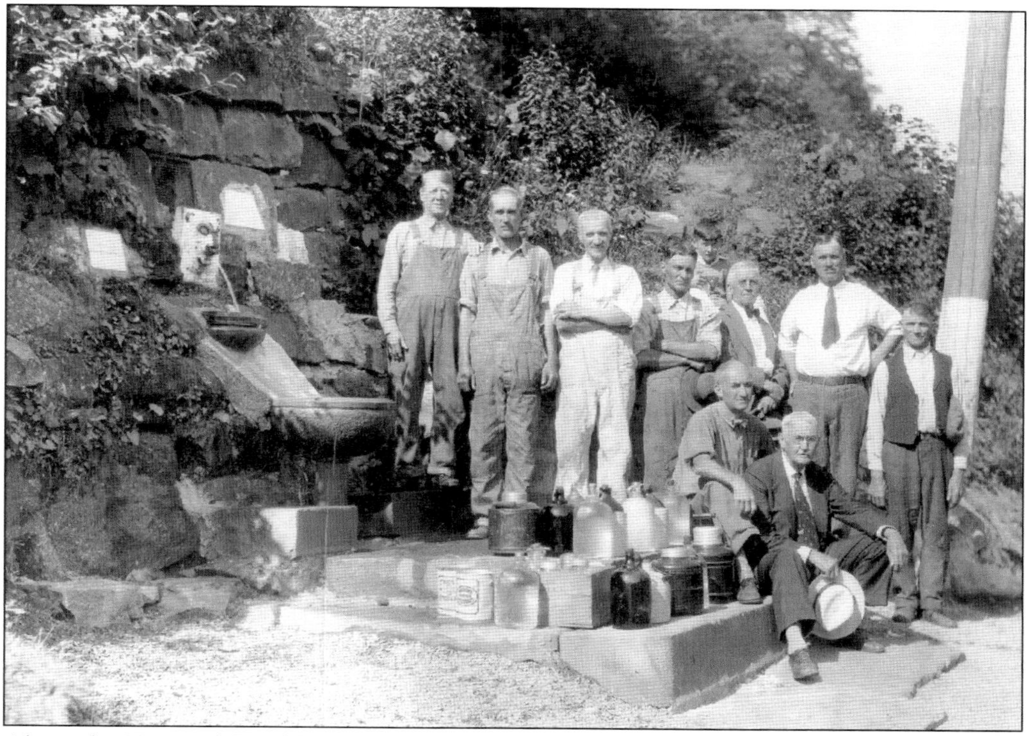

Along the National Road between LaVale and Frostburg was the Lion Head Spring. Water continuously flowed from the spring through a carved lion's head. A plaque offered "water pure and water free... a drink for you and a drink for me."

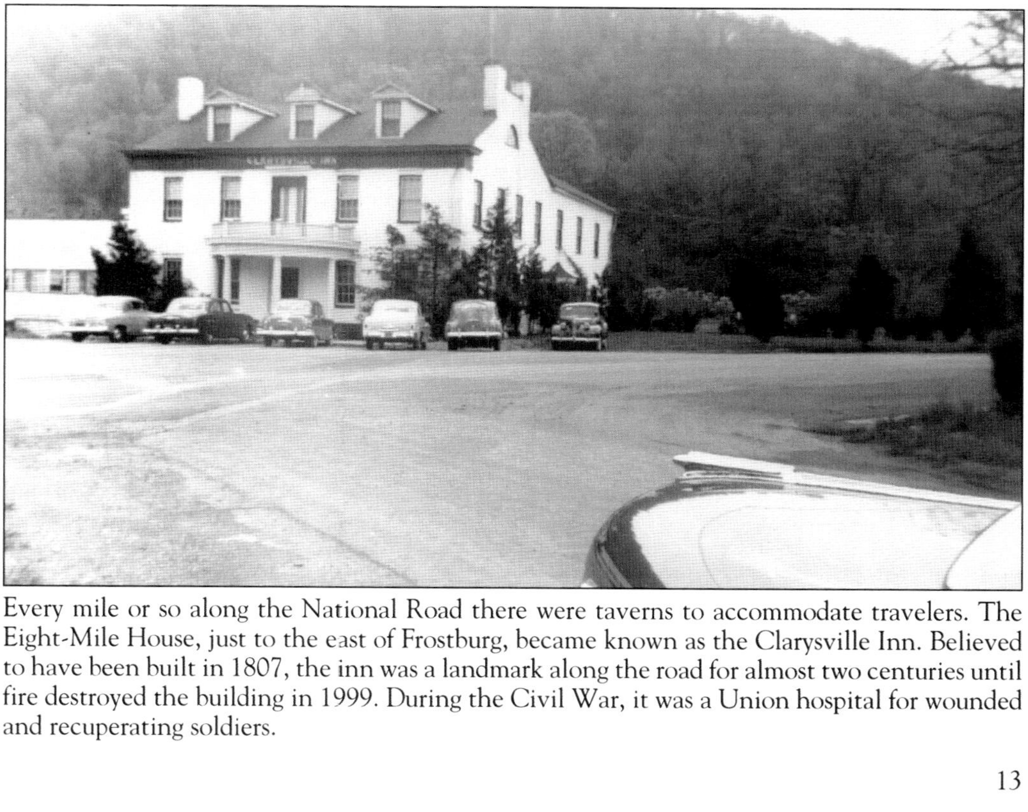

Every mile or so along the National Road there were taverns to accommodate travelers. The Eight-Mile House, just to the east of Frostburg, became known as the Clarysville Inn. Believed to have been built in 1807, the inn was a landmark along the road for almost two centuries until fire destroyed the building in 1999. During the Civil War, it was a Union hospital for wounded and recuperating soldiers.

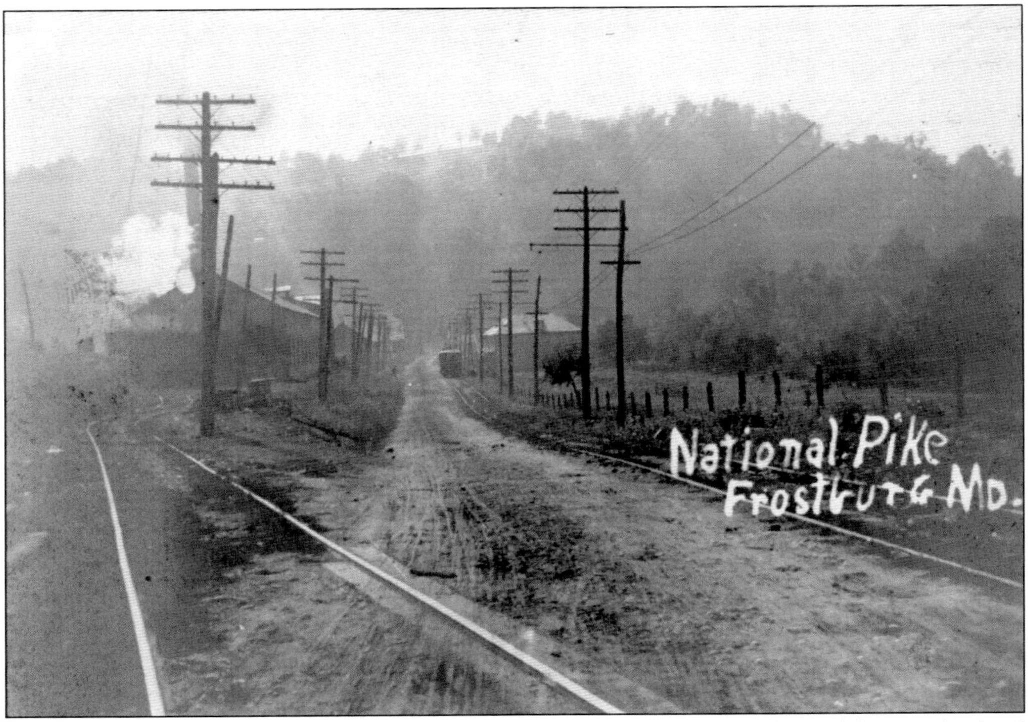

Sharing space along the National Road towards Frostburg is the trolley line of the Cumberland and Westernport Electric Railway, which ran electric trolley cars between Cumberland and Westernport in the George's Creek area. Here, at Clarysville, is the car barn, repair shops, and power station for the electric railway.

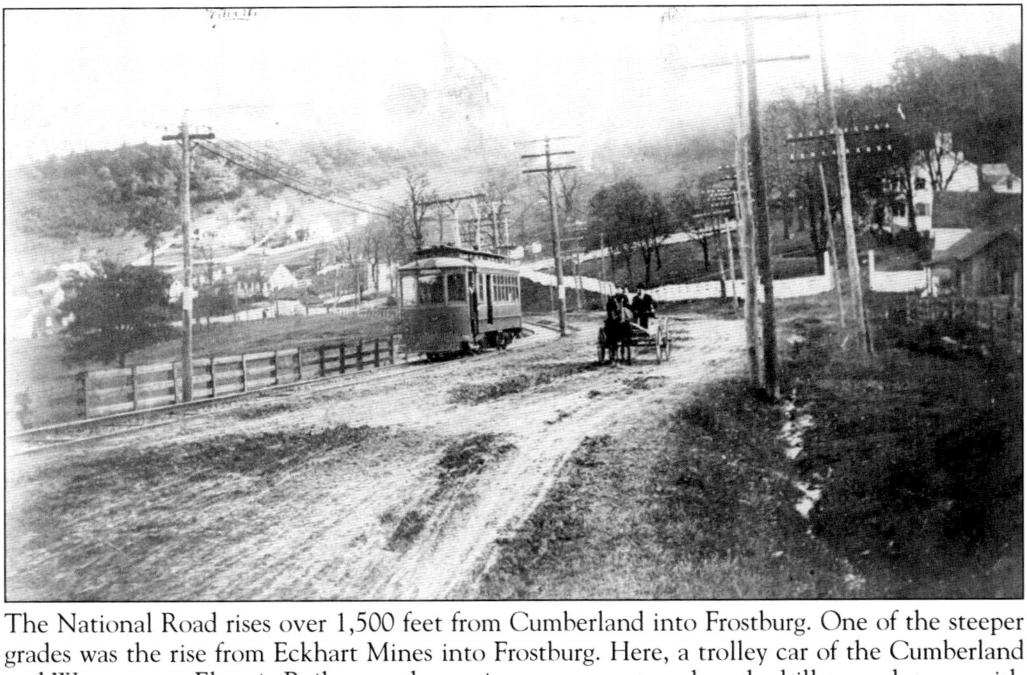

The National Road rises over 1,500 feet from Cumberland into Frostburg. One of the steeper grades was the rise from Eckhart Mines into Frostburg. Here, a trolley car of the Cumberland and Westernport Electric Railway and a carriage creep westward up the hill towards town with the mining village of Eckhart Mines below.

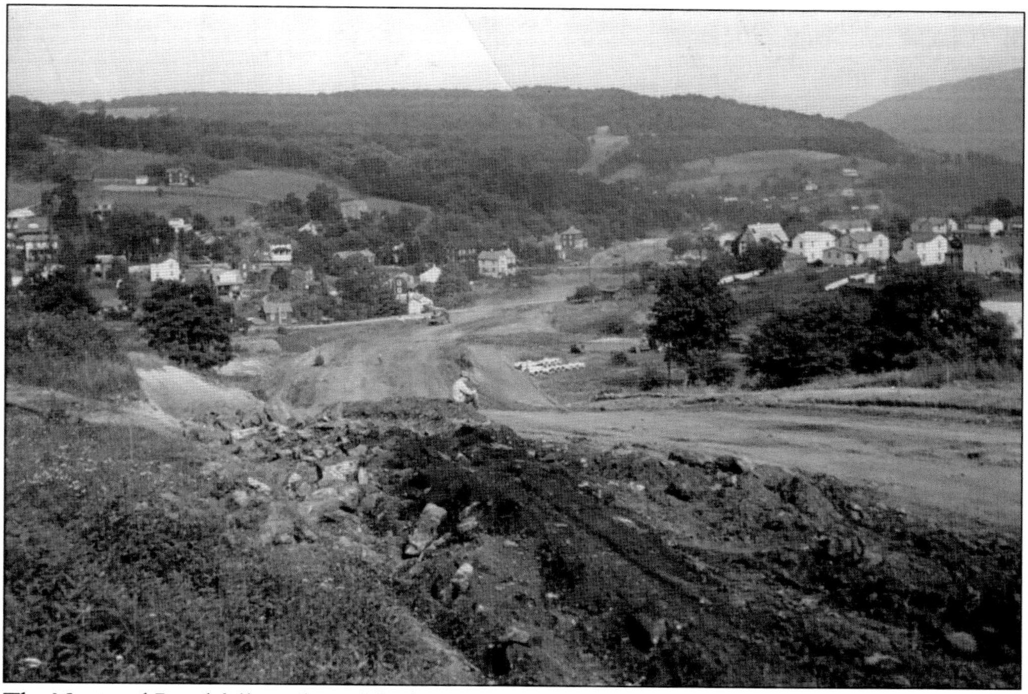

The National Road followed roughly the same roadbed from the 1808 into the 1940s. Following World War II, a new route through Eckhart Mines replaced the old road up the steep grade seen in the previous photograph. Here construction has begun on the new cut, with the Parkersburg Road section of Eckhart to the left. (Courtesy of Karen Delaney.)

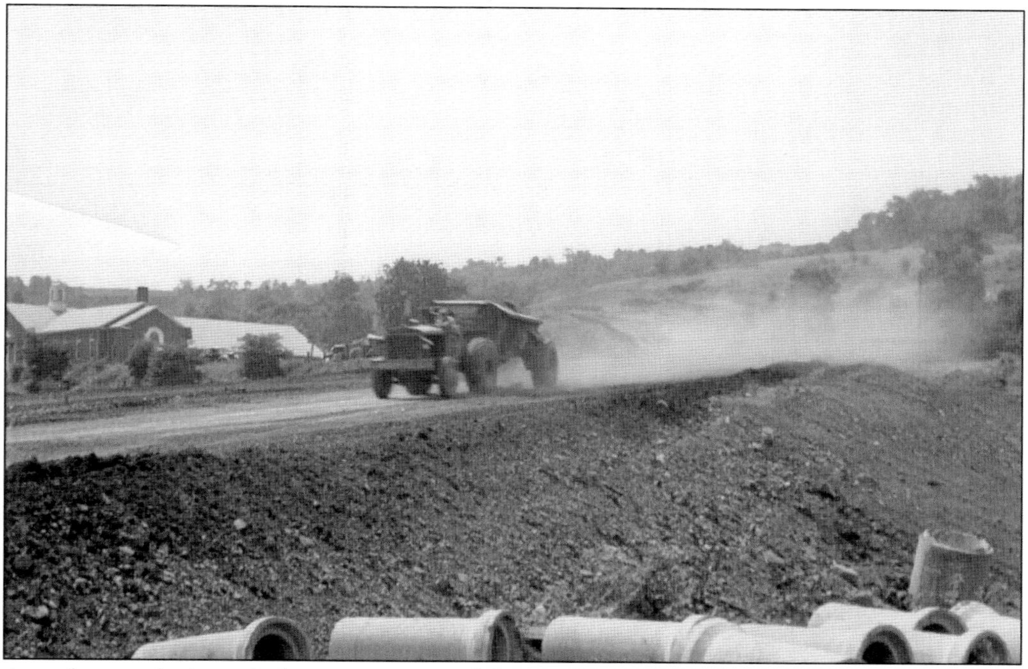

A grader travels through the construction of the new Route 40, with the Eckhart School in the background. An underground walkway was built under the road so the schoolchildren did not have to cross the new highway. (Courtesy of Karen Delaney.)

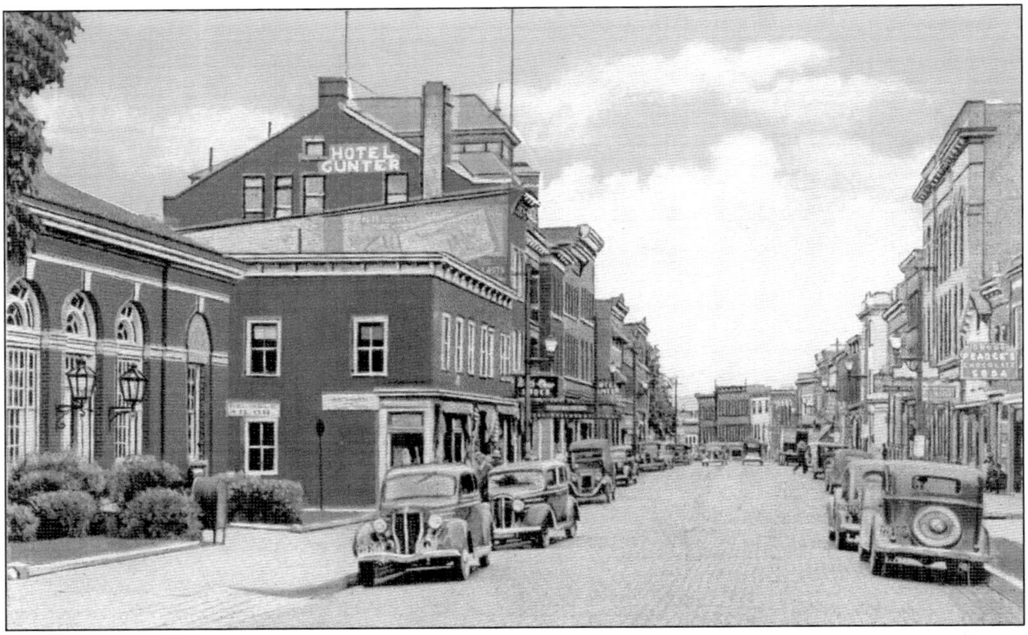

By the 20th century, the National Road was designated US Route 40, the National Highway, one of the major thoroughfares east and west across the United States. Travelers on 40 passed through the business district of Frostburg until the construction of Route 48 (later Interstate 68) which is located to the south of town.

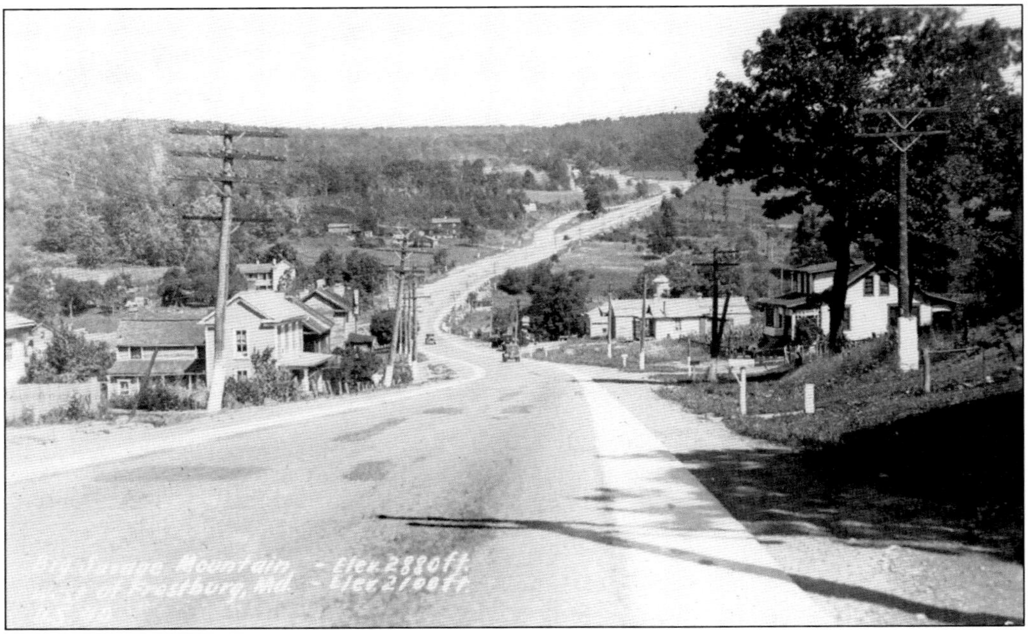

Just to the west of town, the National Road creeps up Big Savage Mountain, climbing to 2,800 feet above sea level. The downgrade into Frostburg was steep and caused several devastating accidents involving run-away tractor-trailers. In 1955, a truck lost its brakes on the mountain, sped through town, and ran eight and one-half miles to the LaVale, near Cumberland, before crashing into another truck and car and killing five.

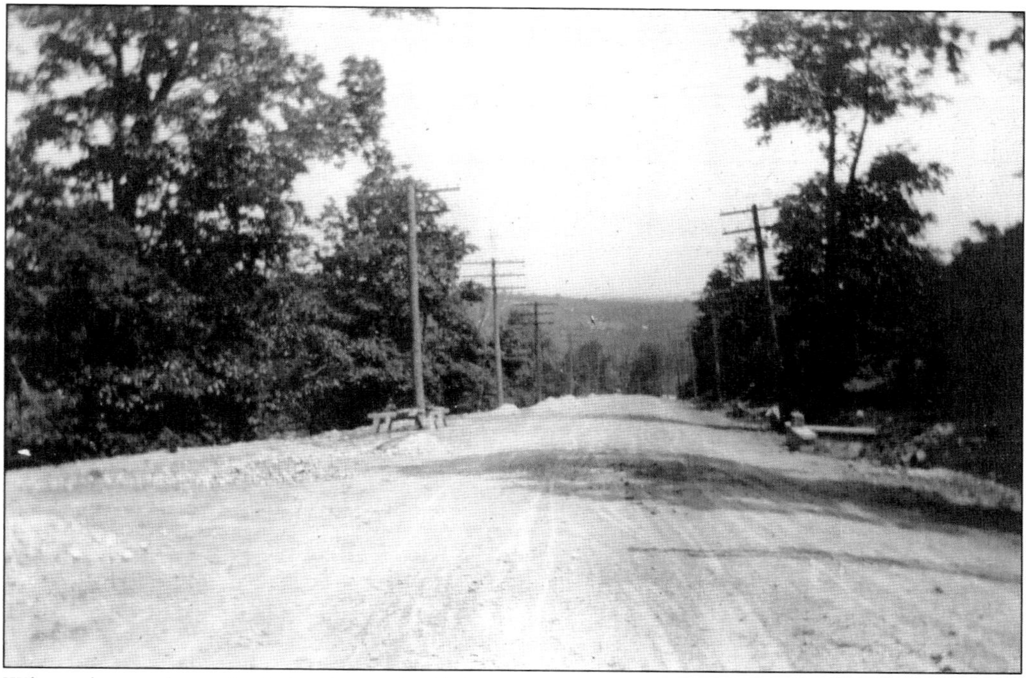

When the road was built in the early 19th century, it was built with a 60-foot right-of-way, which still maintains today. This early 20th-century photograph shows that the road surfaces of today were not always the norm, but the National Road was one of the earliest "metaled" or surfaced roads.

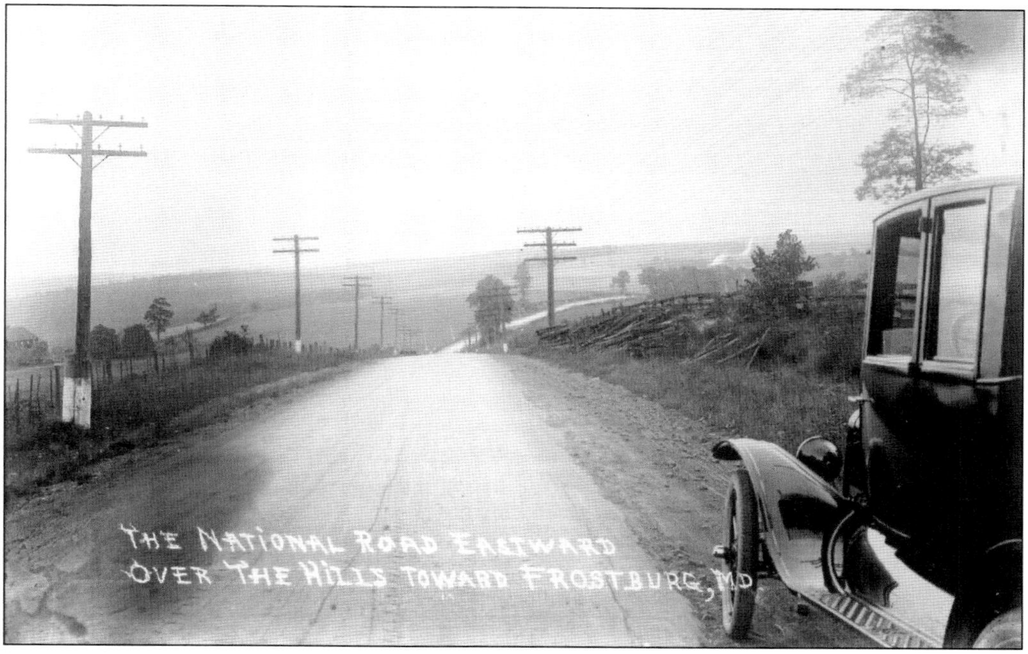

During the 1920s, a prominent Frostburg businessman, W.E.B. Hitchins, traveled along the National Road taking photographs and creating a travelogue of his journey. Here is one of his photographs of the National Road as it dips and climbs over the hills just to the west of Frostburg.

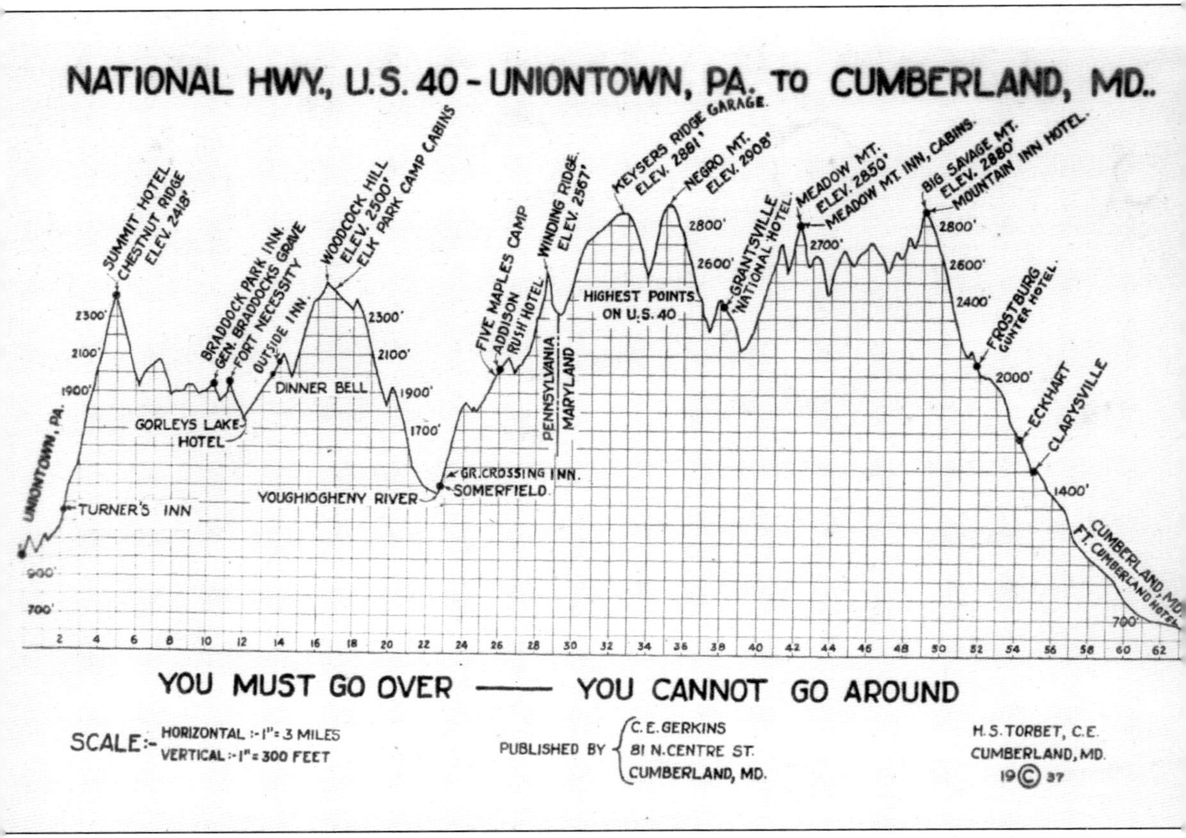

This is a 1937 postcard showing the peaks and valleys along the National Highway from Cumberland to Uniontown, Pennsylvania. This journey can be made on the same road today, albeit a bit faster and fraught with less hazards than a traveler would have faced almost 70 years ago.

Two

Alma Mater

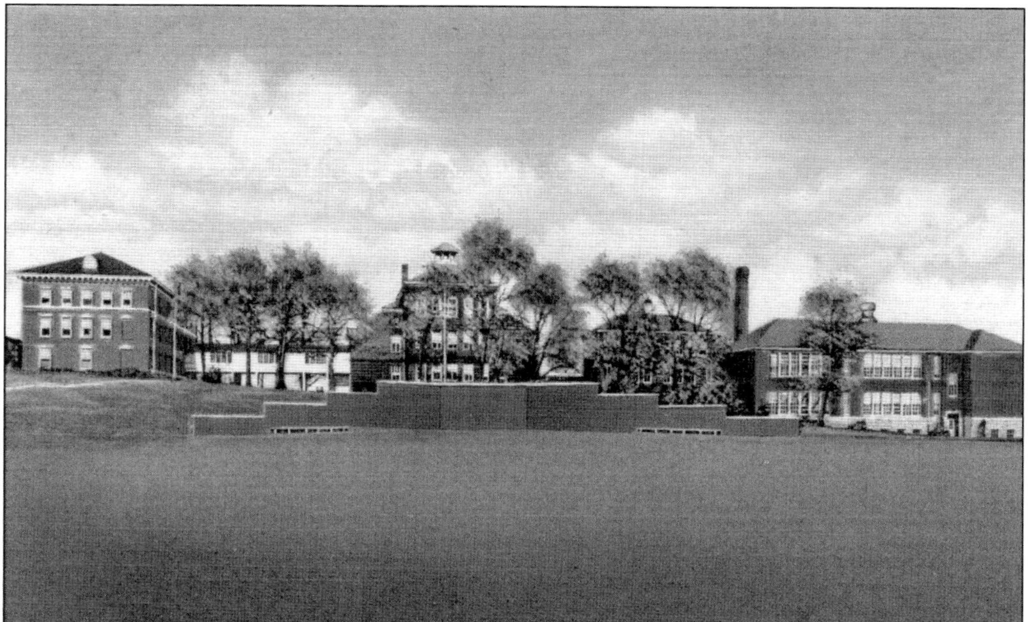

This postcard view shows the original buildings that made up what was, by 1935, the State Teachers College at Frostburg, which became Frostburg State College in 1963, and later Frostburg State University in 1987.

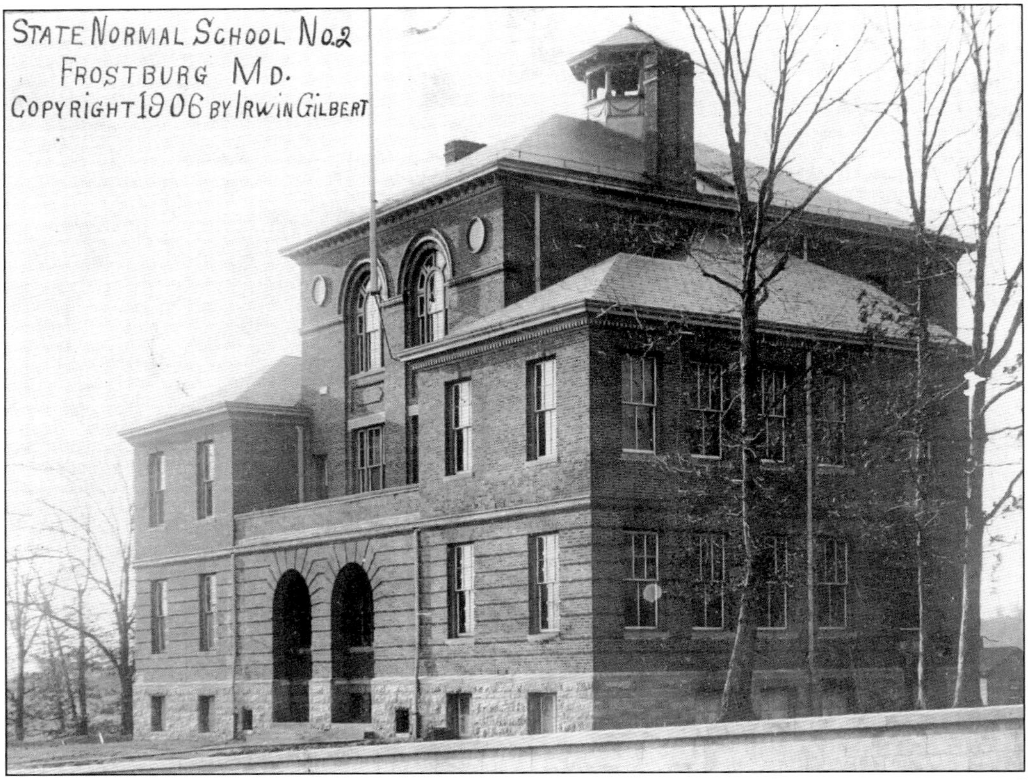

Founded in 1898 and opened in 1902 as Normal School # 2 in Frostburg, Old Main was constructed to house not only classrooms, but the library and other services for the original 57 students.

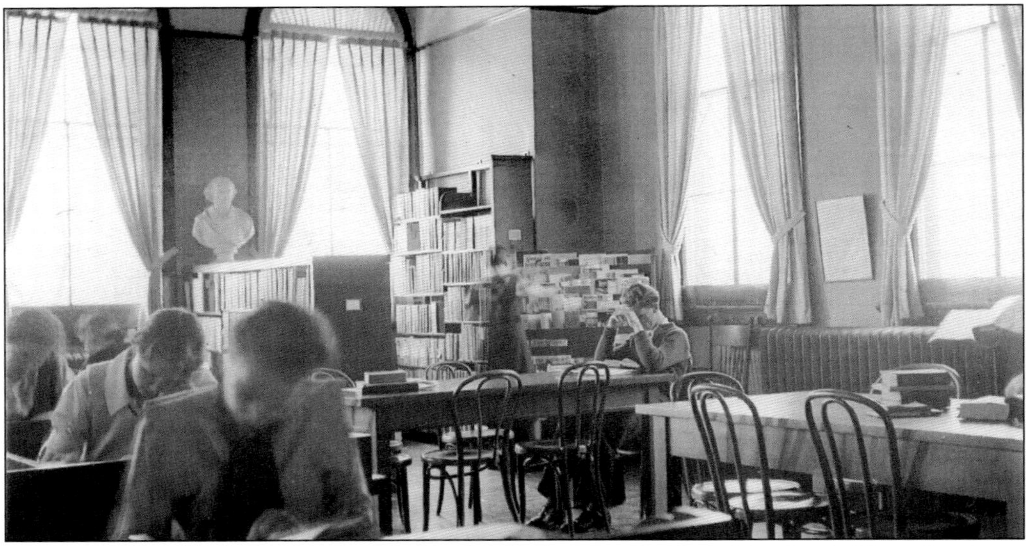

The library in Old Main was reputed to be the best in Western Maryland. The school was initially a two-year training school for elementary teachers and later became a three-year, then four-year school, still emphasizing elementary teacher education. In 1934, a bachelor of science degree in education was authorized and in 1947 junior high school education was added to the curriculum. (Courtesy of FSU Special Collections.)

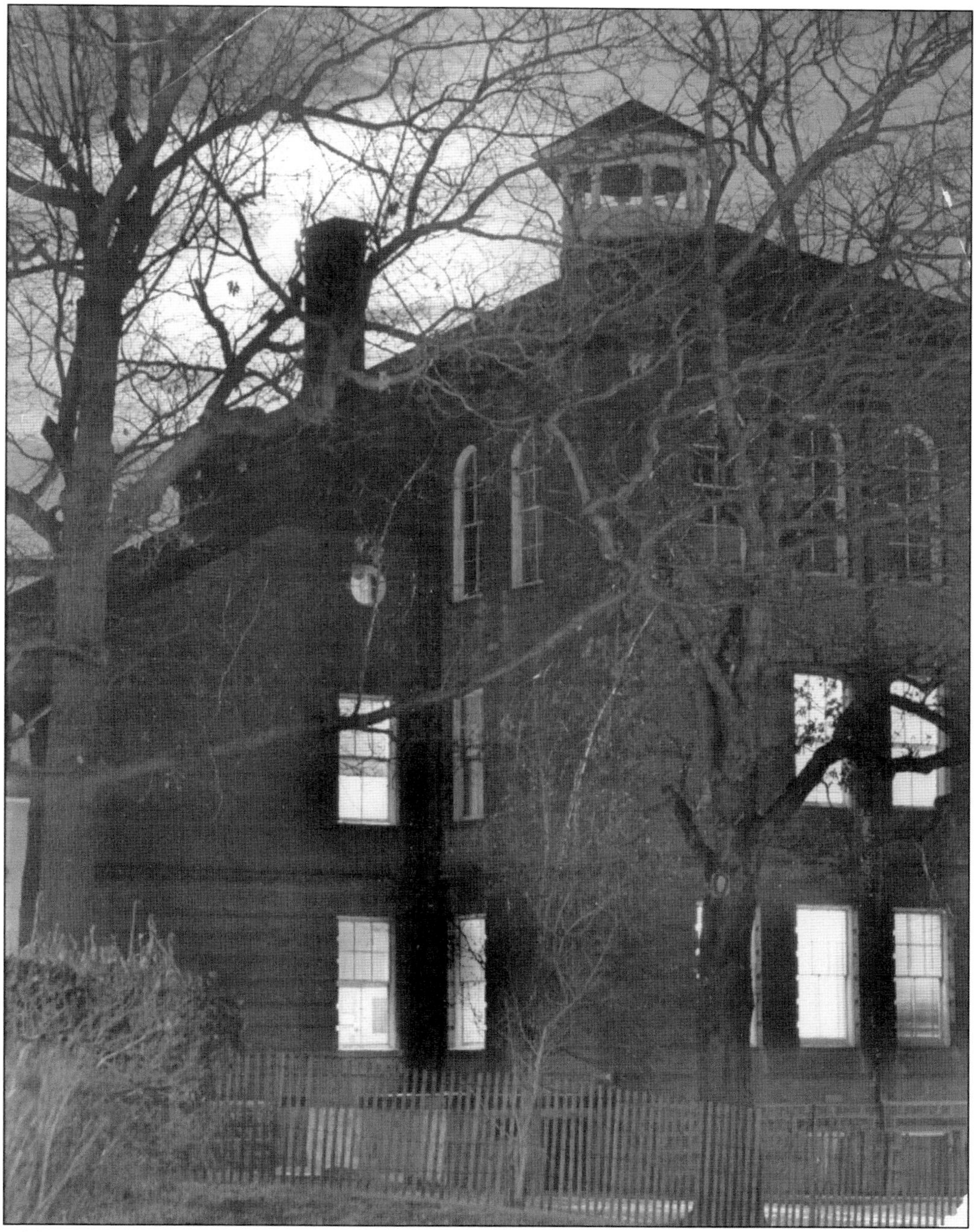

Old Main, silhouetted in the winter's moonlight, shows the midnight oil burning. From the original 57 students, enrollment did increase to 94, but by the 1940s, that number had slipped to merely 60 and the school was in danger of closing. With the insistent urging of Frostburg residents, college president Lillian Compton was persuaded to keep the school open and, over the past 50 years, the school has enjoyed tremendous growth. (Courtesy of FSU Special Collections.)

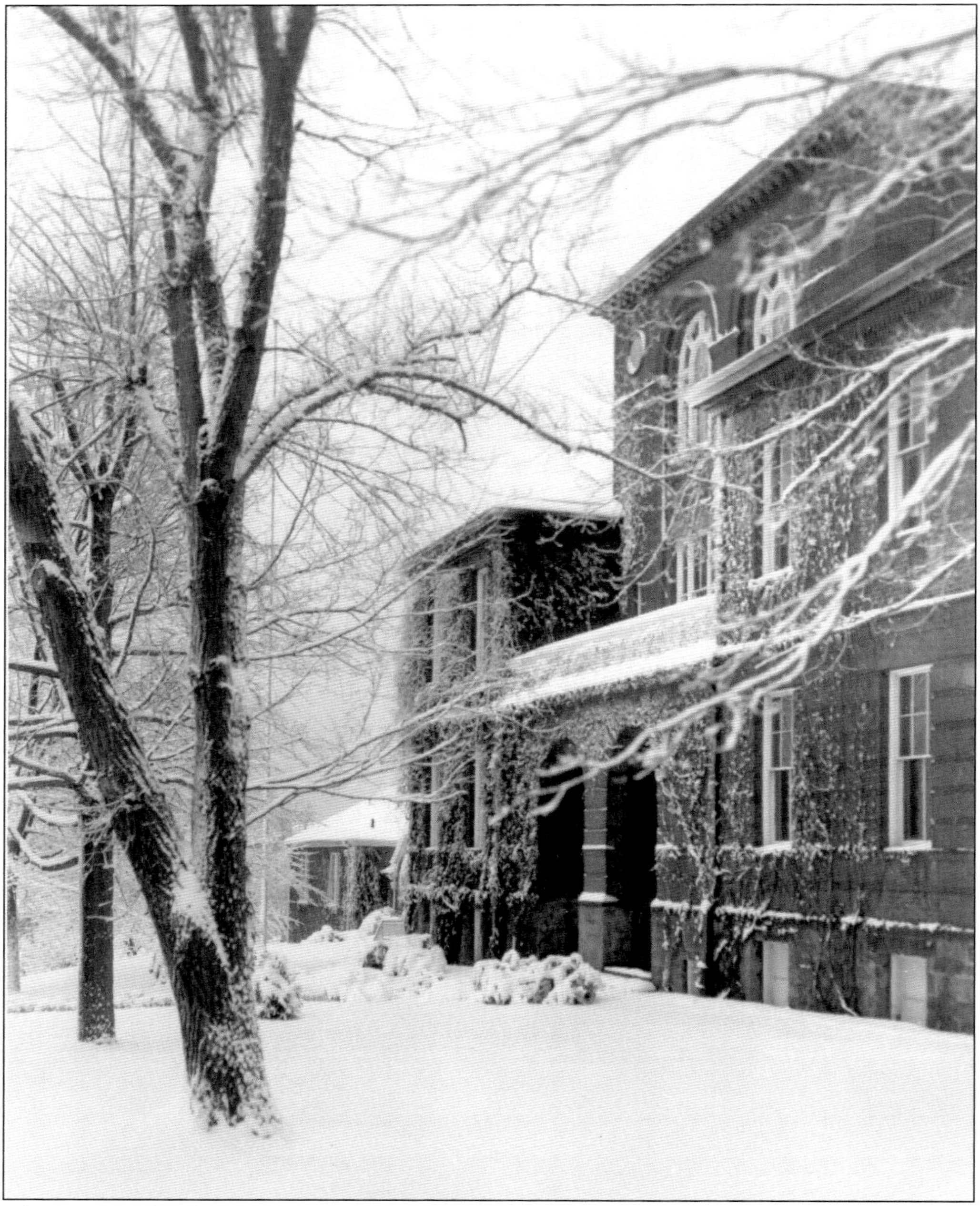

This scene is familiar to many students who have spent the winter on campus. Photographs such as these can still conjure feelings of the cold, bitter winds coming off the mountain and blowing wet snow against red noses and frozen cheeks! (Courtesy of FSU Special Collections.)

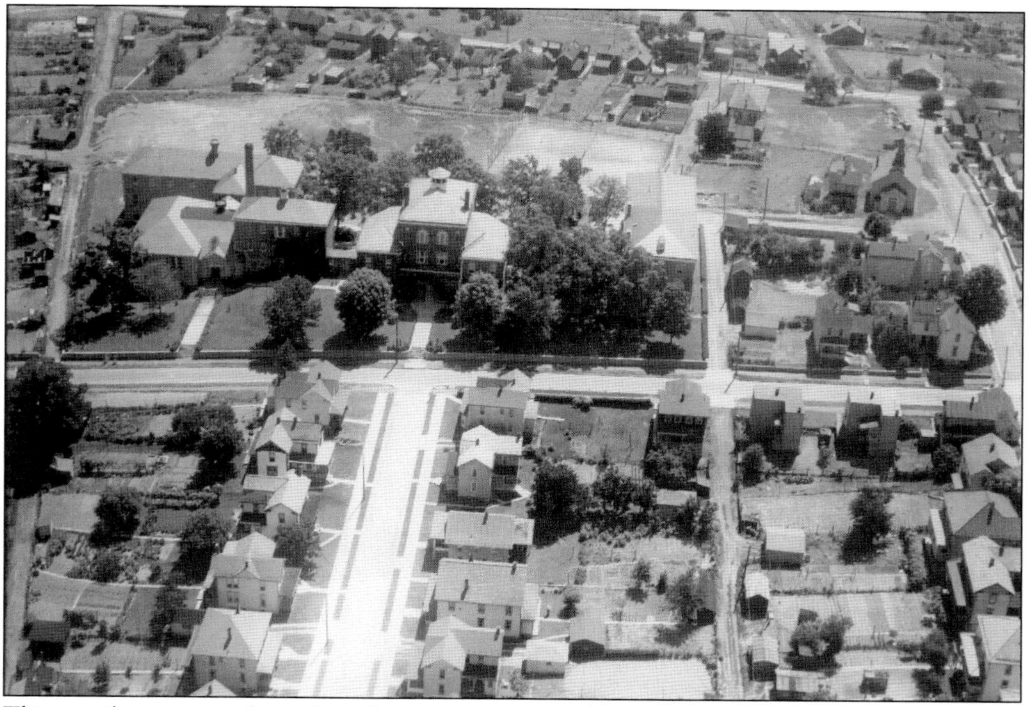

This aerial view was taken when the campus was simply a cluster of buildings along Loo Street (later College Avenue). Construction of other classroom and dormitory buildings had not yet begun, nor had the demolition of houses and buildings to the right of and behind the college buildings in order to make way for expansion. (Courtesy of FSU Special Collections.)

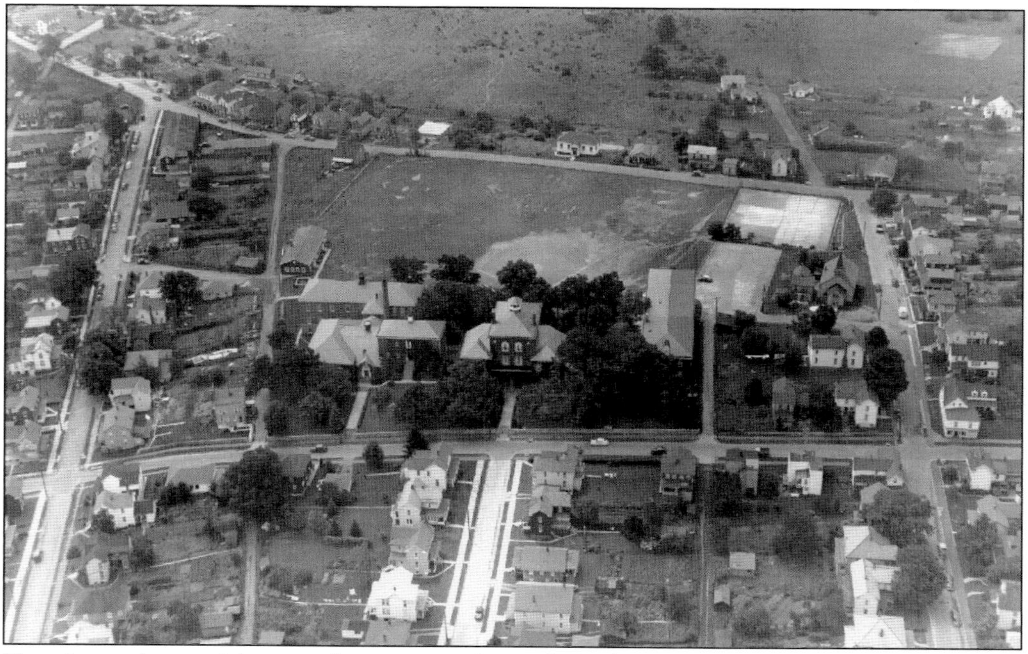

Here is another aerial view of campus in the early 20th century with the tennis courts and a makeshift baseball diamond in the quad behind the classroom buildings clearly visible. (Courtesy of FSU Special Collections.)

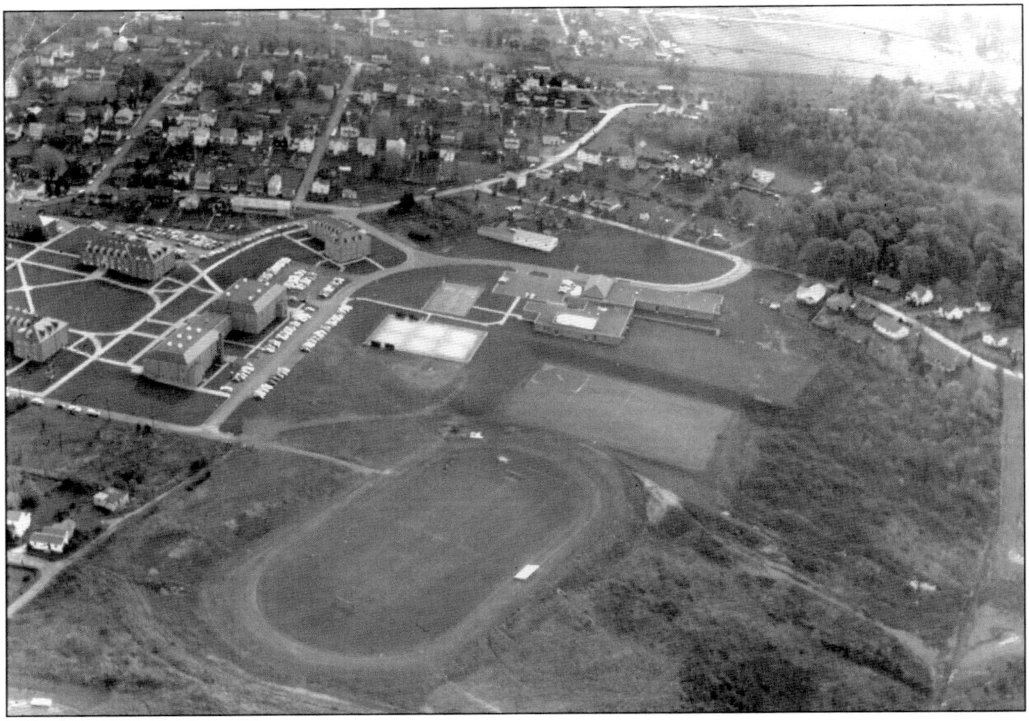

By the 1960s, campus expansion had grown by several classroom buildings and dormitories. At one time, athletic fields and the Pullen School formed the boundaries of the campus. (Courtesy of FSU Special Collections.)

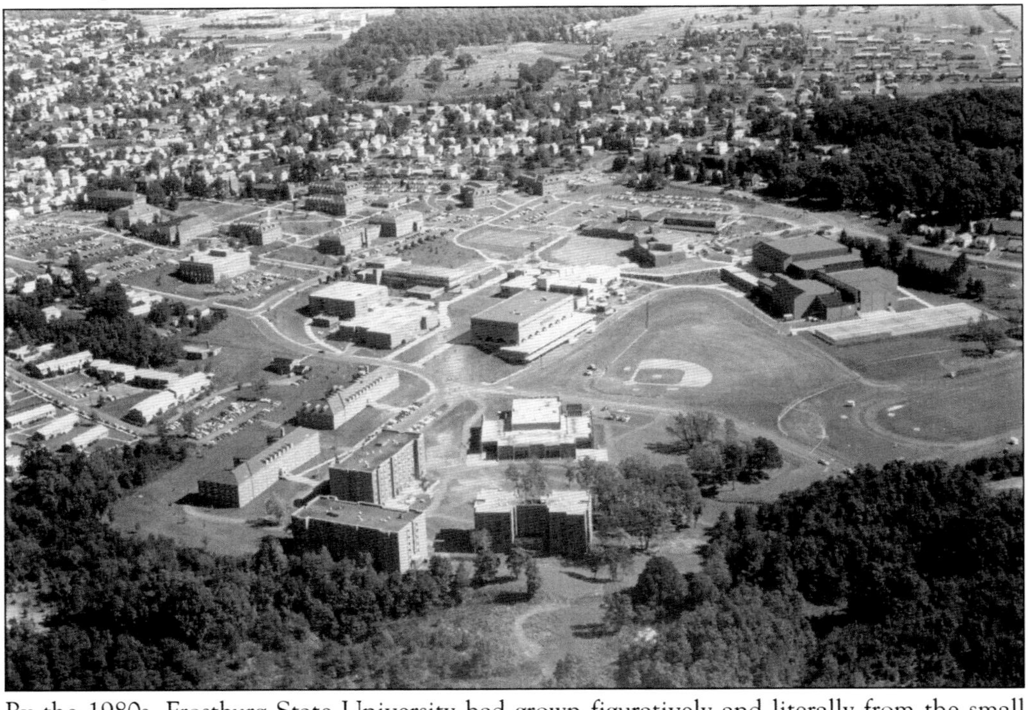

By the 1980s, Frostburg State University had grown figuratively and literally from the small cluster of buildings on College Avenue. (Courtesy of FSU Special Collections.)

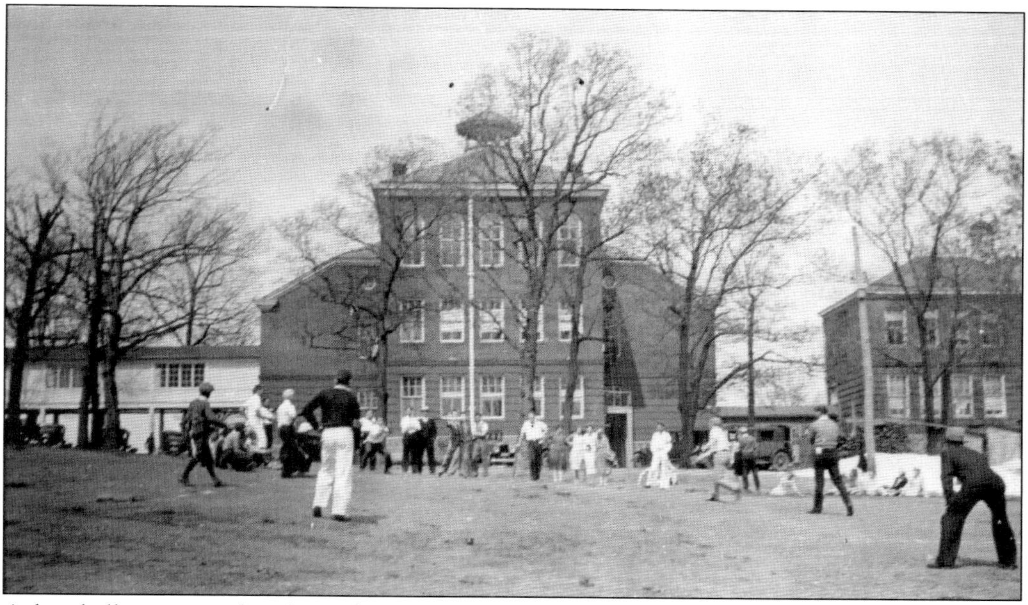

A baseball game is played on the quad behind old Main in the 1920s. The quad area has witnessed many activities, from athletic events to commencement and even sunbathing! (Courtesy of FSU Special Collections.)

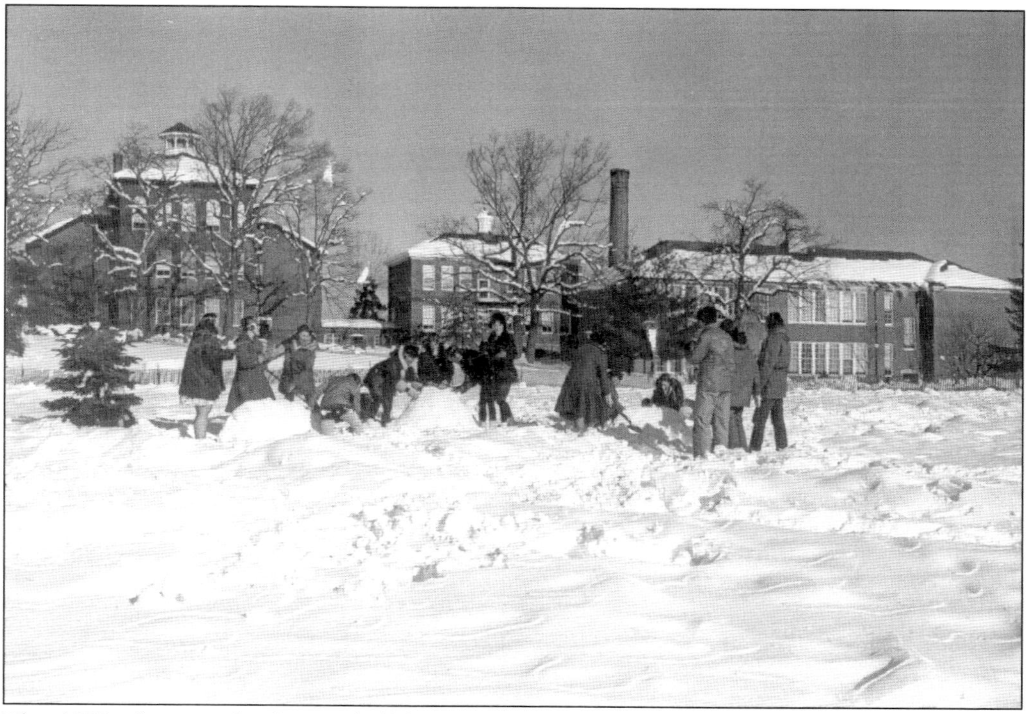

This 1970s photograph of a snowball fight and snowman building in the winter depicts clothing and hairstyles quite different from the 1920s. The buildings behind, however, do not seem to have changed. (Courtesy of FSU Special Collections.)

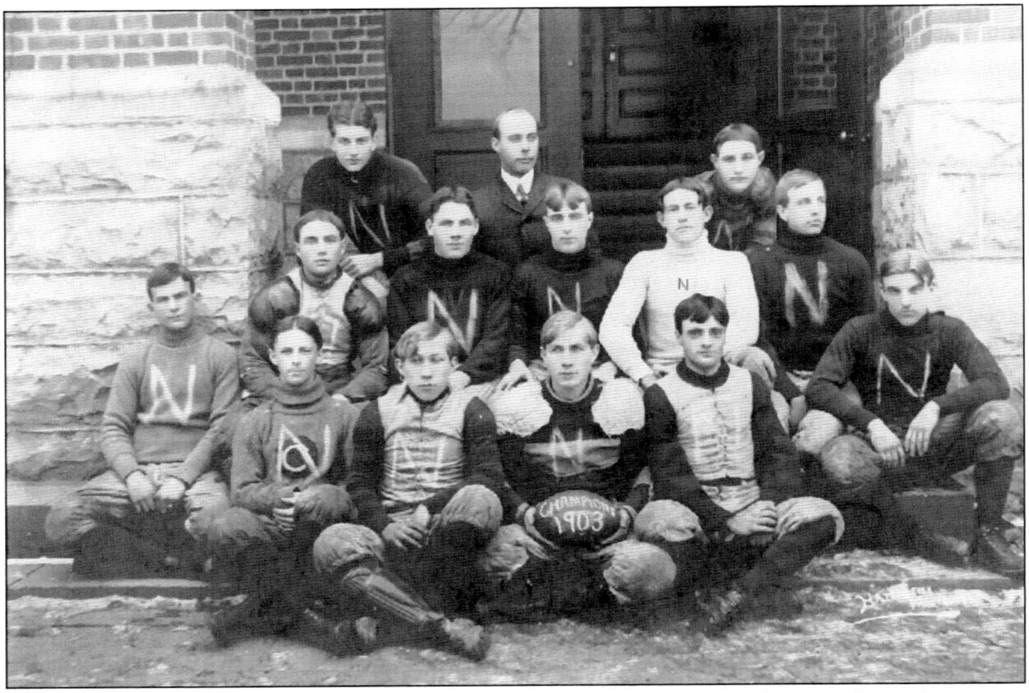

A group of students posed on the steps of Old Main with a football proclaiming them champions in 1903. The makeshift uniforms and equipment show a different view of college football in the first years of the 20th century.

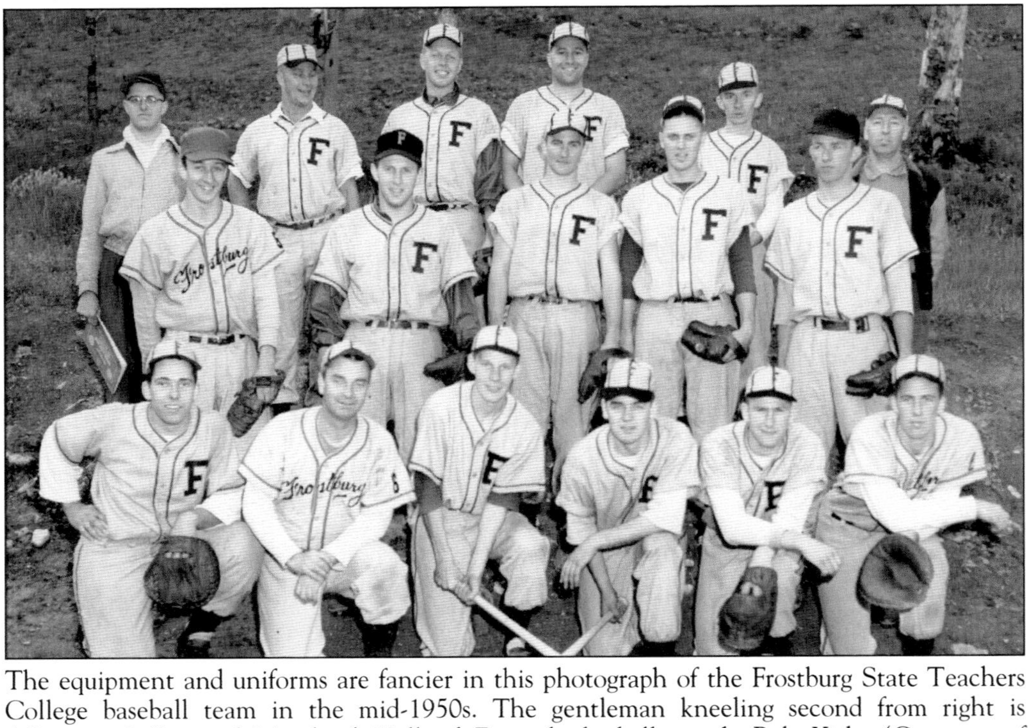

The equipment and uniforms are fancier in this photograph of the Frostburg State Teachers College baseball team in the mid-1950s. The gentleman kneeling second from right is Allegany College of Maryland Hall of Fame basketball coach Bob Kirk. (Courtesy of FSU Special Collections.)

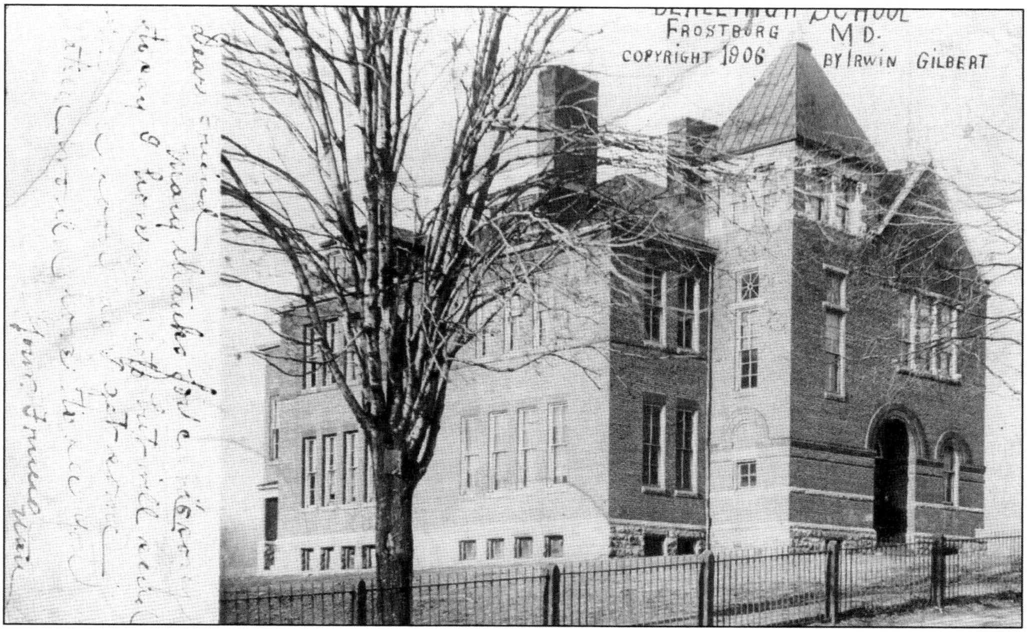

The original Beall High School was at the corner of College Avenue (Loo Street) and Broadway. This building first opened its doors in September 1868. By 1890, the school had expanded and by 1910, another addition was added.

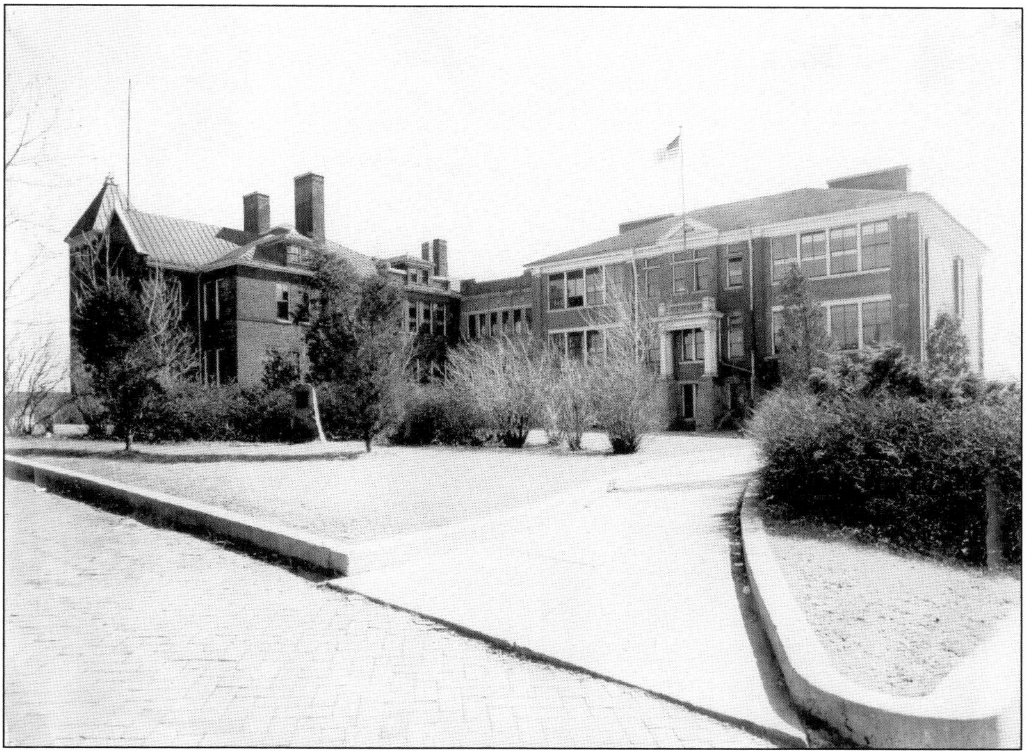

This is Beall High as it looked in the early 1930s. By the late 1930s, however, a new high school was needed. The class of 1940 was the last to graduate from this location.

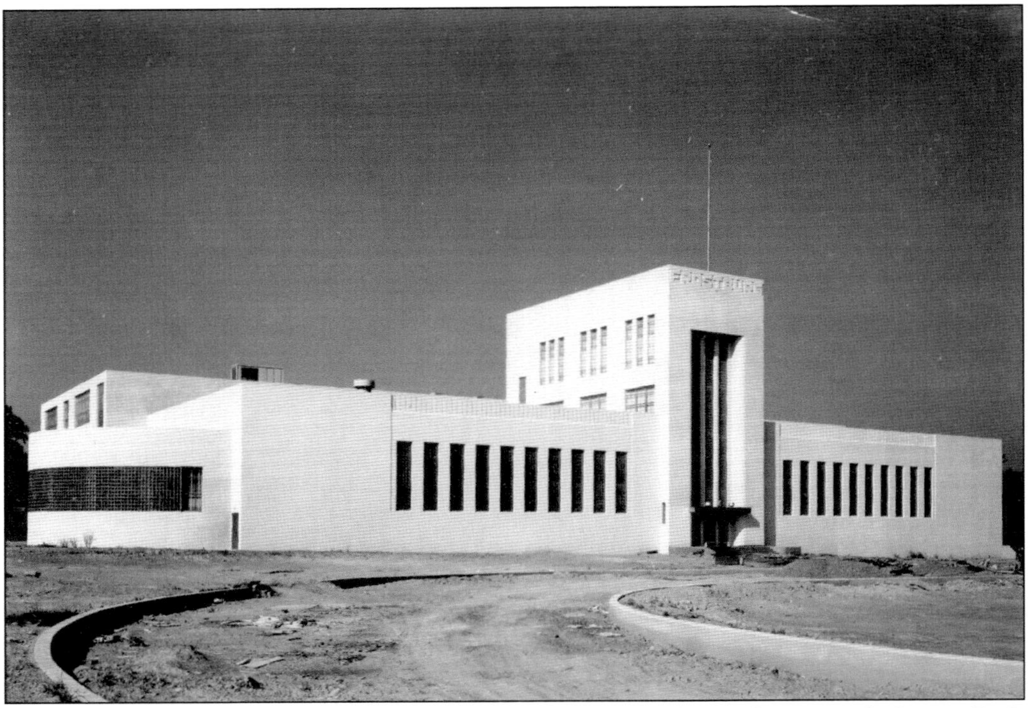

The new Beall High School is under construction on Eckhart Flat on the east end of town. Built on land honeycombed by coal mines, Beall High was made with modern architectural concrete that was supposed to minimize the risk of the entire school collapsing if there was subsidence from unstable ground. The cost of construction in 1940 was $415,506!

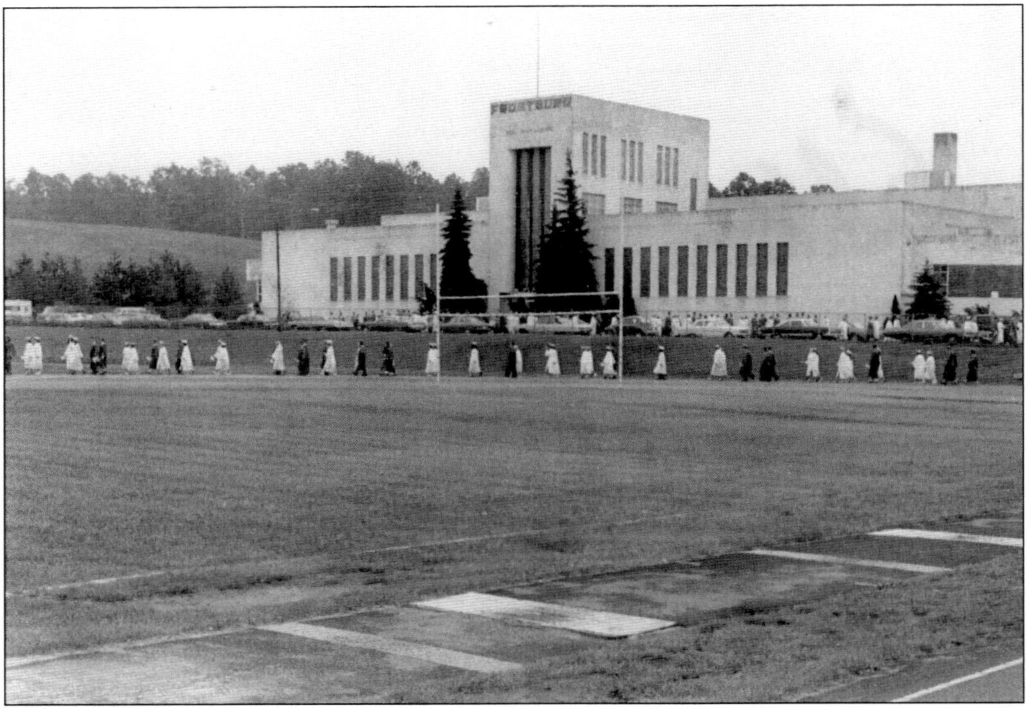

A Beall High School graduation was held in the athletic field during the late 1960s.

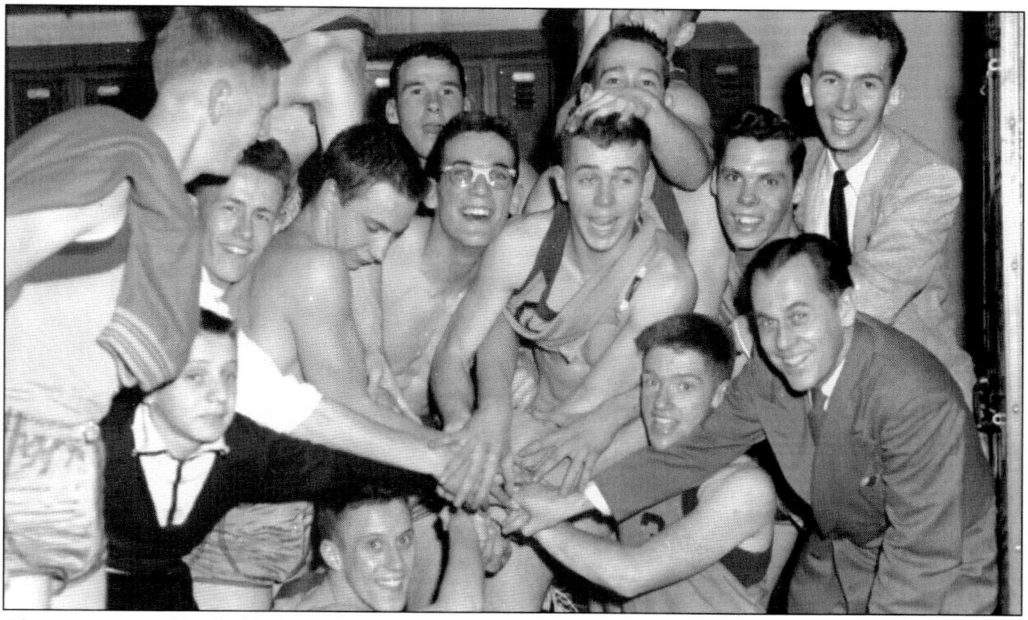

The victorious Beall High Mountaineer Basketball team is photographed after winning the Western Maryland Interscholastic Class A title in 1955. According to the school paper, the *Beall High Chime*, the title was "the first to come to the Mountain City for 31 years." The ebullient coach to the right is Coach Ebbie Finzel, himself a Beall High graduate.

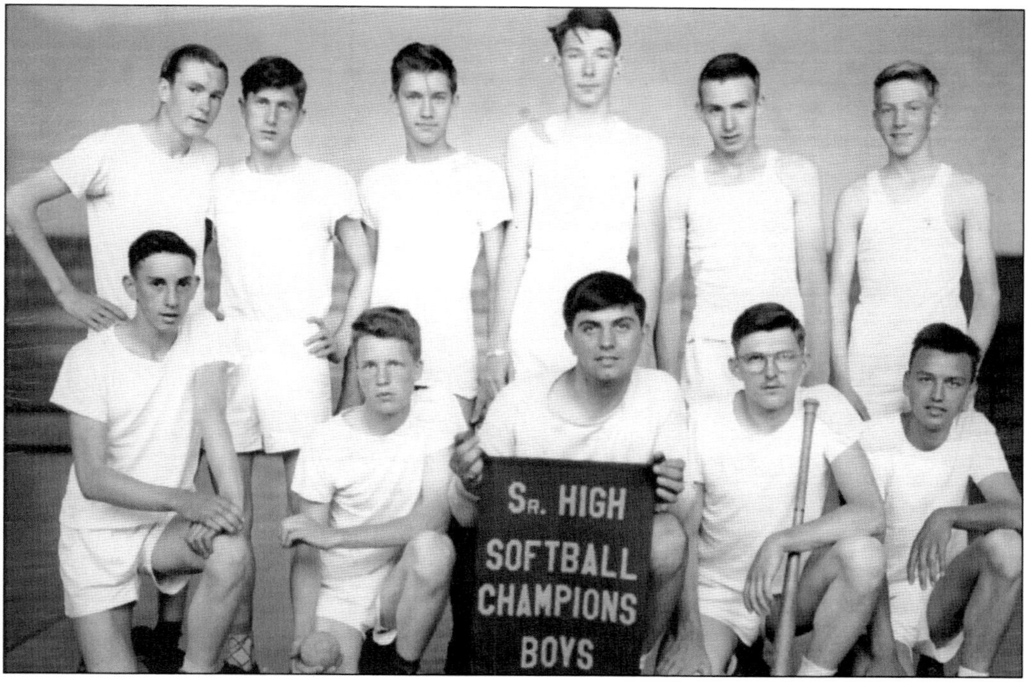

As physical education teachers and coaches have always told us, "sports helps build character and leaders!" Here are the 1950 Beall High intramural softball champions. The young man kneeling in front, holding the banner, is Enardo "Moose" Arnone. Arnone has become a leader in the community as a teacher and school administrator. Arnone is currently a member of the board of education.

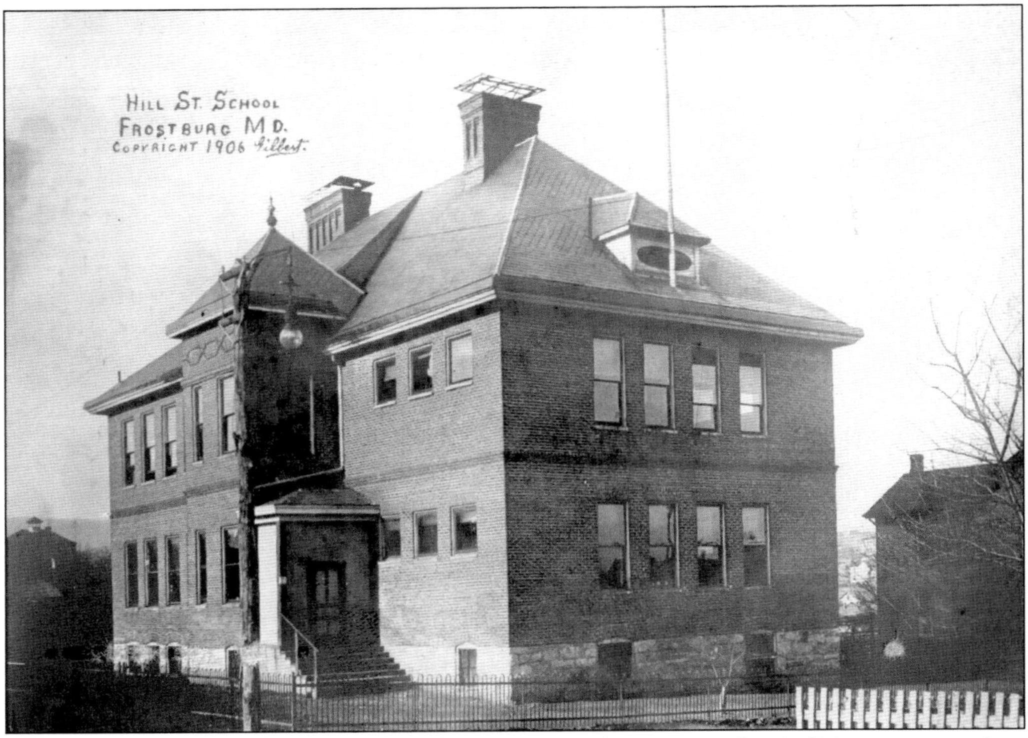

Hill Street School was erected in 1899 as a six-room elementary school. Other rooms and an auditorium were added around 1914. The school was used into the latter part of the 20th century, but because of the construction of a new elementary school on the site of the old Beall High School, Hill Street closed its doors. The building is now the home of the Frostburg Museum.

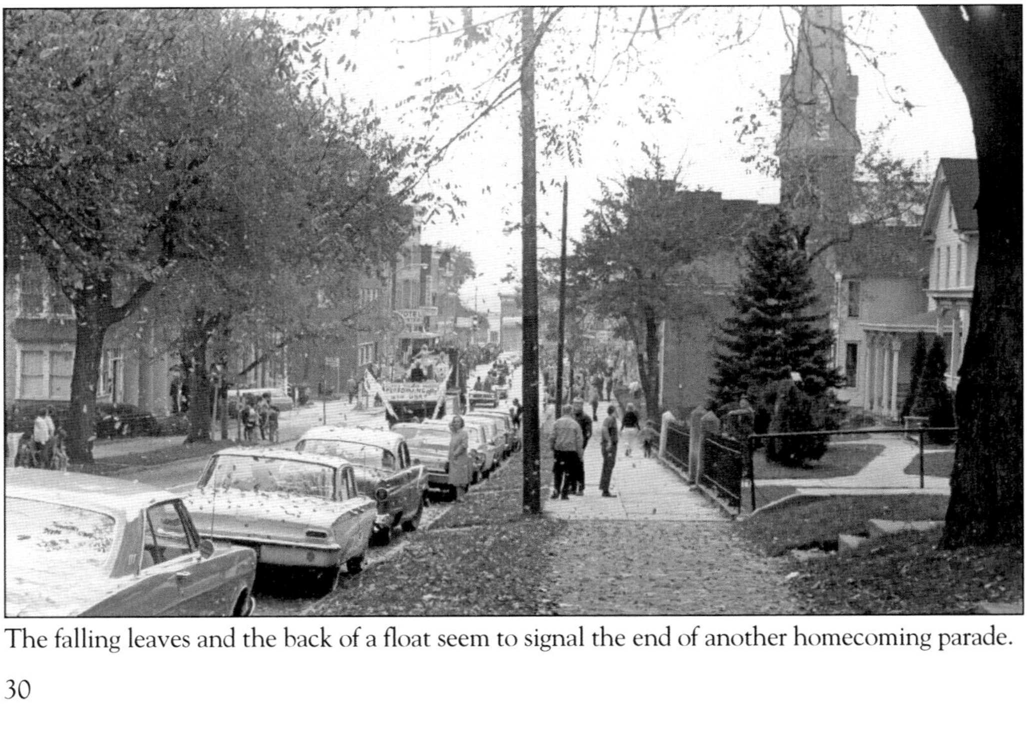

The falling leaves and the back of a float seem to signal the end of another homecoming parade.

Three

When Coal Was King

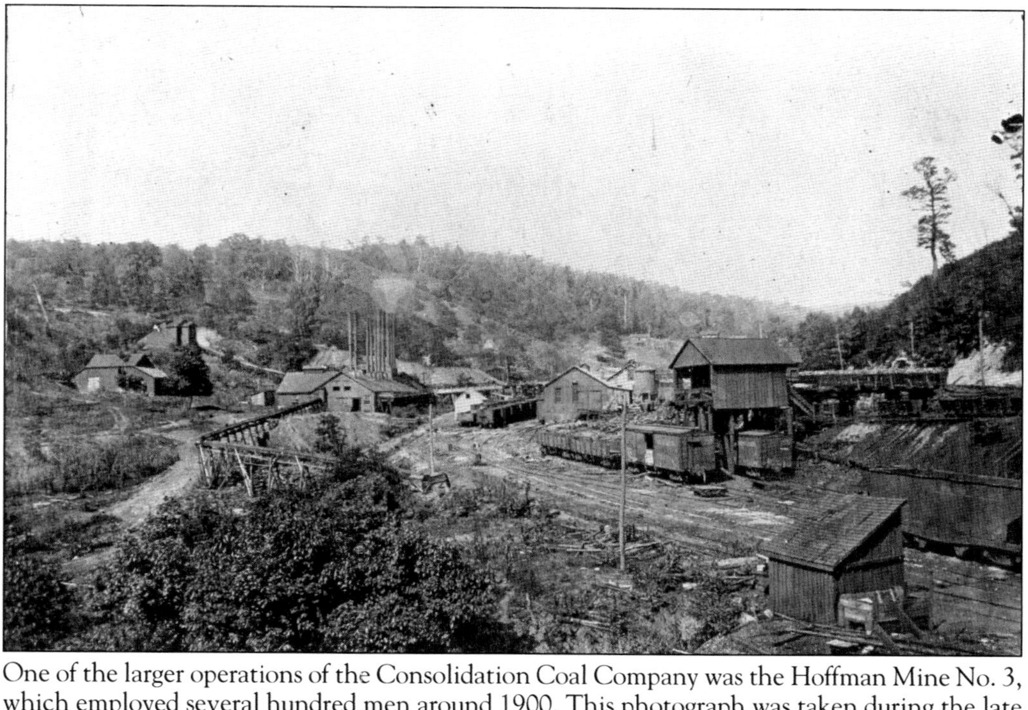

One of the larger operations of the Consolidation Coal Company was the Hoffman Mine No. 3, which employed several hundred men around 1900. This photograph was taken during the late 19th century at the height of the coal industry boom.

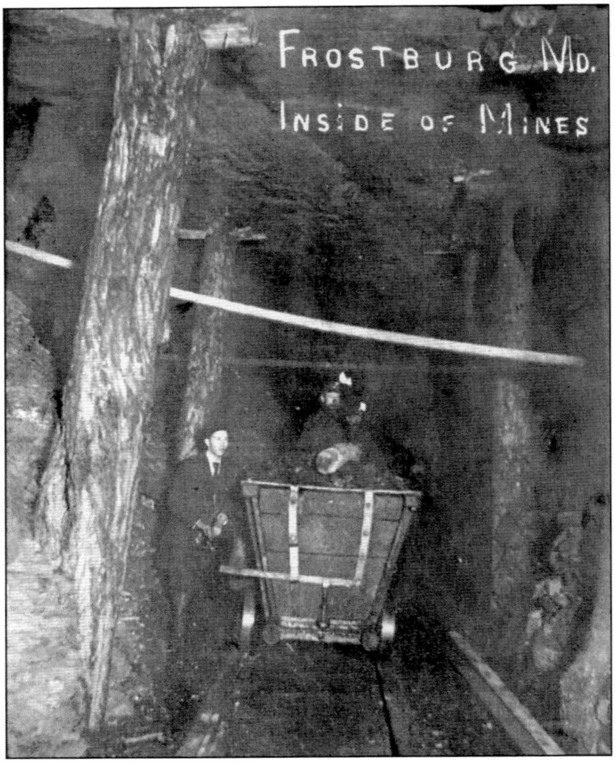

Beneath Frostburg there is a honeycomb of coalmines. The Pittsburgh Vein of bituminous coal was much sought after to fire furnaces of buildings, trains, and steamships. The Georges Creek coal was often used in government buildings and for the United States Navy of the steamship era. The maze of tunnels was so intricate that miners could enter one mine and exit at another mine whose portal was several mines distant.

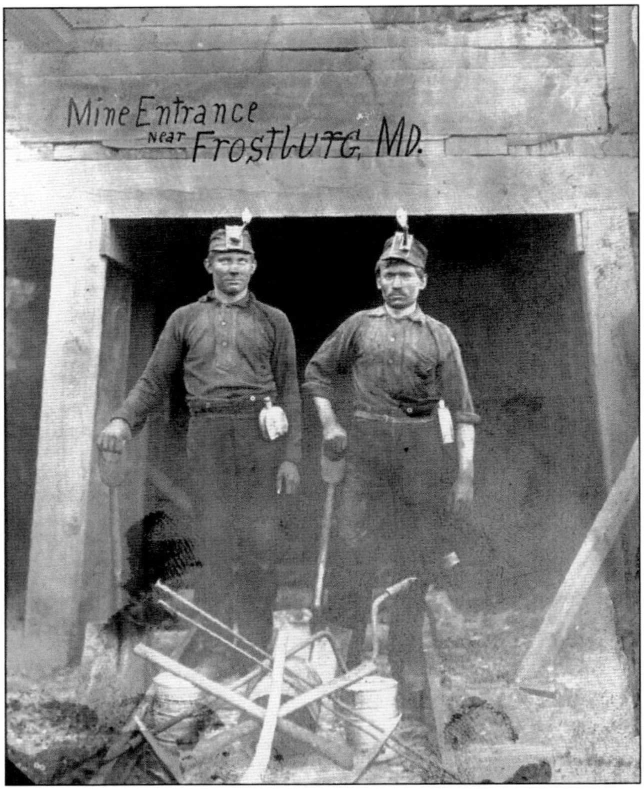

The miners of the Georges Creek region were once described as the "best-dressed miners." The stereotype of depressed conditions and men toiling unceasingly in the earth does not fit the miners of the Frostburg region. Most of the area miners saw mining as a skill and a craft. They owned their own homes and enjoyed a variety of economic and educational advantages that miners in other areas of the country did not.

One of the veins of coal in the region was known as Big Vein coal. So called because it was a large vein of coal (averaging about nine to ten feet in thickness) and high enough that the miners could actually stand in places to dig the coal, rather than work in a crouching or kneeling position that was common with many other veins of coal.

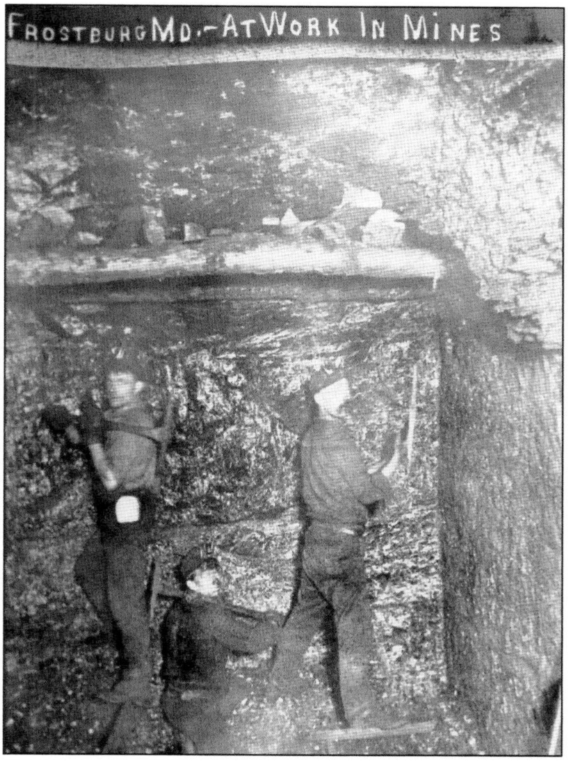

Work underground was hard and often dangerous, to be sure. Timbers propped up the tons of earth above them and pumps and fans tried to keep the work area as dry and free of dangerous gasses as possible. The Georges Creek coal mining region was spared the numbing disasters that occurred in other mining areas.

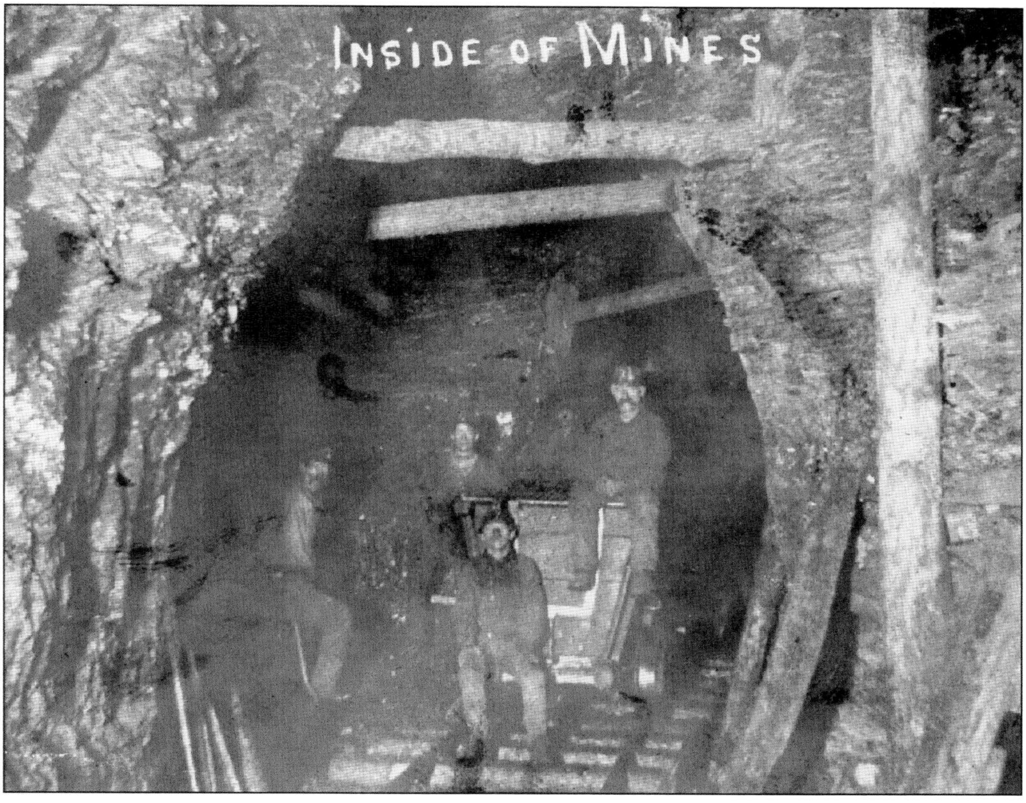

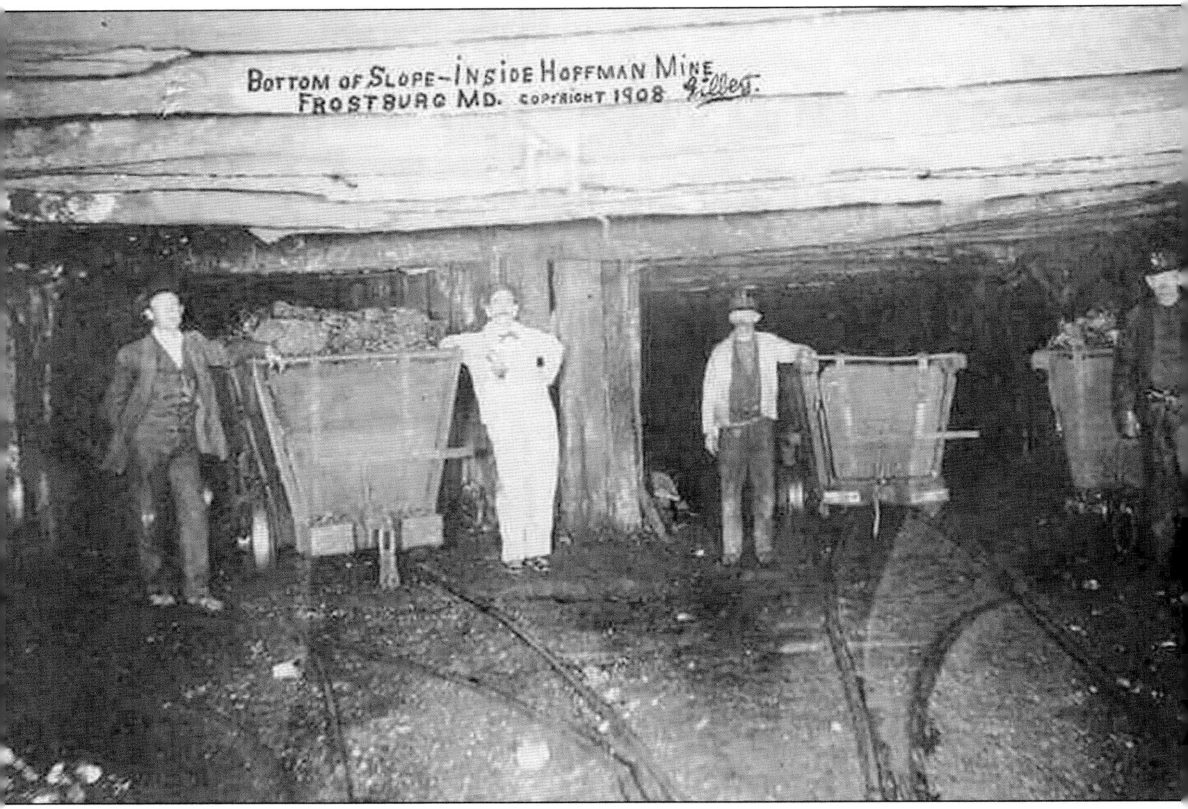

These loaded coal cars are inside the Hoffman Mine. Coal was dug or blasted out of the coalface and hand-loaded into coal cars for removal from the mine. The miner would be paid by the tonnage he dug by weighing the coal in the cars. Most of the mines of the area were slope or drift mines, meaning that the mine went into the hillsides rather than drop into deep shafts. It was in the Hoffman Mine in 1901 that Consolidation Coal Company installed the first ventilating fan for safety.

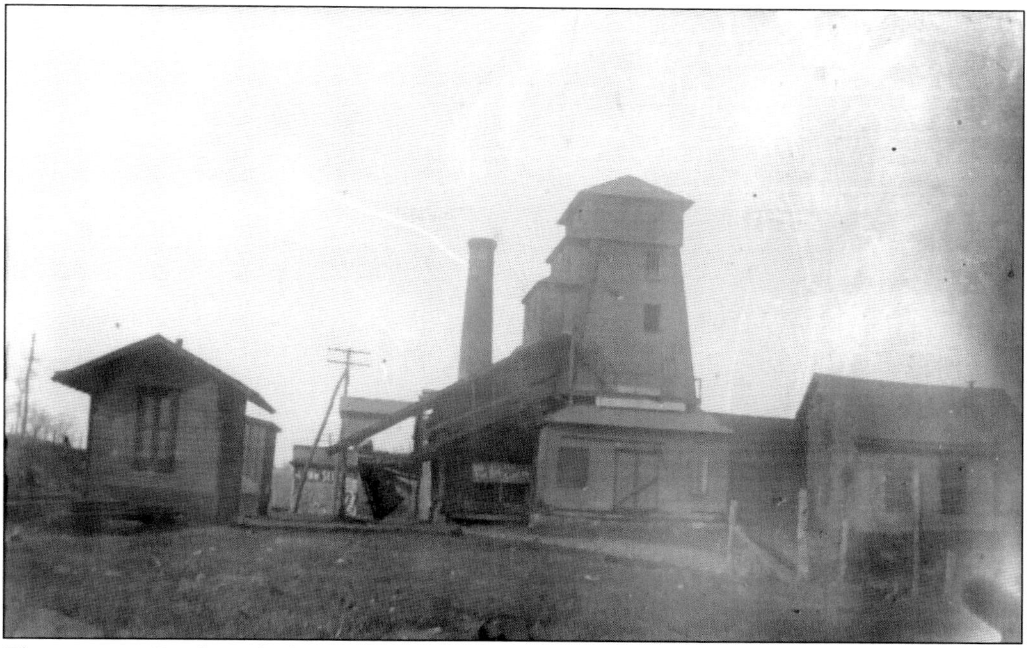

The mine at Borden Shaft was one of the exceptions to the more common drift and slope mines of the area. Sunk in 1859 by the Borden Mining Company, this shaft mine was worked until 1889. The shaft was 150 feet deep and had two compartments lined with wood. The tall building in the center is the hoist house that allowed entrance and exit from the shaft for coal and miners.

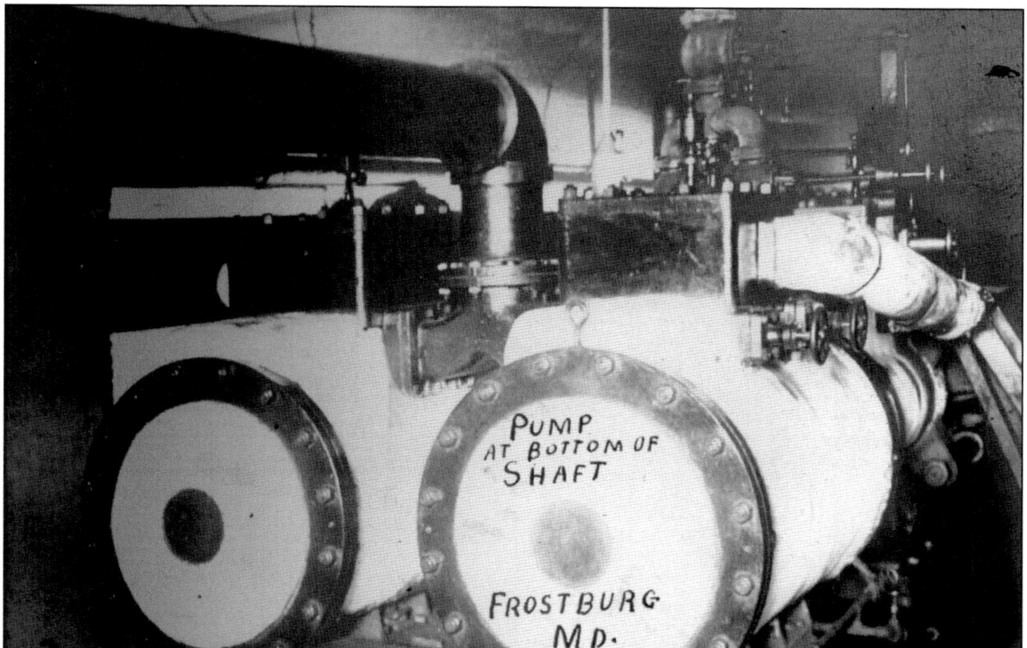

Even with pumping machinery such as this, problems with water drainage forced Borden Shaft's closure in 1889. It stood idle until 1911 when the Consolidation Coal Company was able to drain it by use of the Hoffman Drainage Tunnel (see page 38) and the mine was reopened.

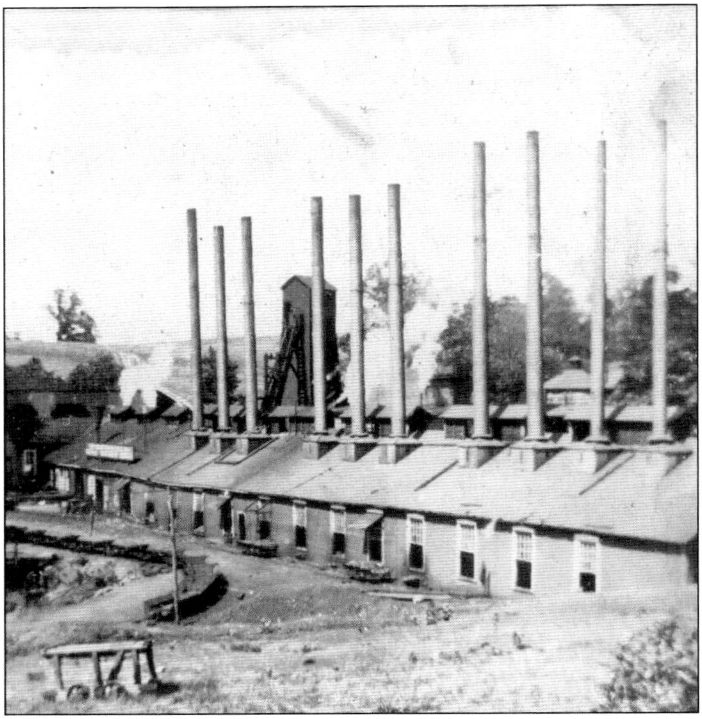

The new shaft mine of the Consolidation Coal Company was originally built as a pumping station to pump water out of the mines. With the building of the Hoffman Drainage Tunnel (see page 38), the need for the pumping station was unnecessary, so the company began to mine coal out of the shaft. Located on the Little Vein of coal (approximately four feet thick as opposed to the nine or ten feet of Big Vein), by 1910, this mine was viewed as "a model of coal mining efficiency."

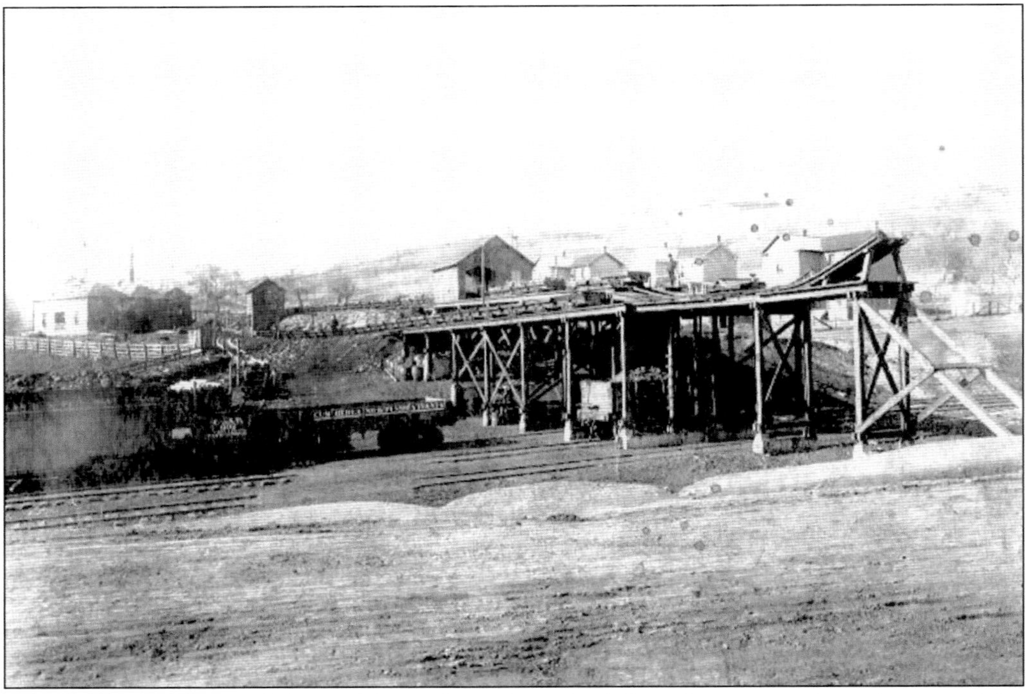

The Brophy Tipple at Eckhart Mines shows how loaded coal cars were brought out of the mines and dumped into waiting railroad cars below the tipple. Once the coal cars were emptied, gravity slid them back towards the mine. The building in the middle of the tipple is the weigh house, where loaded coal cars were weighed to determine how much the miner was paid for his toil.

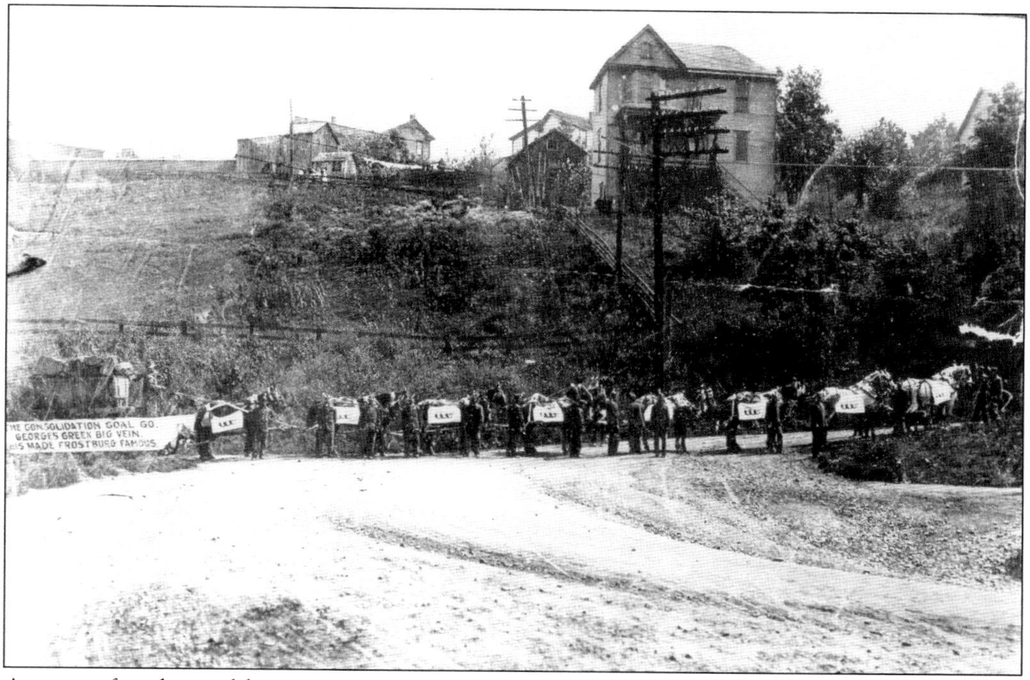

A team of mules and horses prepare to pull a wagon with a loaded coal car up Depot Street to take part in the Centennial Parade of 1912. Consolidation Coal Company, founded in the Georges Creek area in 1864 with the "consolidation" of several small mining companies, was the largest coal company in the area well into the 20th century.

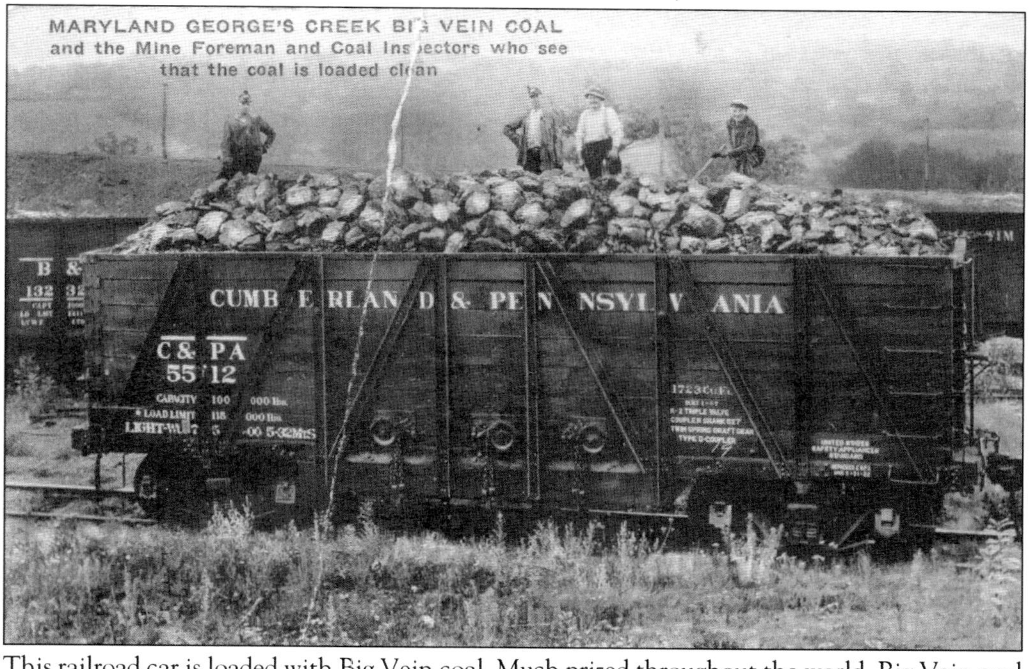

This railroad car is loaded with Big Vein coal. Much prized throughout the world, Big Vein coal made its way into the furnaces of some international customers. A single block of Big Vein coal, measuring four-by-four-by-ten feet and weighing five tons became a world attraction and was on display at the International Fair in Milan, Italy in 1924.

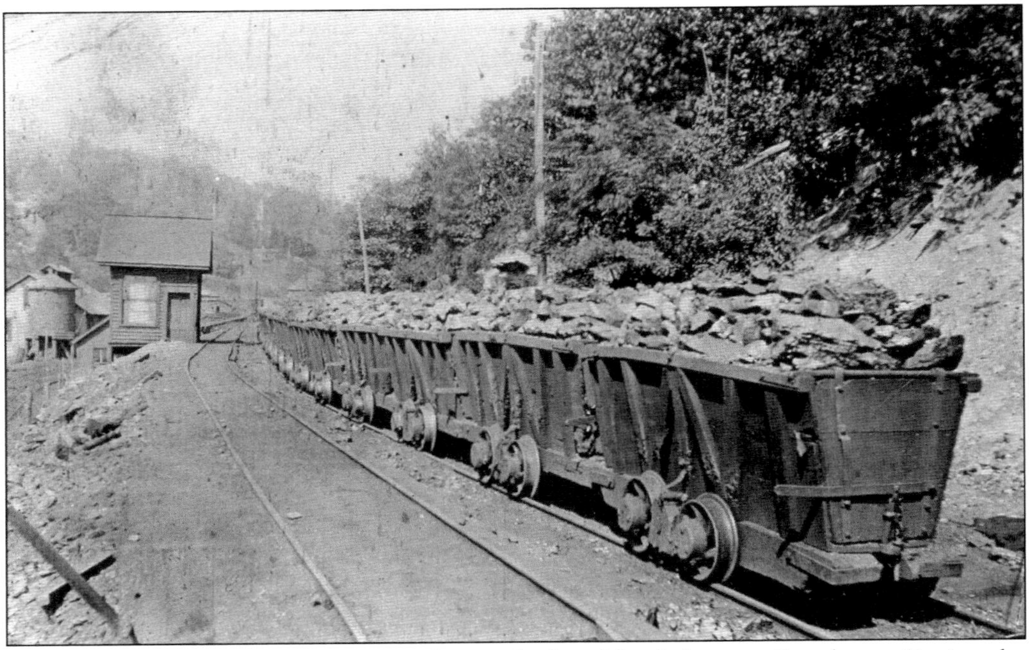

These loaded coal cars are waiting to be weighed and loaded into railroad cars. During the boom time around the turn of the last century, the Georges Creek region was one of the major producers of coal. The mines of the Consolidation Coal Company in the region alone extracted 1,770,844 tons of coal in 1899.

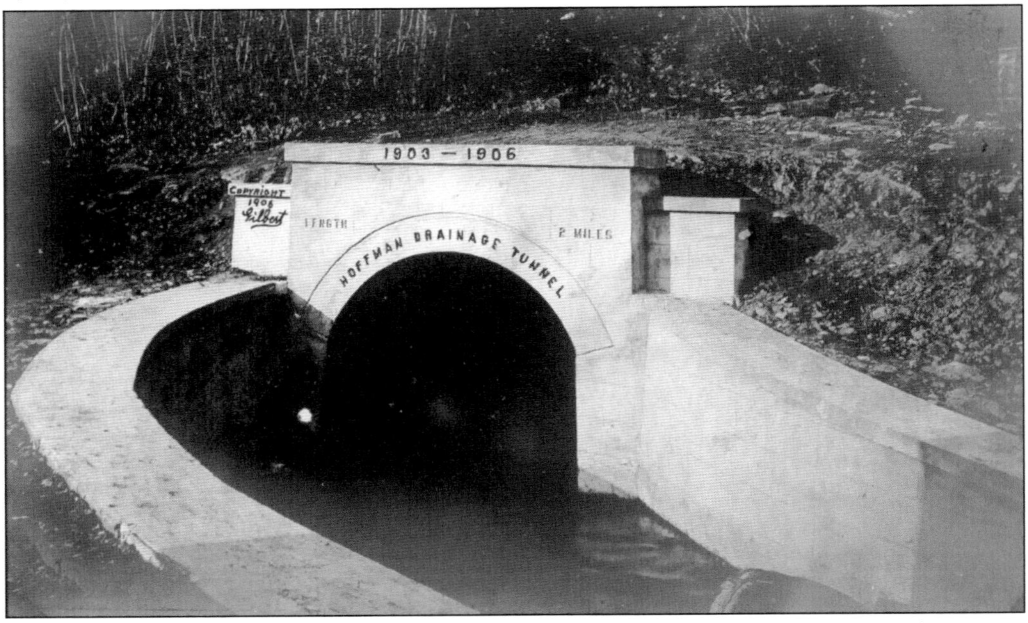

The Hoffman Drainage Tunnel helped alleviate the problem of excess water in the mines. Costly pumps ran constantly to keep groundwater from filling the mine works, but in 1903 the Consolidation Coal Company contracted Welsh immigrant Philip Jenkins and his four sons, William, Edward, James, and Philip Jr. to begin digging a tunnel to allow water to drain naturally out of the mines. Almost two mines long and costing $300,000 the drainage tunnel was such an engineering success that water continues to drain from the portal shown here.

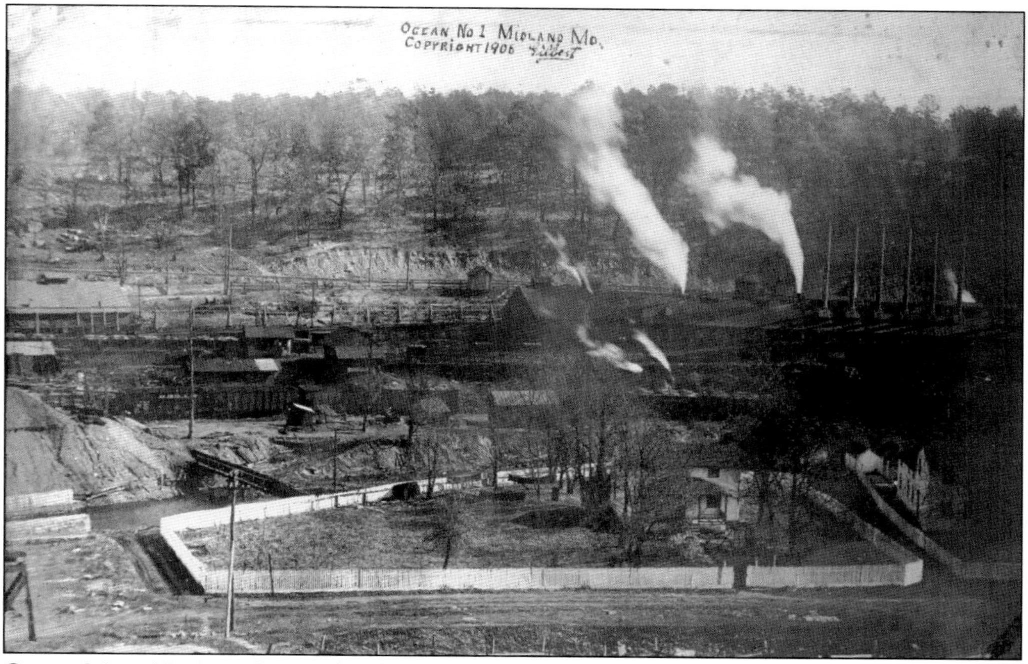

Ocean Mine No.1 works south of Frostburg, near Midland, and was one of Consol's larger operations. While a rather strange name for a series of coalmines in the mountains of Western Maryland, the name is derived from the original Ocean Steam Coal Company that was founded by William Aspinwall. Aspinwall was a steamship operator who appreciated the qualities of Georges Creek coal for his and other steamships. Consolidating into the Consolidation Coal Company, the Ocean mines were integral parts of Consol's operations in Western Maryland.

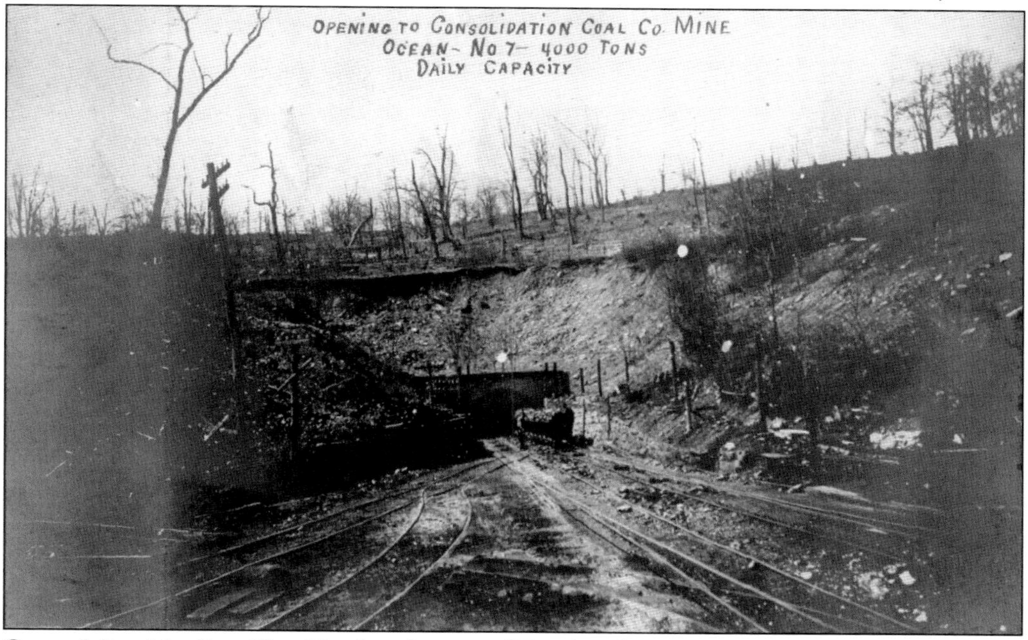

Ocean Mine No. 7 at Klondike (south west of Frostburg) was reported to be the largest slope mines ever worked in the Georges Creek region. Operating from 1897 to 1924, this mine once employed over 1,000 miners and often mined over 5,000 tons a day at peak production.

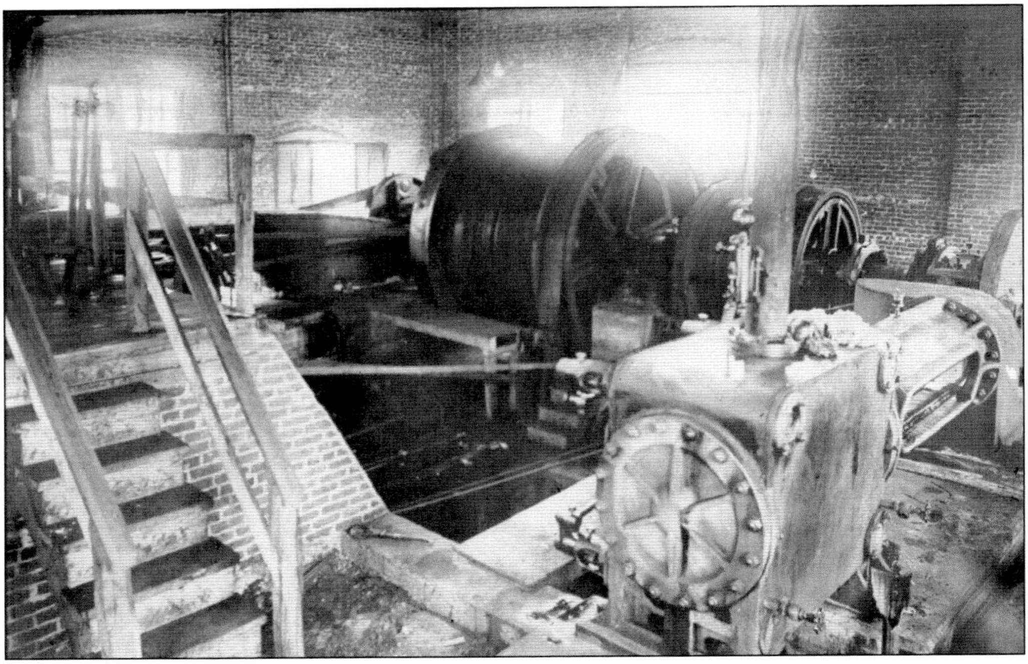

While mules commonly brought loaded coal cars out of the mines, by the 20th century new methods of transportation for safely working the mines became more common. The "new engine" at Ocean No. 7 mine could haul a trip of 50 loaded coal cars from the bottom to the top of the mine within six minutes, while lowering 50 empty cars to the work area at the same time

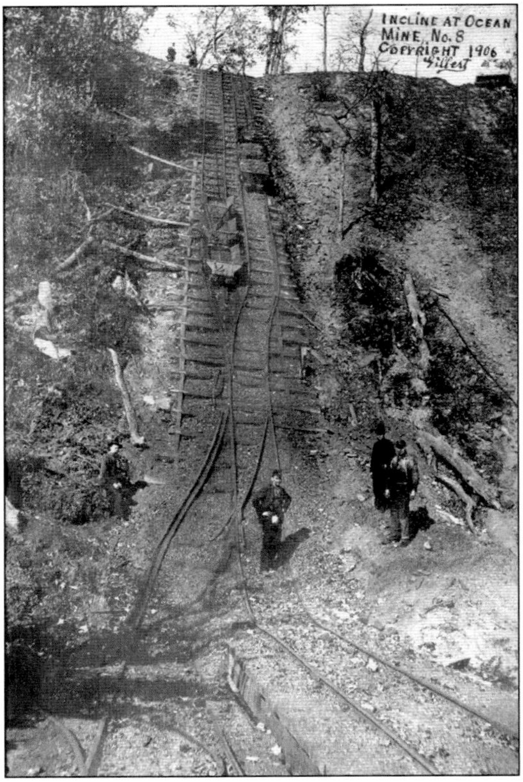

The incline at Ocean No. 8 mine used gravity to move loaded and empty coal cars around the facility. As the loaded cars were pulled to the top, the empties ran back down. A close look at the photograph shows the loaded cars to the right and the empties sliding down on the left.

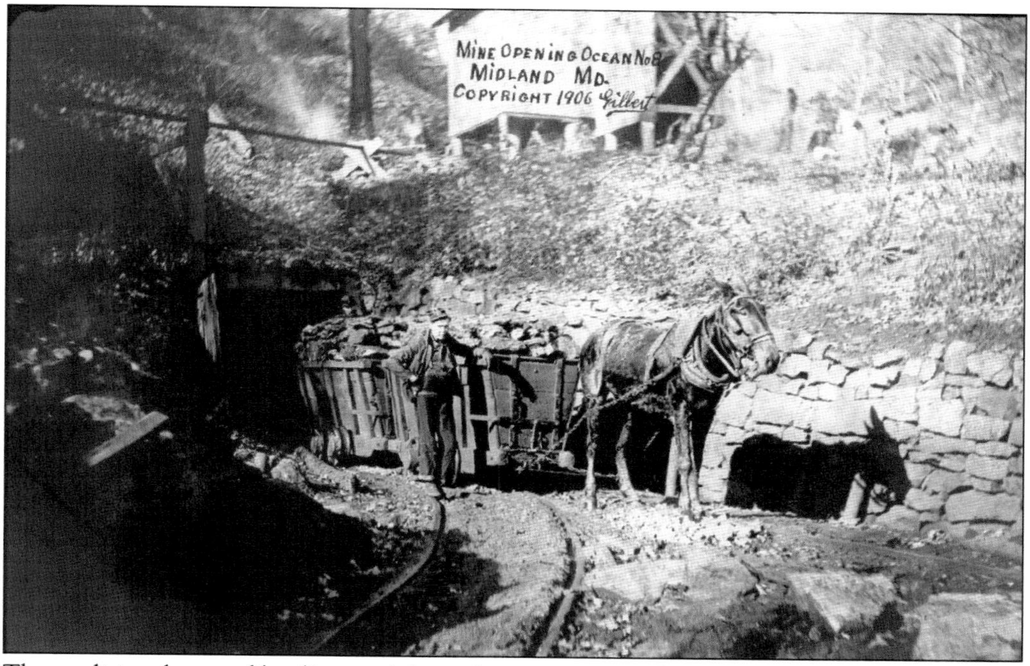

The traditional way of hauling coal from the mine was mule-power. A driver and his mules would work as a team. After years of pulling coal cars, mules got used to pulling a certain weight. Stories abound on how a mule, hooked to several cars, would listen to the number of "thumps" the cars made as he began to pull. If there was just one more thump than he was used to, the mule would often stop until the driver unhooked the extra cars!

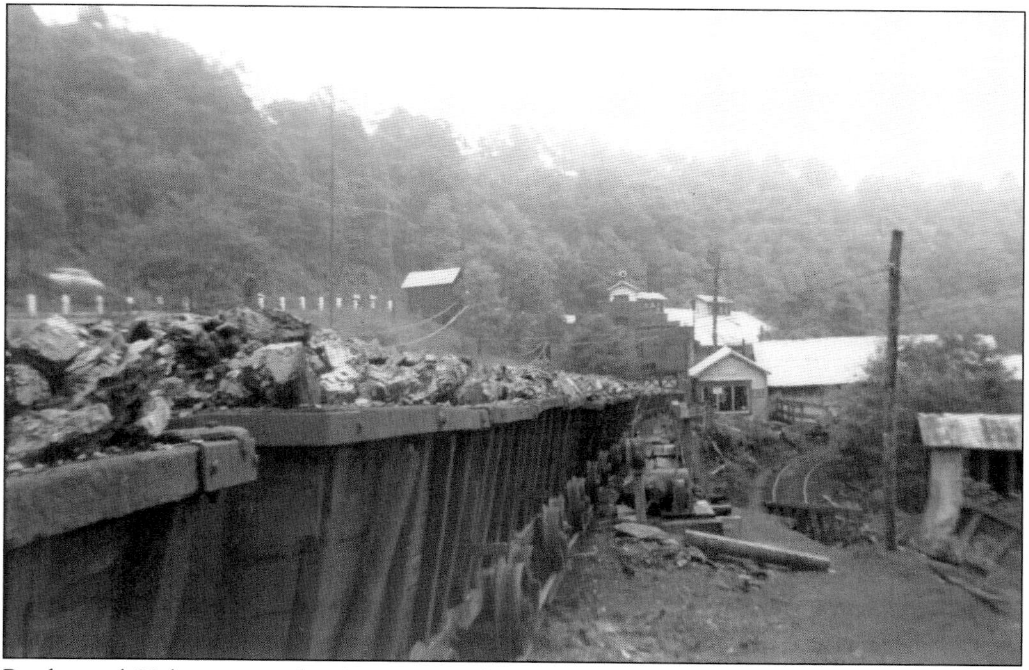

By the mid-20th century, the Georges Creek region was in decline as a major coal producer. However, as this 1950s photograph shows, coal was still being mined in some areas of the region. (Courtesy of FSU Special Collections.)

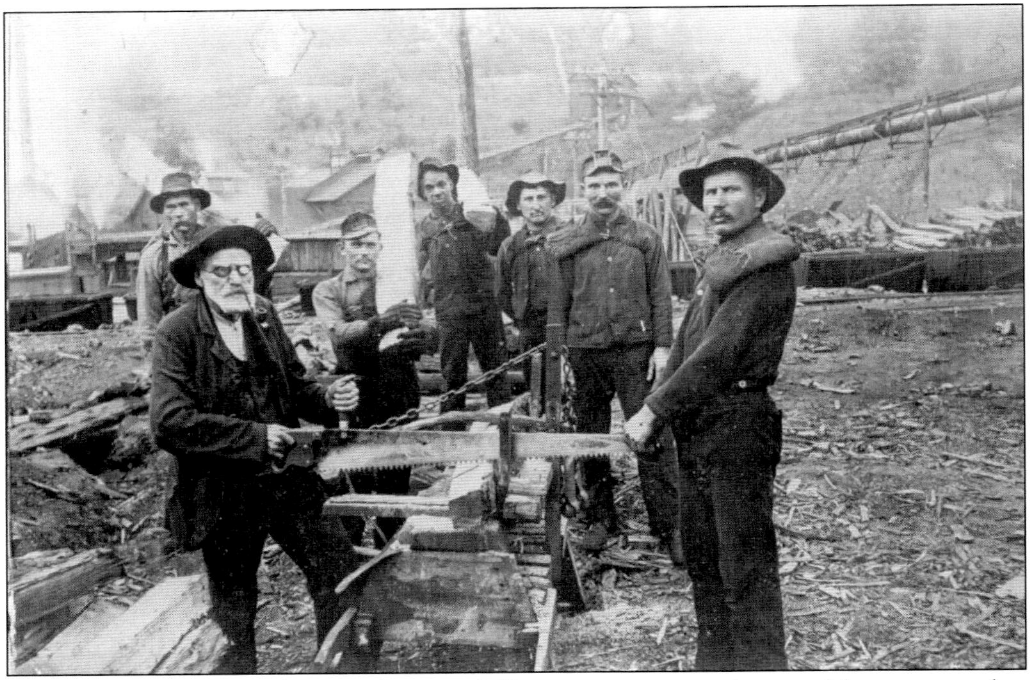

Not all of the miners work was underground. Here, sawyers are cutting wood for props or other uses in the mines.

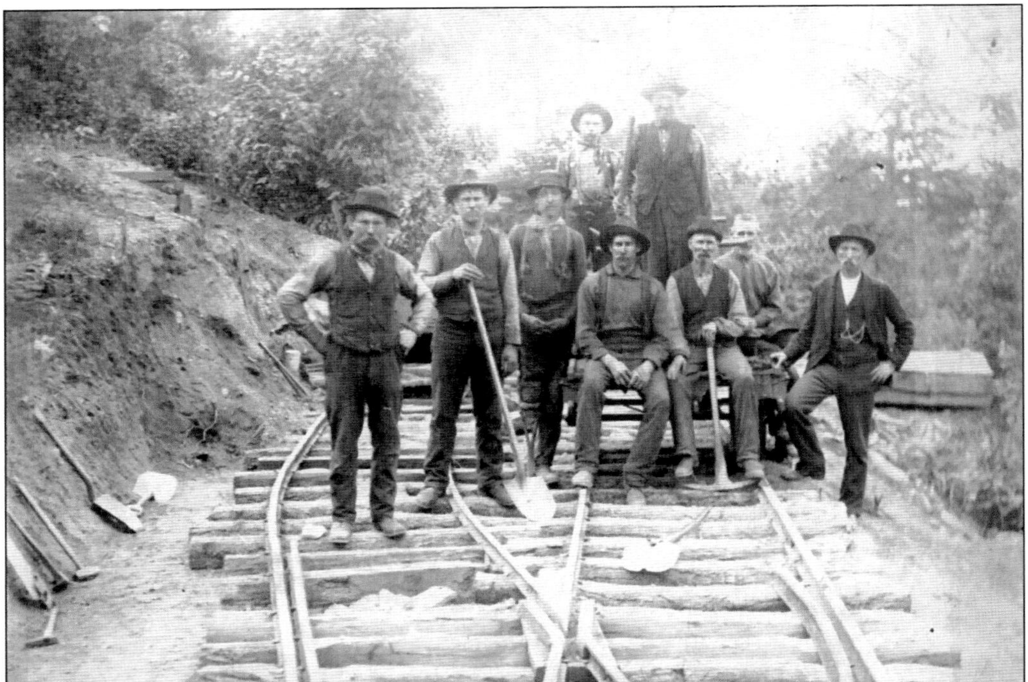

Miles of track were necessary for moving coal cars and miners through the mines and to the waiting railroad cars. Here, trackmen are at work on a switch outside of Eckhart Mines in the late 19th century.

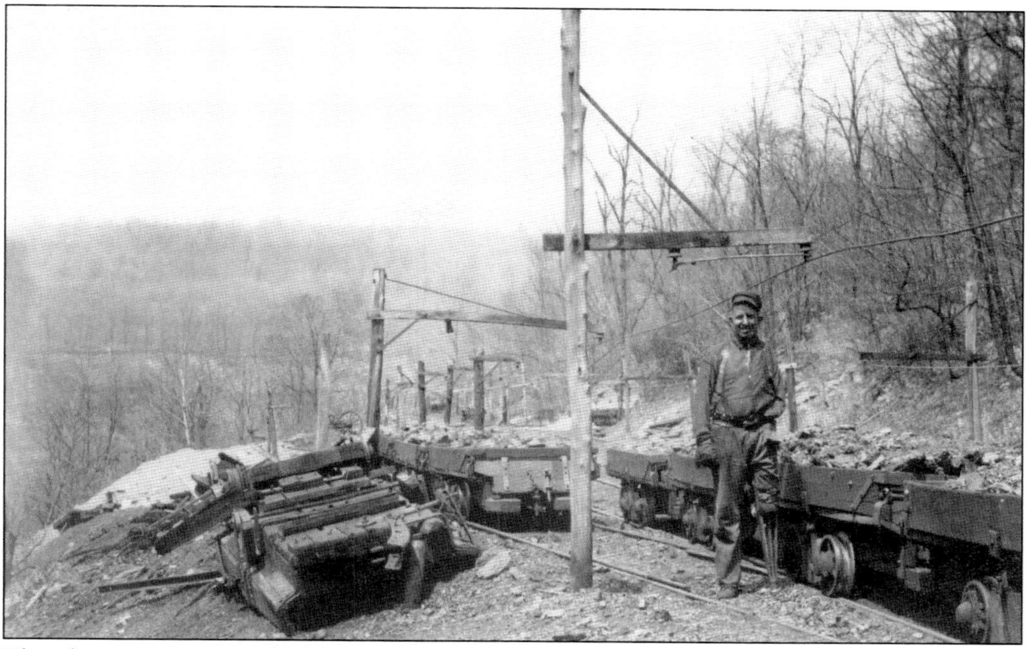

The electricity was supplied by the wires running overhead. By the 20th century, electricity was replacing mule power to move the loaded cars out of the mines. Notice the left arm and leg of the miner, depicting the dangers of work in the coal industry! (Courtesy of FSU Special Collections.)

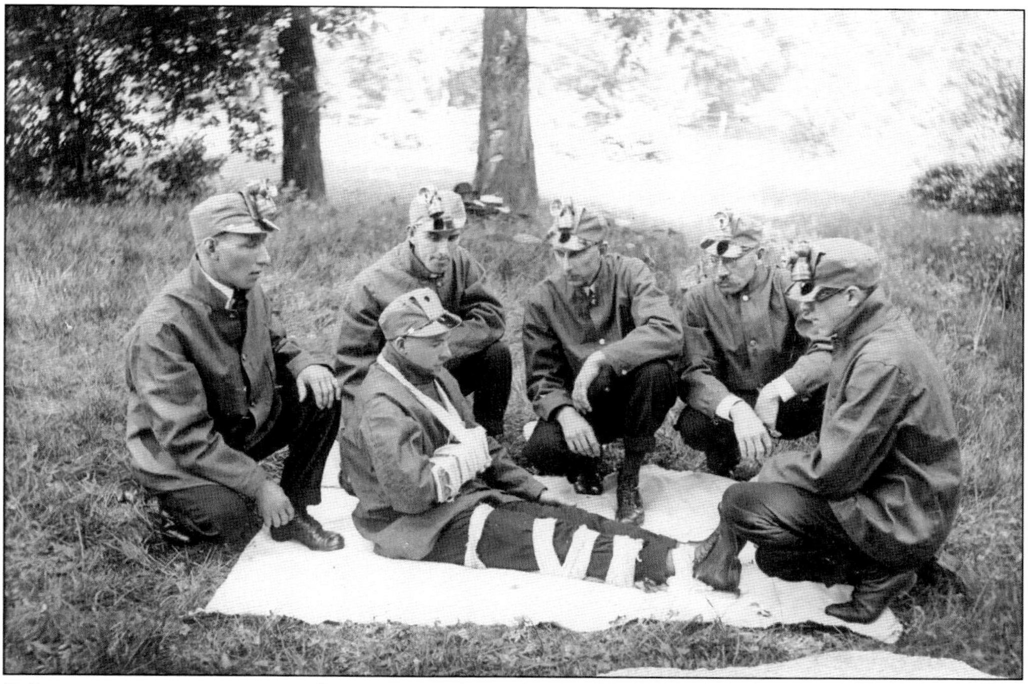

Safety was a major concern for miner and employer alike. Safety drills were common. There were even competitions between different company safety teams. For several years in the 1920s, Consolidation Coal safety teams walked away with many trophies and honors. Here is a photograph of a Consol team practicing in the early 20th century.

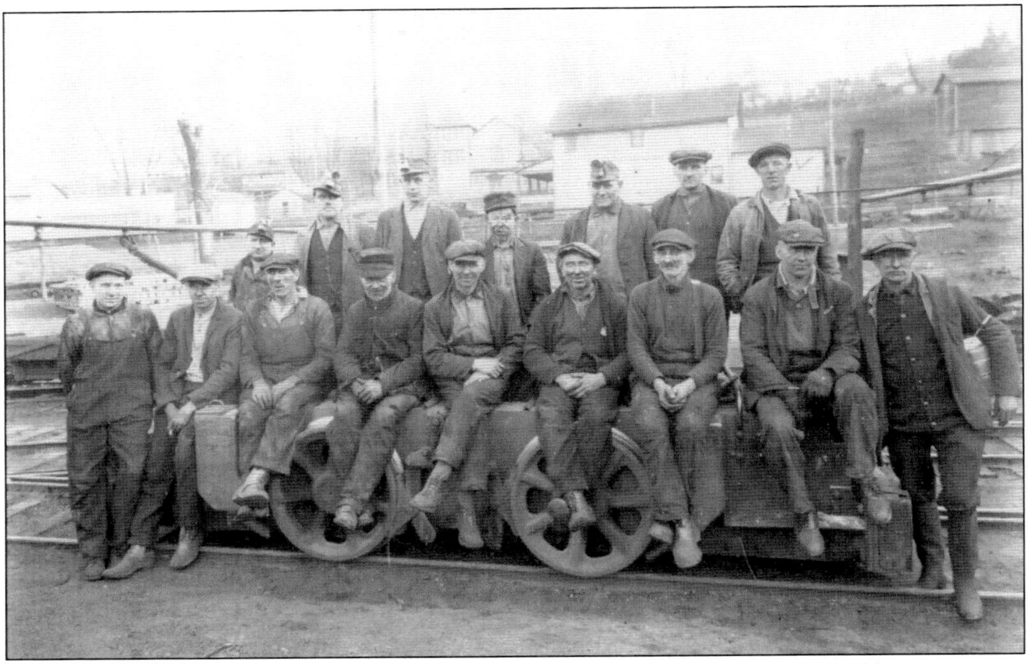

Miners are photographed at Consolidation Coal Company's No. 4 mine at Eckhart Mines in the early 20th century. Mine No. 4 was opened by the Maryland Mining Company around 1835 and was operated intermittently until the early 1950s.

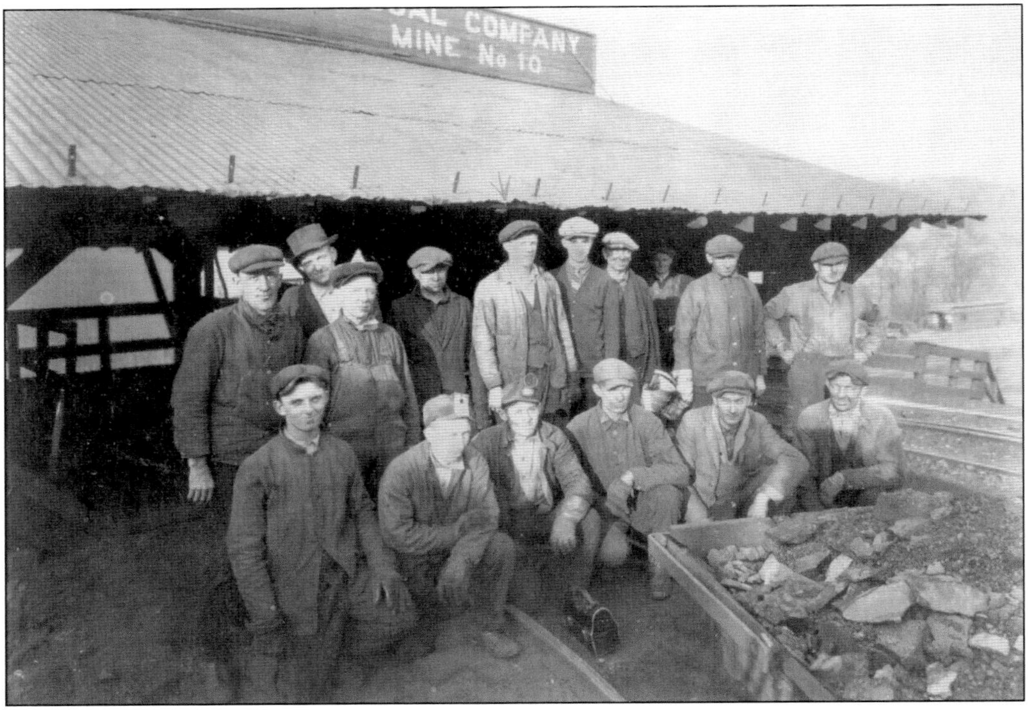

Consolidation Coal Company mines No. 4 and No. 10 had portals near each other in Eckhart Mines. While No. 4 was Big Vein coal, No. 10 was Little Vein coal. Here is another group of Consol miners who worked the company's Eckhart Mines.

A motorized "man-trip" is bringing miners out of Consolidation Coal Company's No. 10 mine at Eckhart Mines in the early 1920s. The engine's trolley can be seen contacting the electric lines, giving the juice needed to power the man trip. Such advances were welcomed by the miners, saving miles of walking to and from the underground work-faces.

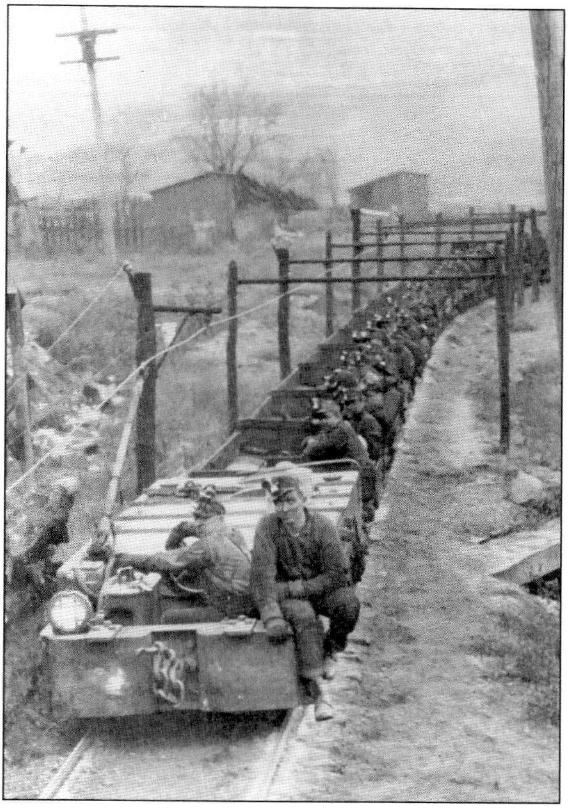

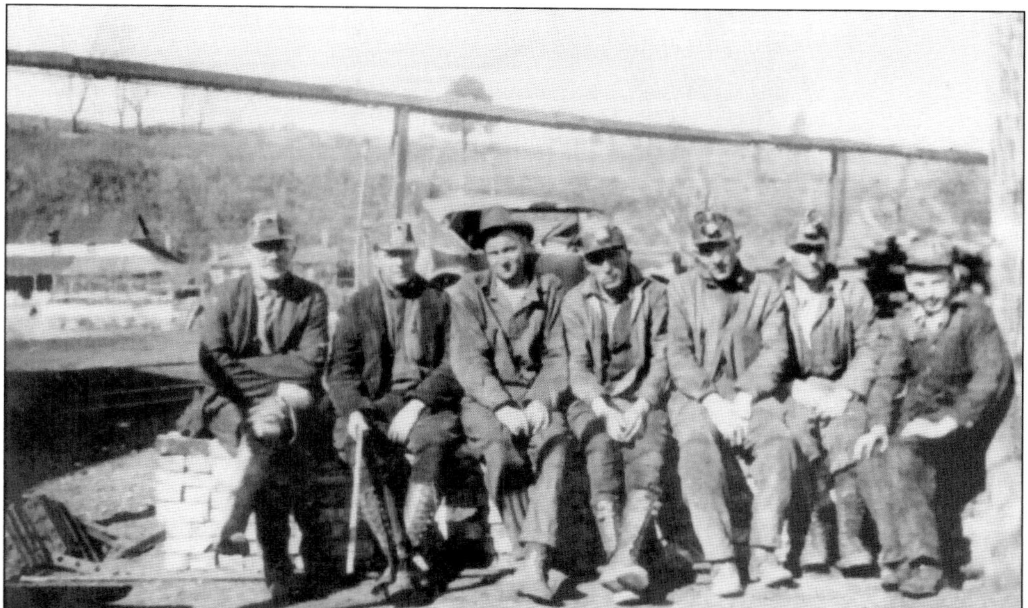

Some later 20th-century miners are pictured here at Eckhart Mines. The clean faces show that their shifts have not yet begun!

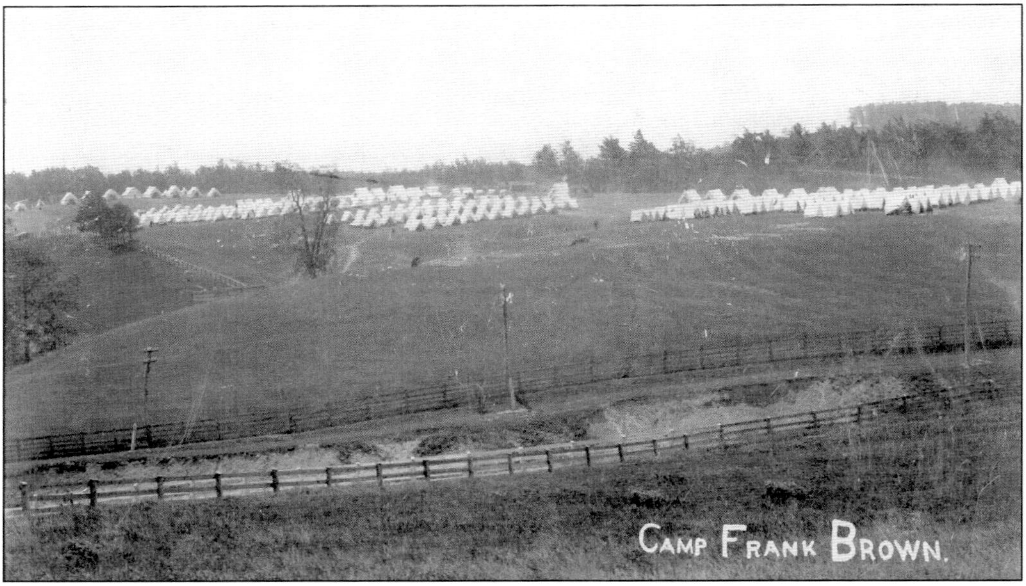

In June of 1894, the Frostburg coalmining region found itself in the throes of a major strike. As strikebreakers were brought in to keep the mines open, striking miners took to acts of vandalism and violence. At the order of Governor Brown, regiments of the Maryland National Guard were sent to the area to maintain order. During the month of June, the Guard was encamped at what was named Camp Frank Brown, after the governor.

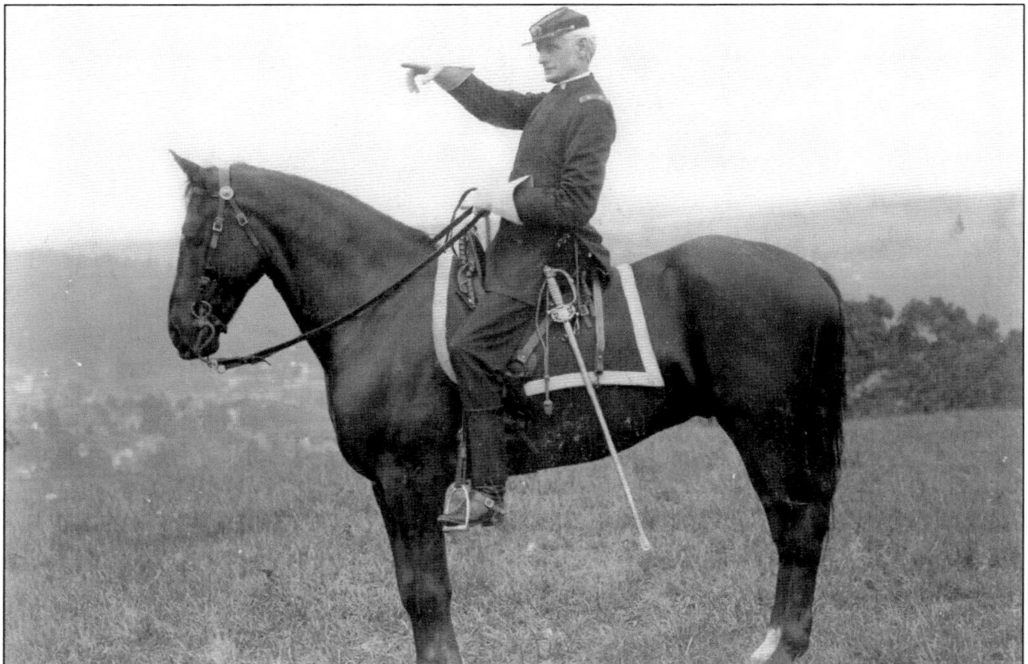

Maj. Gen. H. Kyd Douglas commanded the National Guard troops. Kyd Douglas was a college graduate and lawyer who joined the Confederate forces in the Civil War and gained some notoriety as a member of Stonewall Jackson's staff, all of which he related in his embellished autobiography, *I Rode with Stonewall.*

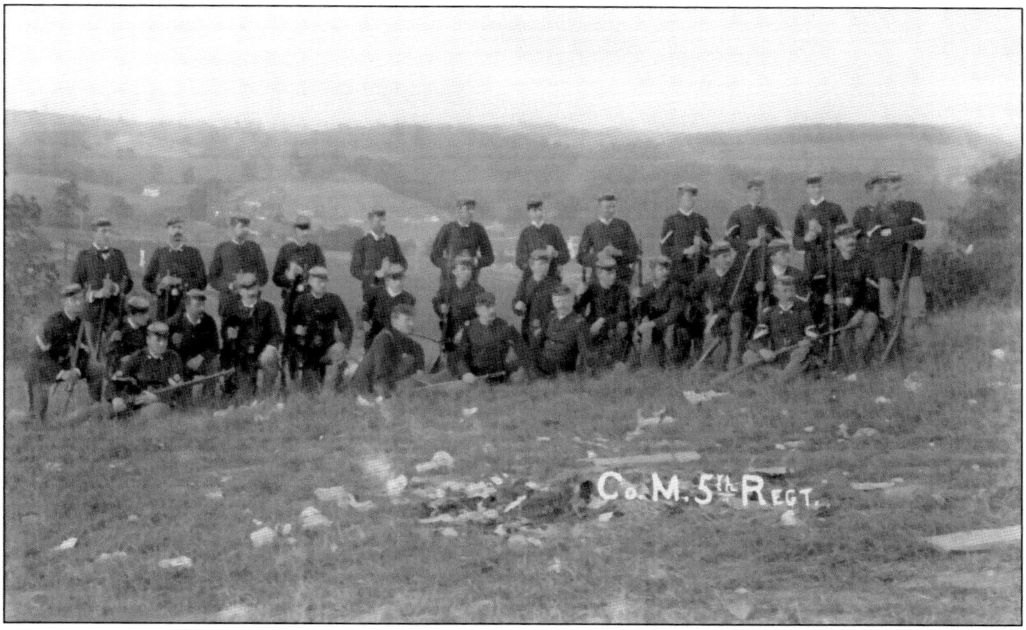

Members of the Fifth regiment of the Maryland National Guard are pictured here during the June 1894 encampment at Camp Frank Brown. While there was no need for force by the troops, it was reported that the thousand or so troops who spent time in Frostburg "behaved like boys at summer camp." Many were away from home for the first time and made the best of their time, often "consorting" with local girls who were attracted by men in uniform!

THE HOFFMAN MINE SONG

By

Robert Simpson of Frostburg, Maryland, (1900)

We are asking one another as we pass the time of day,
Why men resort to strikes to gain their proper pay?
And why the labor unions now will not be recognized?
But the actions of the companies must not be criticized.

Chorus

Then the men who fight for justice, none can blame them,
May luck attend wherever they may roam;
And no son of his shall ever live to shame him,
While liberty and honor rule his home.

Oh, the troubles there at Hoffman came about this way:
The grasping corporation had the audacity to say,
If you all deny the union and forswear your liberty,
We'll give you all a chance to live and die in slavery.

See that sturdy band of miners who made a stand that day,
With determination in their faces which surely went to say,
"No men shall drive us from our homes for which we've toiled so long,
"No men shall take our places, for here's where we belong."

A woman with a rifle, her husband in the crowd;
She handed him the weapon, they cheered her long and loud;
He kissed her and said, "Mary, you go home till we are through,"
But she answered, "No, if you're on strike, I'm going to stick to you."

Oh, the workmen there at Hoffman knew they were face to face
With a soulless corporation, and they knew it was their place
To protect their wives and daughters, and that they've nobly done;
And the angels will applaud them when a victory they have won.

This folk-song was discovered in a Scrapbook now in the possession of Valley High School, Lonaconing, Maryland. It was printed in a local newspaper. *With the permission of Mr. Jack A. Petry, Principal.*

The Hoffman Mine Song was typical of the songs, poetry, and other writings that came out of the miner's struggle for unionization, better wages, and safer working conditions in the mines.

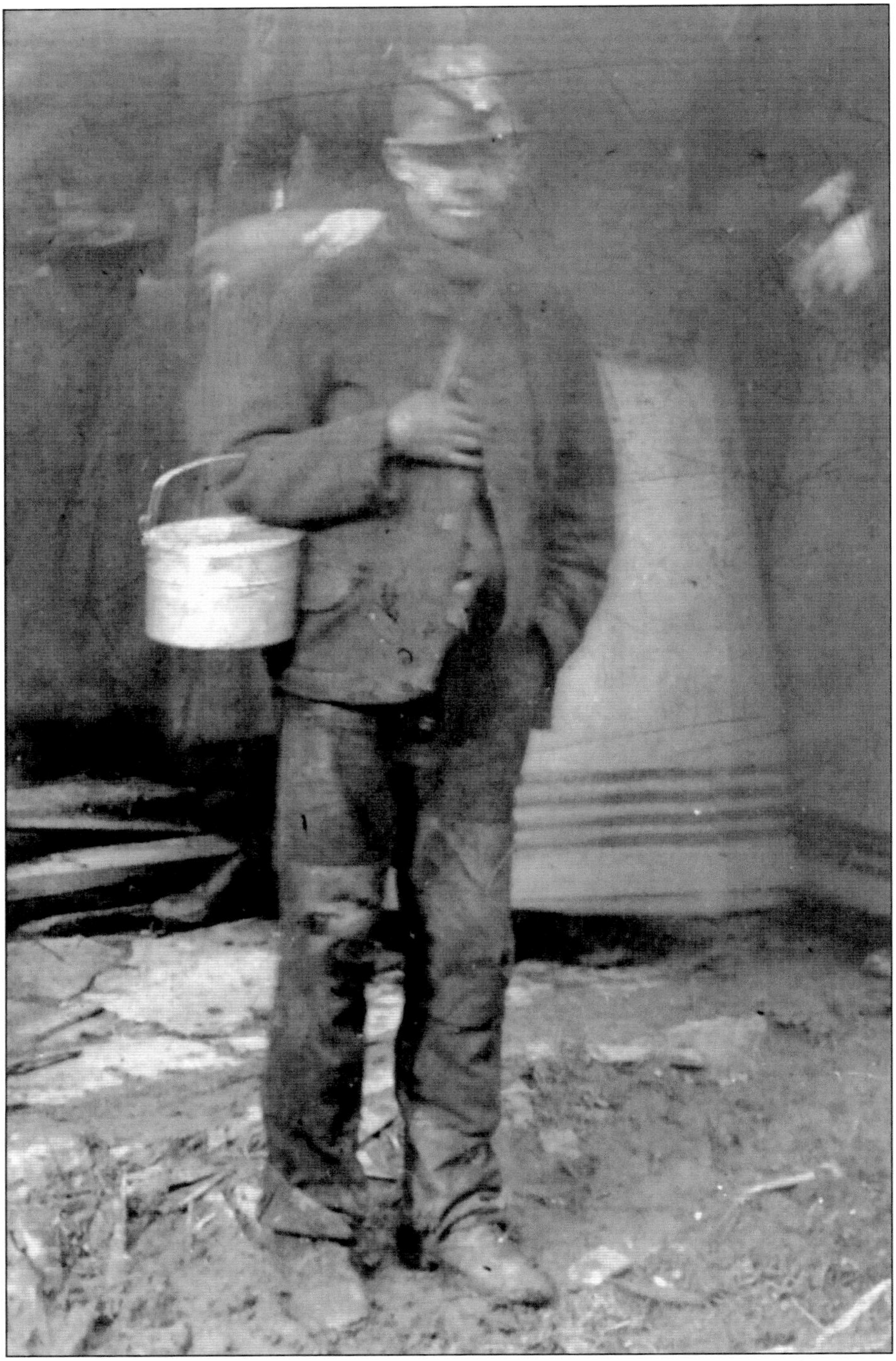

A young miner is caught for posterity as he walks along Water Street in Frostburg in 1891. Typical of many of the young men and boys who worked the mines, he is clutching his circular lunch bucket with his mining lamp on his head. Patches on the knees show he toiled in the lower Little Vein coal seam. Thousands like him worked long, hard hours in a harsh environment that demanded skill and caution. Much of the success that Frostburg enjoyed as a coalmining center is owed to young men like this one.

Four

Going "Up Street"

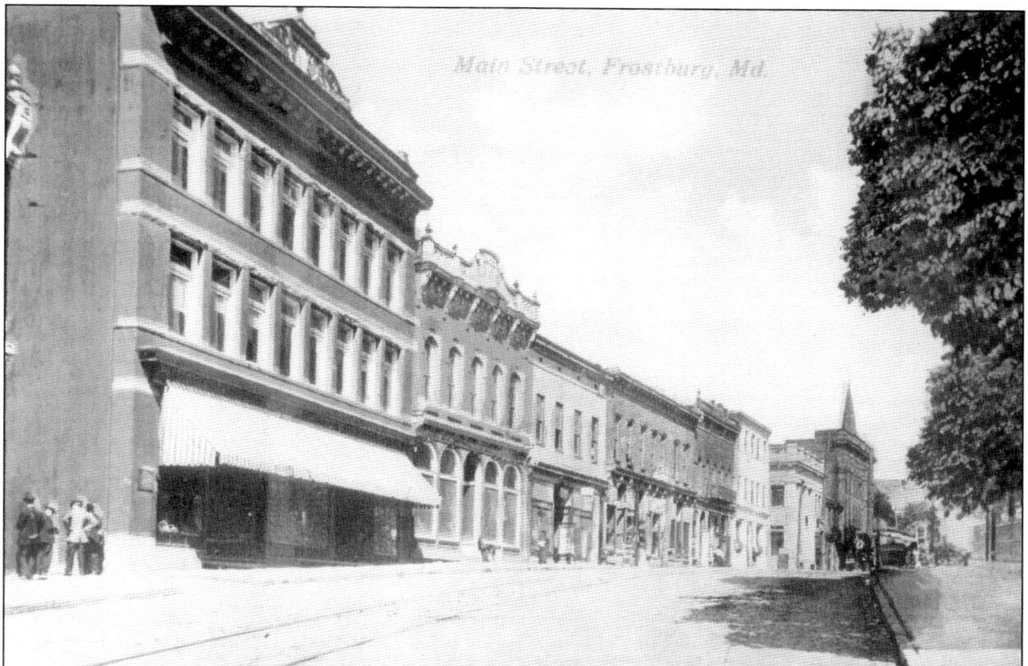

Looking toward the central business district of turn-of-the-century Frostburg, the tracks of the electric railway can be seen in the cobblestones of what was once referred to as Union Street. The Hitchins Brothers store is to the left and the trees in St. Michael churchyard are visible on the right.

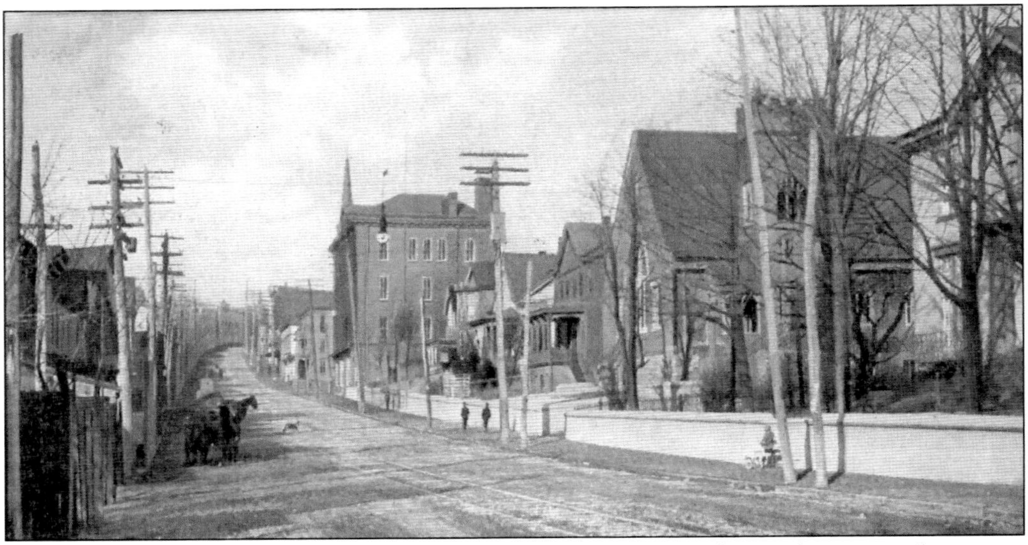

Looking toward "up-street" from near Bowery Street, the opera house dominates the center of this turn-of-the-century postcard, with the First English Baptist Church seen to the right. The trolley car tracks and collection of electric and telegraph poles show a town ready for the new century.

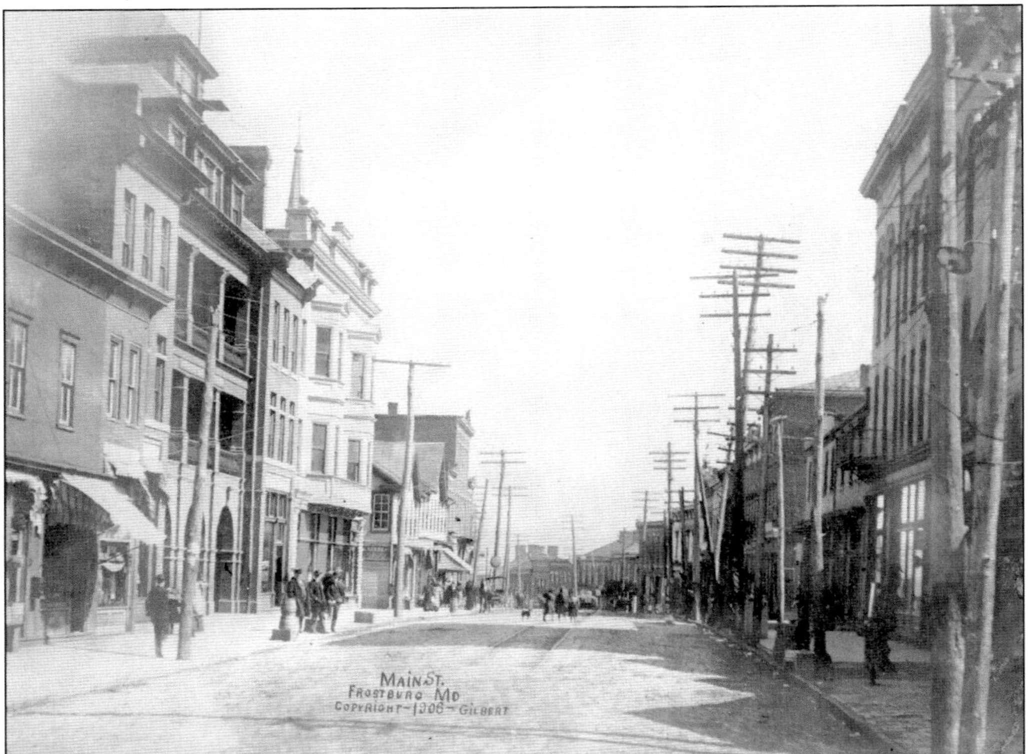

This is the central business district on Main Street looking towards the east in an early 20th-century photograph. The arches and balconies of the Gladstone Hotel stand just to the left of the bay-windowed Shea Building. Across Main Street from the Gladstone stands t he Eleanor Building.

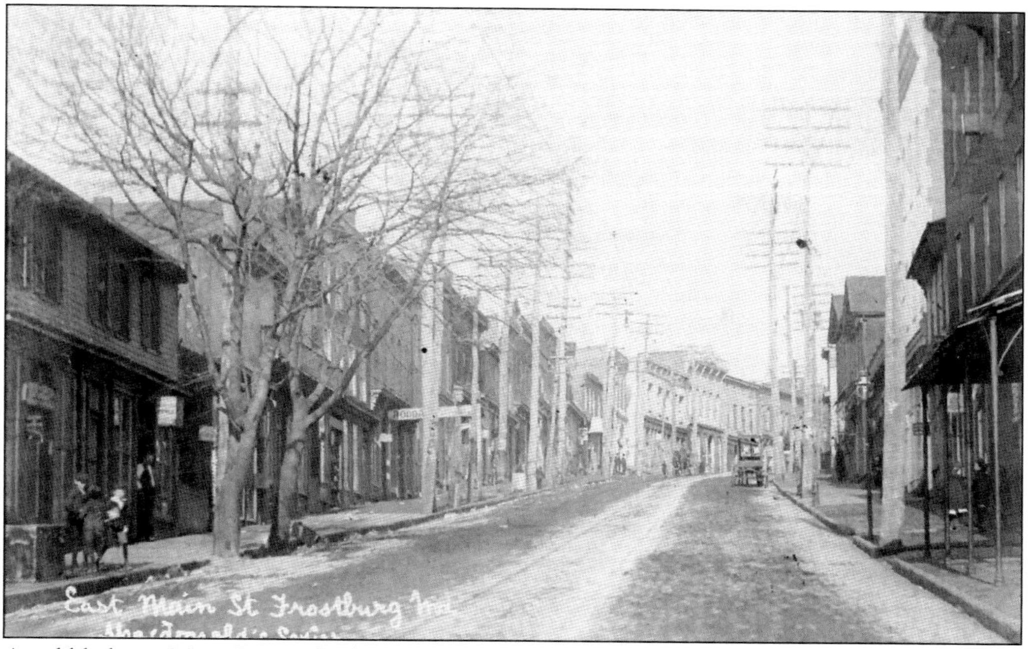

A cobbled east Main Street climbs up the hill toward the central business district. This hill was the location for downhill "ordinary races" (the high-wheeled bicycles without brakes), some wintertime sledding, and is still used today for the annual Fourth of July Soap-Box Derby Races.

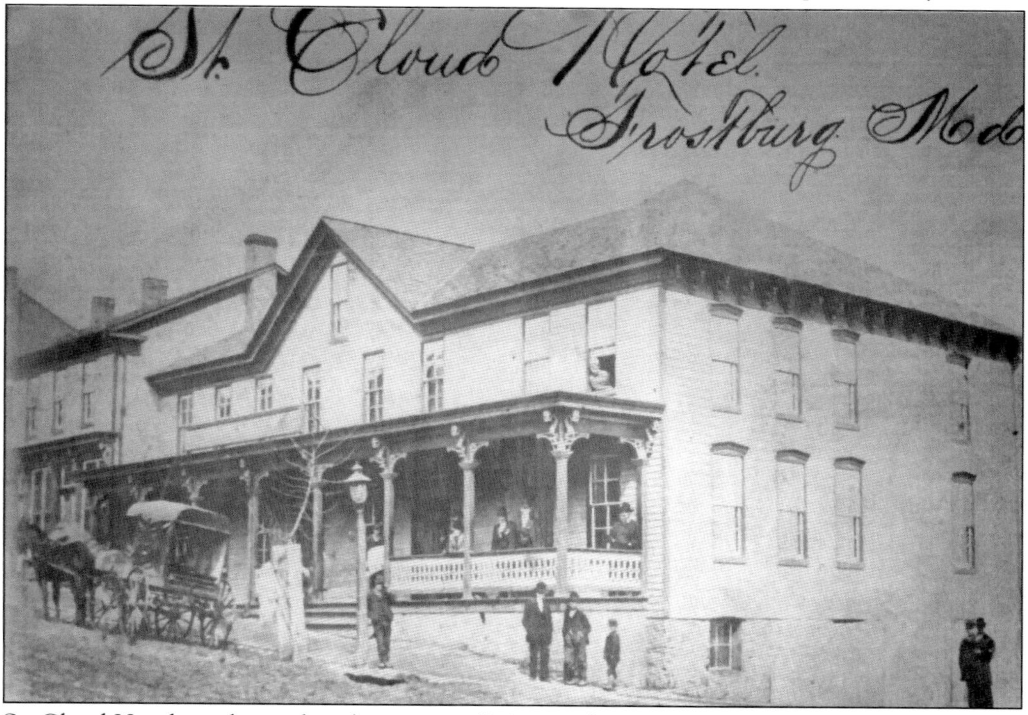

St. Cloud Hotel was located at the corner of Main and Depot Streets. Originally the Frostburg Hotel, the St. Cloud was said to be one of the oldest hotels in Frostburg. In 1887, it boasted 22 bedrooms, a 100-seat dining room and, to show they were truly modern, a large, indoor bathroom. No need to use an outdoor privy or chamber pot!

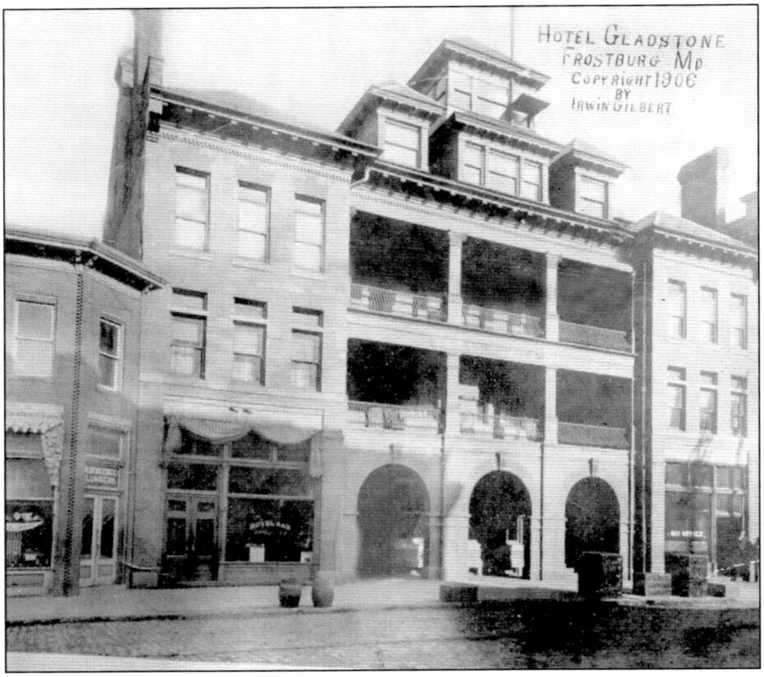

One of the showpieces of turn-of-the-century Frostburg, complete with a ballroom, electric lights, and horsehair mattresses on brass beds, was the Gladstone Hotel. The Gladstone was built in 1896 by William R. Percy and was named for his son-in-law, William Ewart Gladstone Hitchins. In 1925, it was remodeled and operated by the Gunter family as the Gunter Hotel; it is currently owned by the Falinger family.

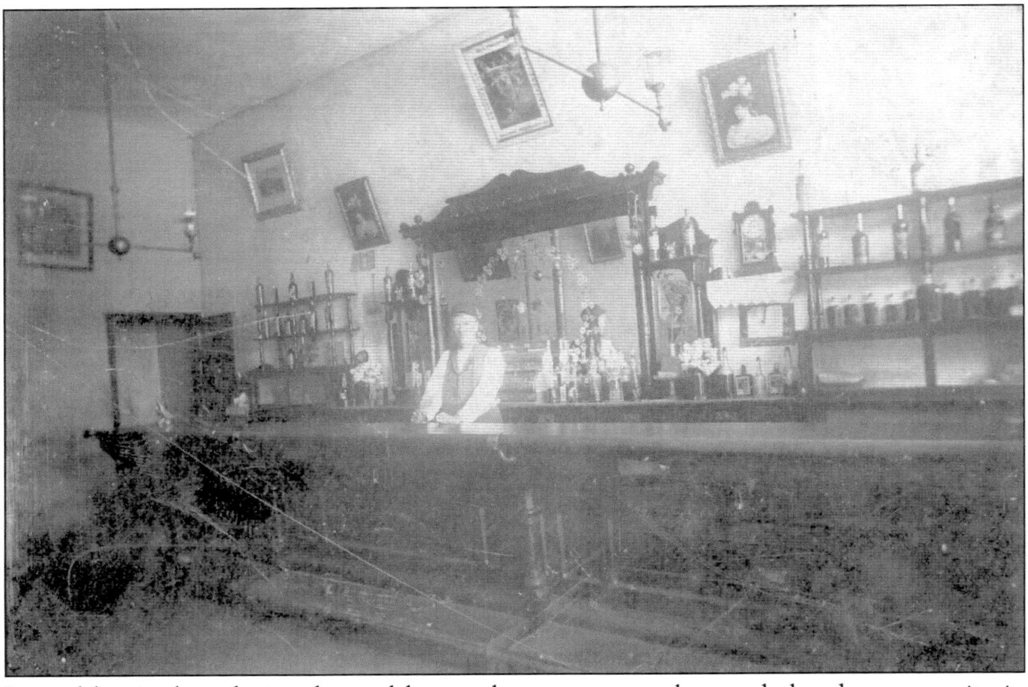

Legend has it that, during the coal boom, there were more bars and churches per capita in Frostburg than in any other town in Maryland. While that was not quite accurate, there never was a shortage of places for residents and visitors alike to wet their whistles, such as this bar that was located in the Gladstone Hotel.

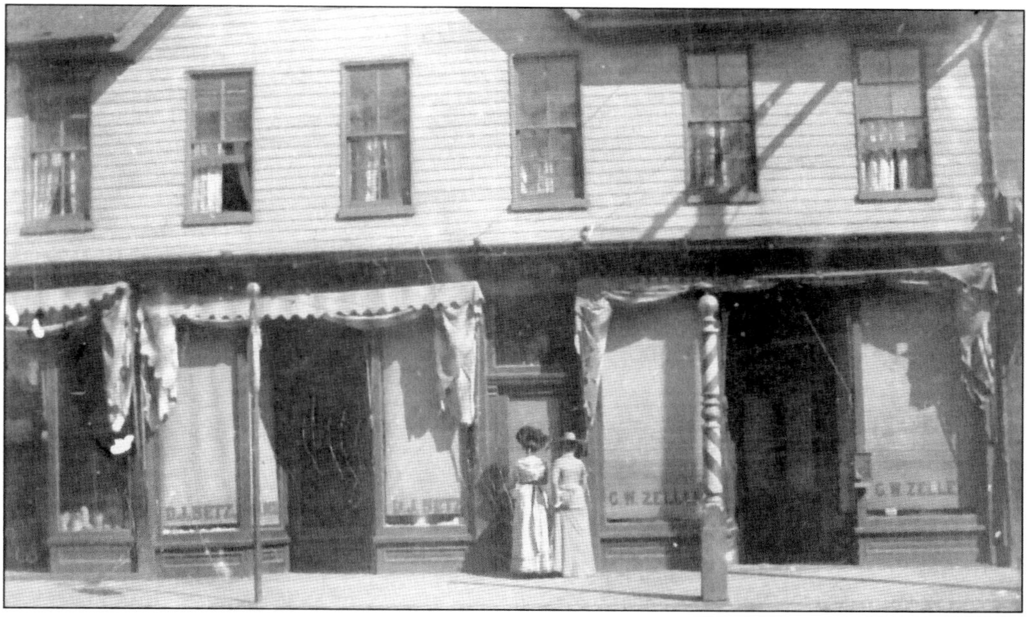

The original Betz Building stood on the north side of Main Street. The two Betz brothers ran a jewelry store and a grocery; they rented another section in the building to various tenants, who operated businesses from groceries to the Zeller Barber Shop seen here. A fire in 1917 destroyed this building (see page 59), but the Betz brothers replaced the frame building with a brick structure that later housed the G.C. Murphy Company for many years.

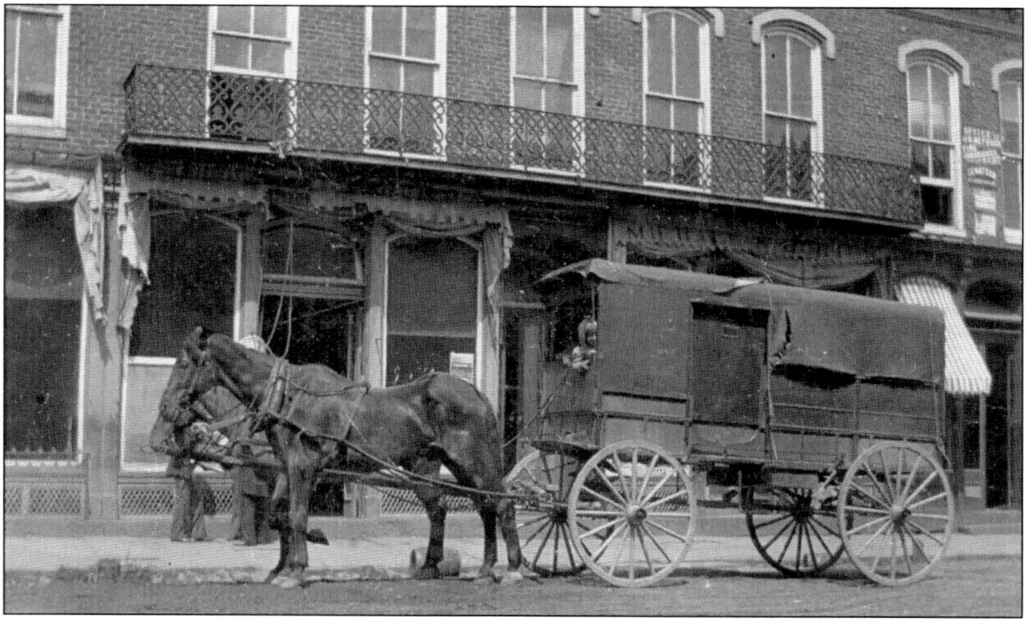

A delivery wagon is pictured on a dirt Main Street in front of Paul's Hall, a brick structure that over time accommodated Stanton's Hardware store, barber shops, saloons and billiard parlors, and even a bank. The second floor was once an auditorium that held stage plays and other shows until it was converted into a dance hall. At one time known as Moat's Opera House, the building would later be known as the Lyric Building when the Lyric Theater was added in the early 20th century.

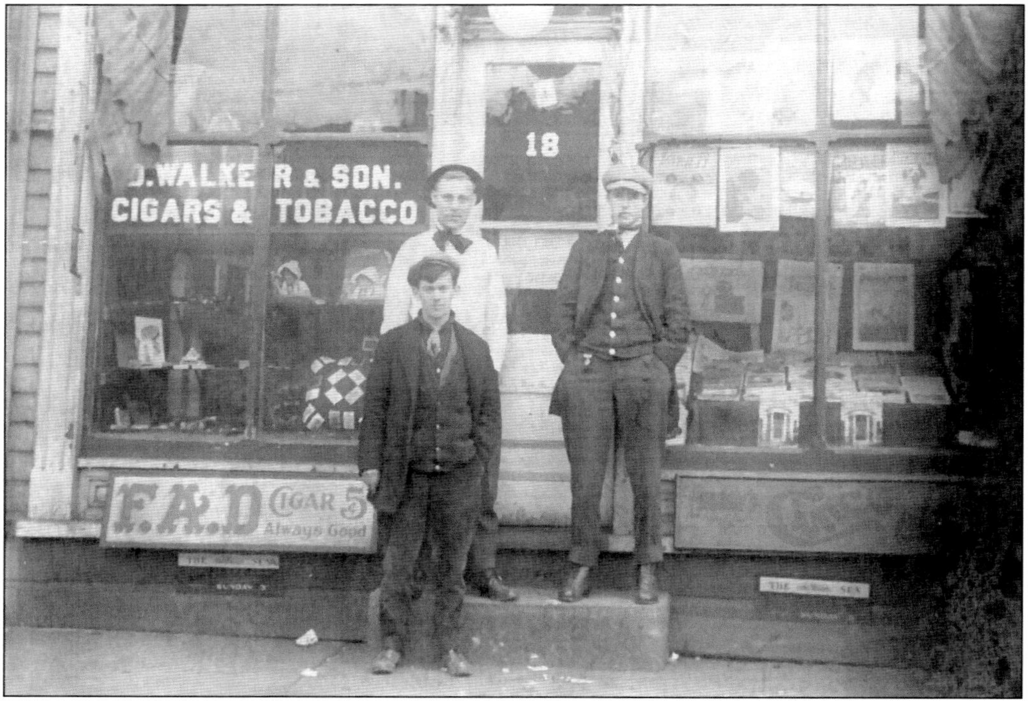

At J. Walker & Sons tobacco shop you can always get a good 5¢ cigar and a copy of the *Baltimore Sun*, according to the signs beneath the window. The *Sun* is still sporting the same logo today, but is no longer only 3¢.

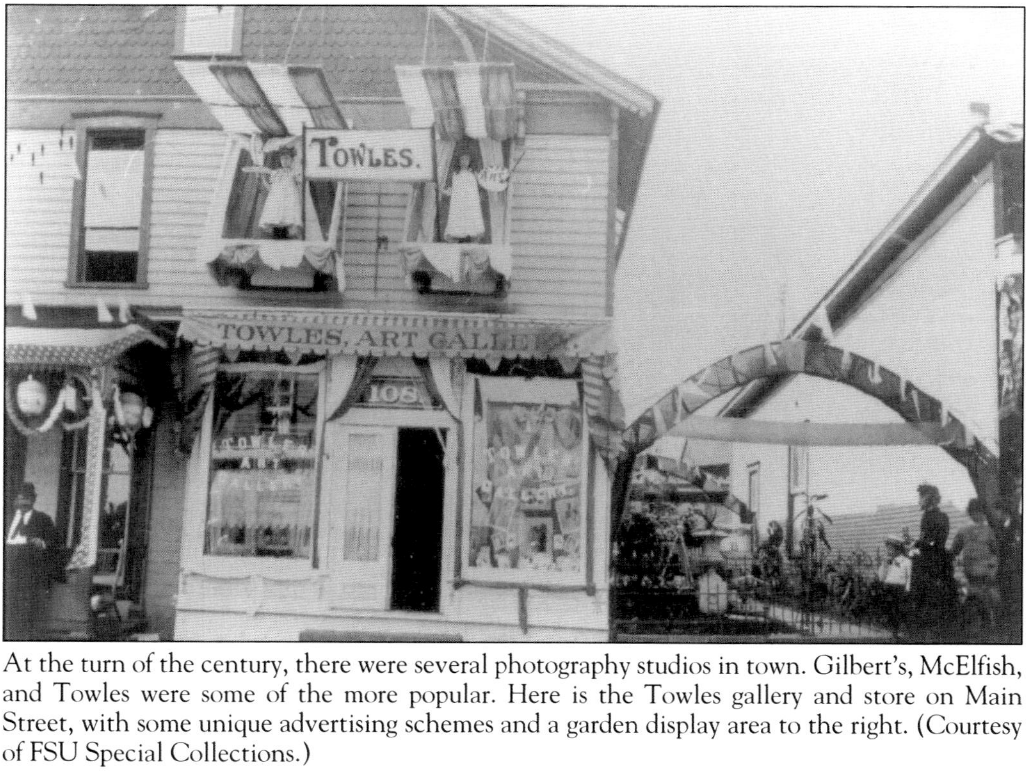

At the turn of the century, there were several photography studios in town. Gilbert's, McElfish, and Towles were some of the more popular. Here is the Towles gallery and store on Main Street, with some unique advertising schemes and a garden display area to the right. (Courtesy of FSU Special Collections.)

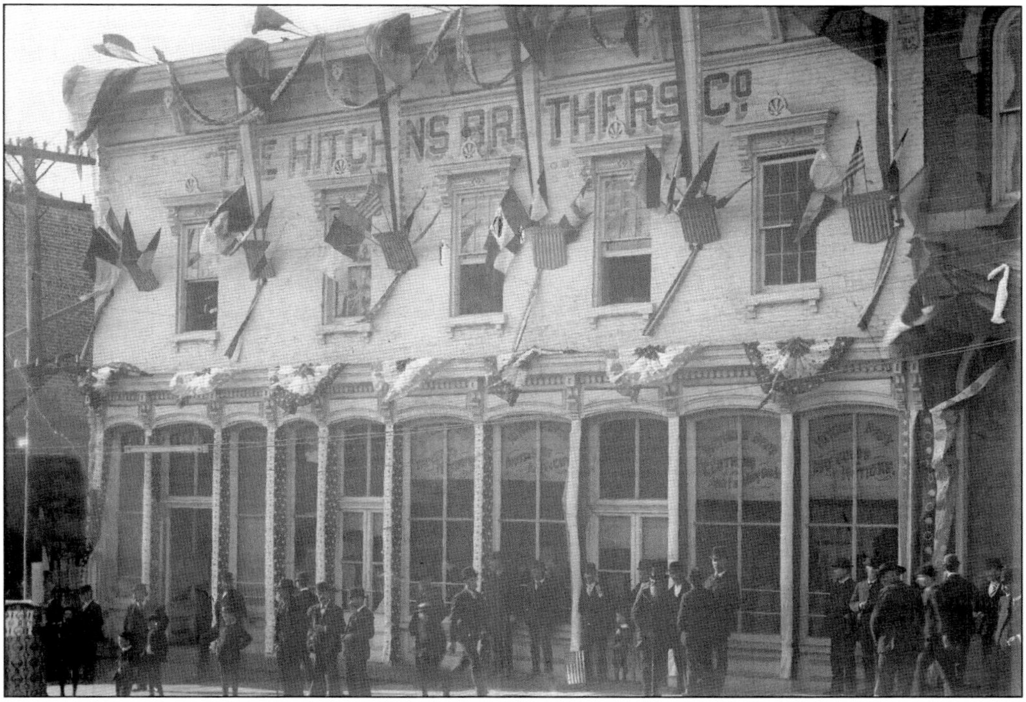

The Hitchins Brothers Store on Main Street (just above the Palace Theater) was one of the major mercantile establishments in town at the turn of the century. The Welsh-immigrated Hitchins Brothers not only operated this general store, but were also very involved the local coal industry and in the manufacture and sale of fire-brick in Olive Hill, Kentucky. They became very prosperous and prominent local businessmen.

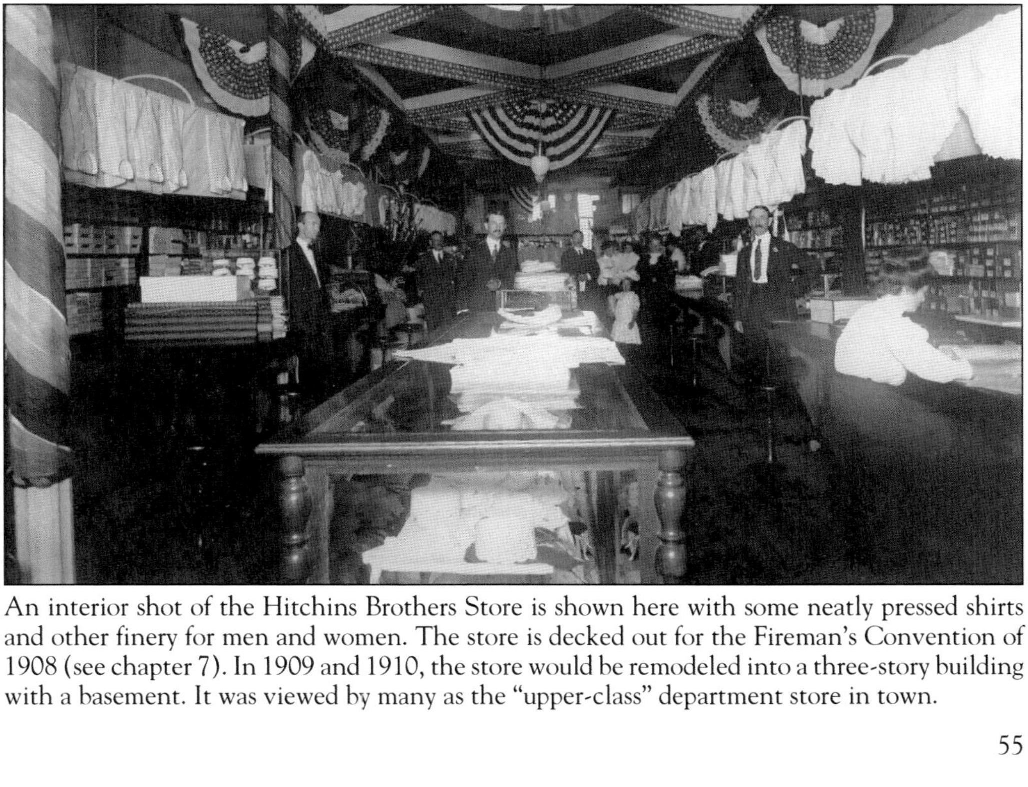

An interior shot of the Hitchins Brothers Store is shown here with some neatly pressed shirts and other finery for men and women. The store is decked out for the Fireman's Convention of 1908 (see chapter 7). In 1909 and 1910, the store would be remodeled into a three-story building with a basement. It was viewed by many as the "upper-class" department store in town.

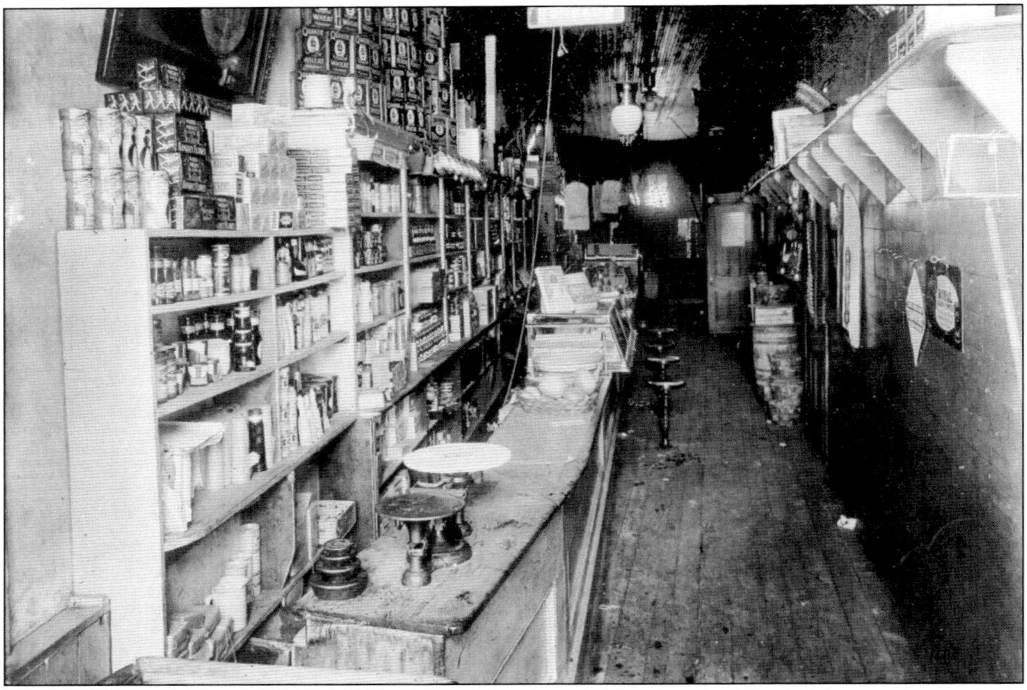

Here are interior views of the Hitchins Brothers store showing a variety of dry goods available in the late 19th and early 20th centuries. A 1912 advertisement for the store boasted that "the company carries a full line of everything needful for the pleasure and well-being of individuals and homes."

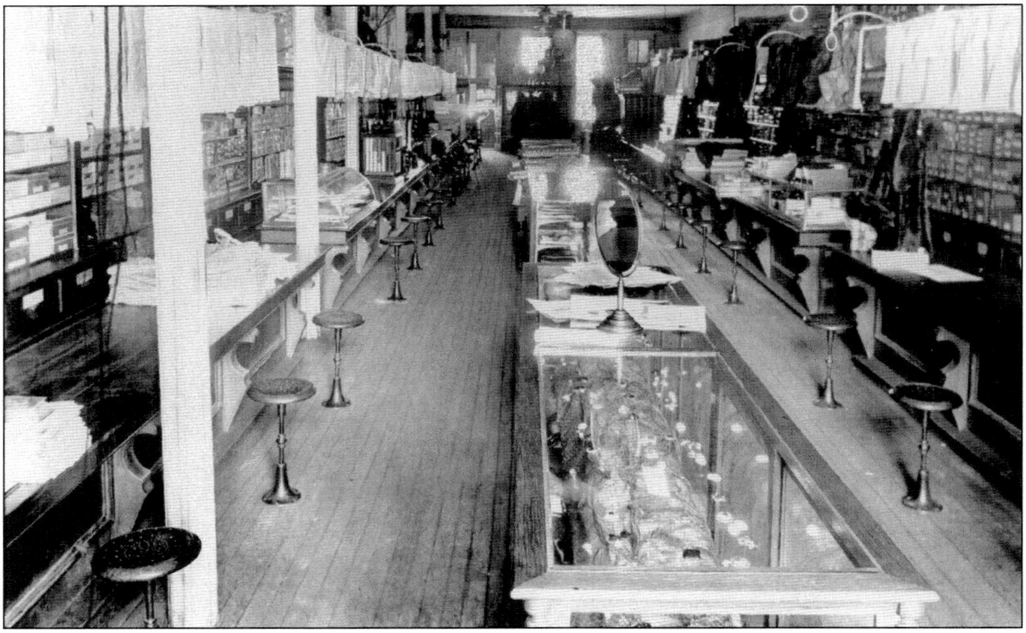

The company also proclaimed that "the store is equipped with all the modern appliances for handling the immense trade which it enjoys." It was also said that "courteous treatment of employees and customers has characterized the dealings of this firm throughout its entire history, and these elements have built up for them the largest business in Western Maryland."

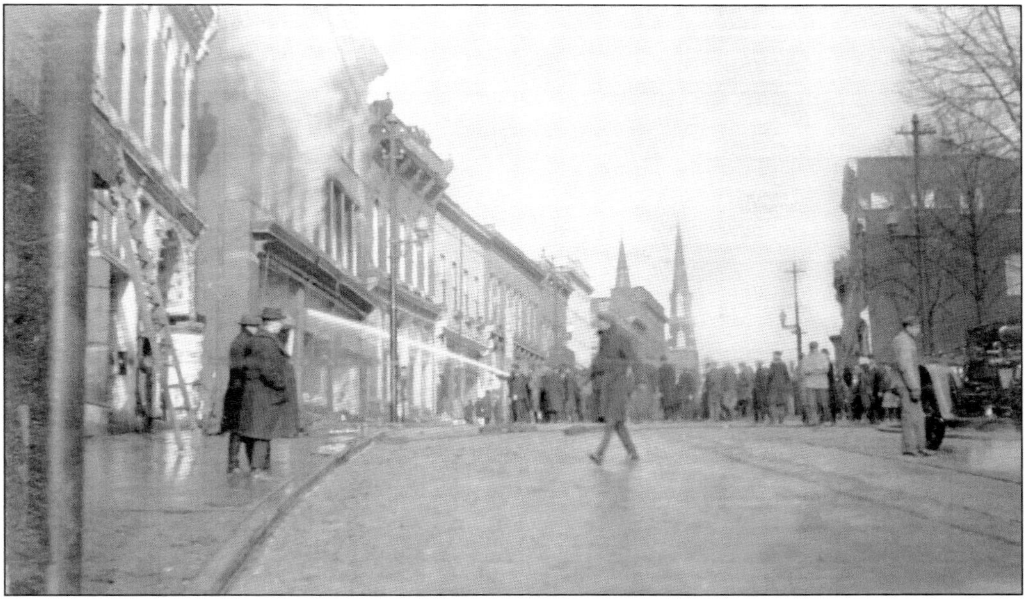

Tragedy struck in early 1925, when a fire broke out in the store, totally destroying the interior and leaving weakened walls and rubble. Before the ruins of the building could be removed, high winds caused the walls to collapse. In the process, it took out the west wall of the neighboring Palace Theater, which was linked to the damaged store by an elevated walkway, causing much damage to the interior of the Palace.

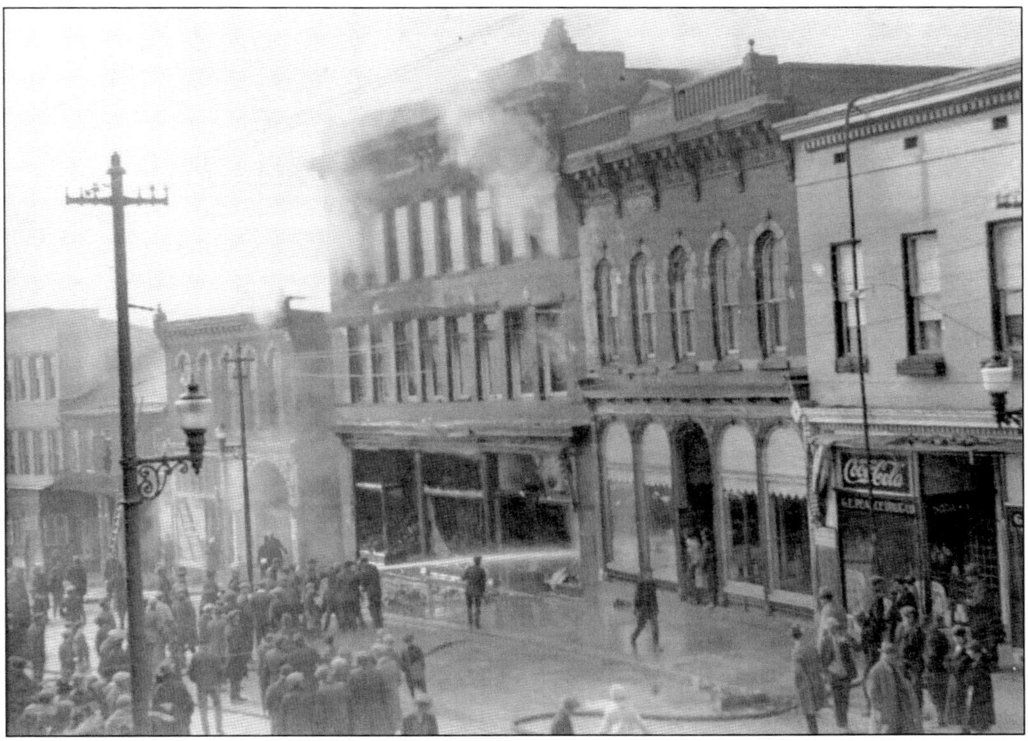

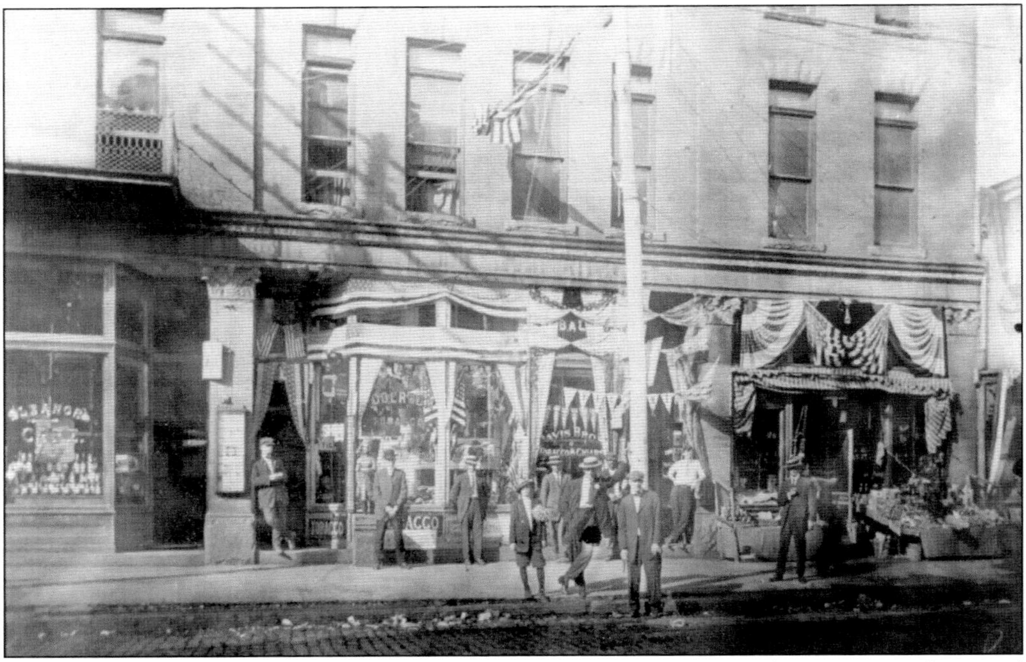

The Eleanor Building, still standing on the south side of Main Street between Broadway and Water Streets, was built in 1900 and owned by Dr. C.C. Jacobs. Dr. Jacobs was reported to be the first physician in Western Maryland to use x-rays. Interestingly, Dr. Jacobs did not name the building after his late wife, Huldah, or his new wife, Fannie, or even for his daughter, Grace, but for his mother-in-law, Eleanor McCulloh Taylor!

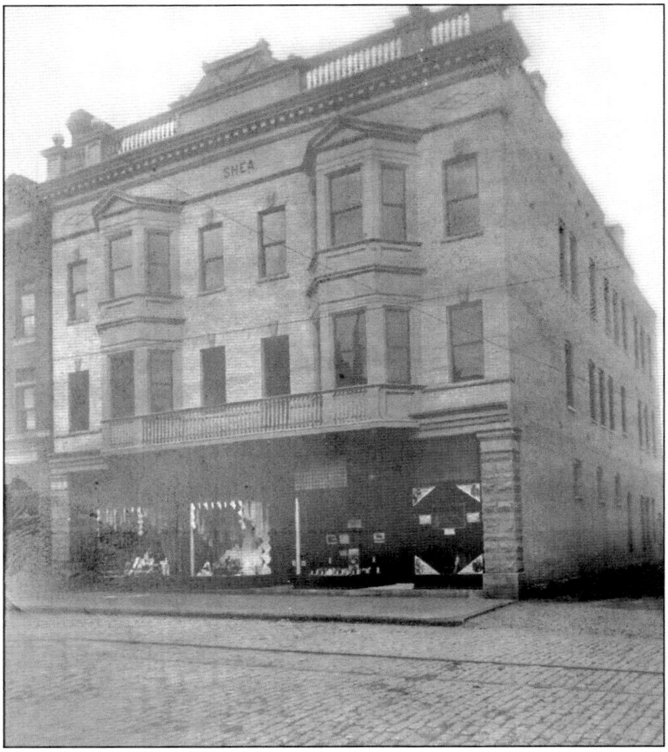

The Shea Building, on the north side of Main Street next to the Gladstone Hotel, housed several businesses. The Shea Drug Store (advertised to be the oldest druggist in Frostburg) and a McCrory Five & Ten Cent Store (reported to be one of the most pretentious in Western Maryland!) were on the ground floor, several coal company and attorney offices and the Elias Tailor shop were on the second floor, and the Frostburg Aerie of the Fraternal Order of the Eagles was on the third floor.

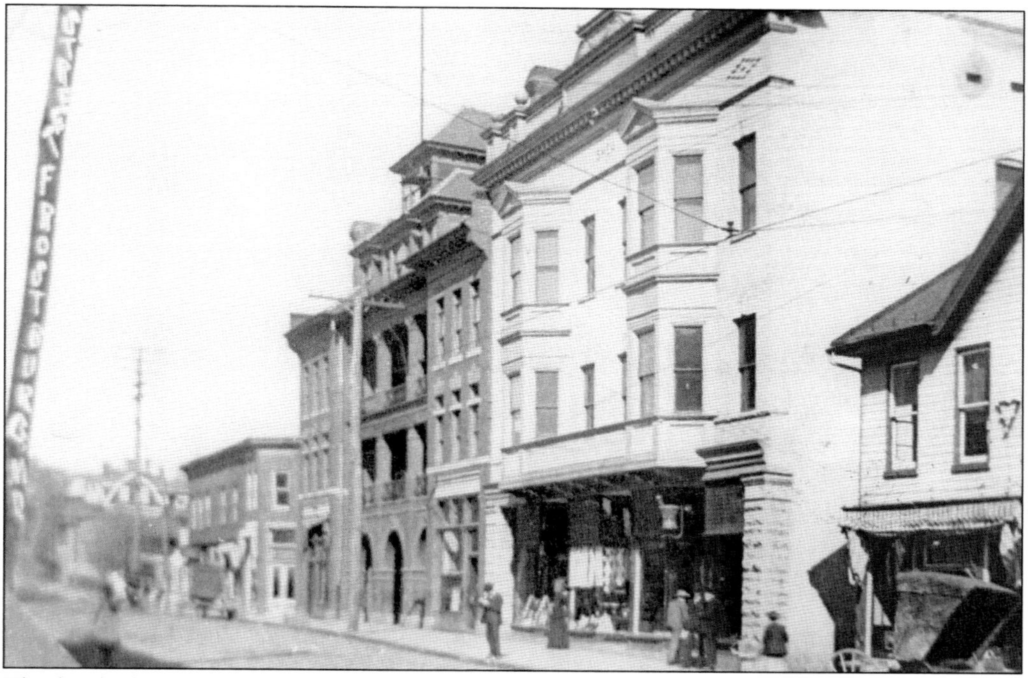

The bright brick and brown stone Shea Building in the foreground, and the dark, red brick Hotel Gladstone on the north side of Main Street are pictured in the early 20th century. The mortar and pestle of the Shea Drug store can be seen in the front of the Shea Building.

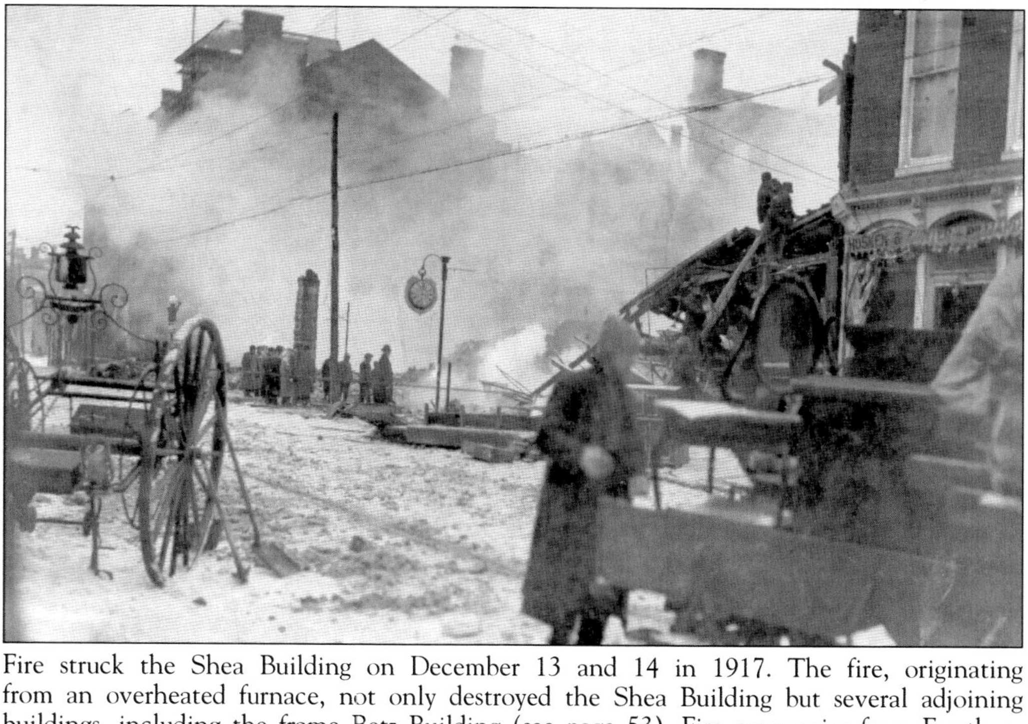

Fire struck the Shea Building on December 13 and 14 in 1917. The fire, originating from an overheated furnace, not only destroyed the Shea Building but several adjoining buildings, including the frame Betz Building (see page 53). Fire companies from Frostburg and neighboring Cumberland, Lonaconing, and Midland fought the blaze, fueled by high winds. The loss of the Shea Building was estimated between $150,000 and $200,000.

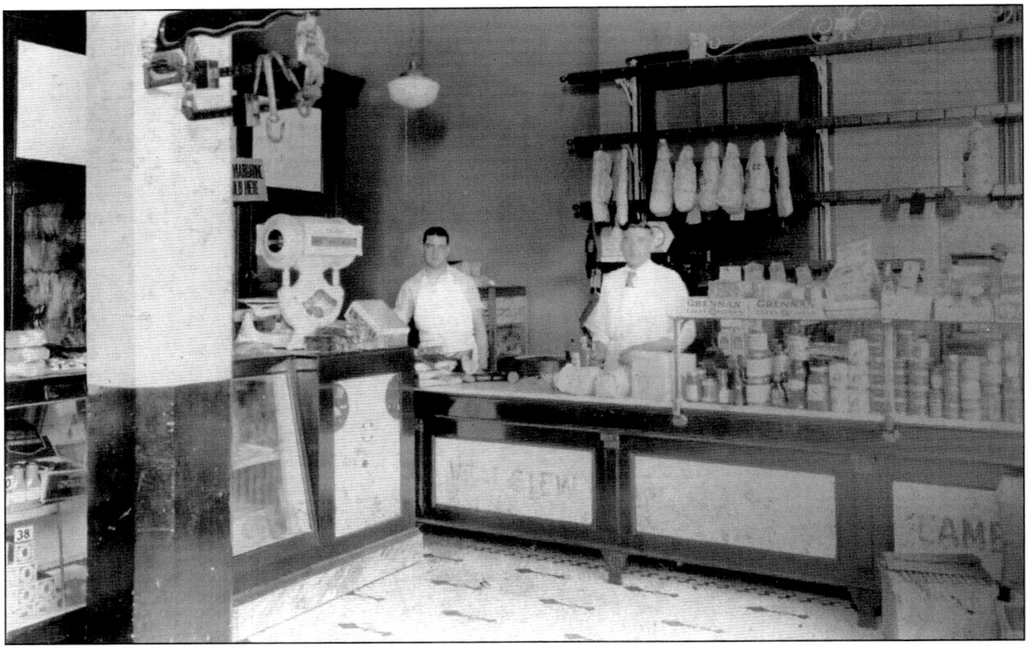

The Engle Butcher Shop was one of Frostburg's most popular butcher shops in the early 20th century. The Engle or Frostburg bologna, a rather spicy concoction of meats sold sausage-style, became an area favorite. The bologna is still being sliced for sandwiches and snacks today.

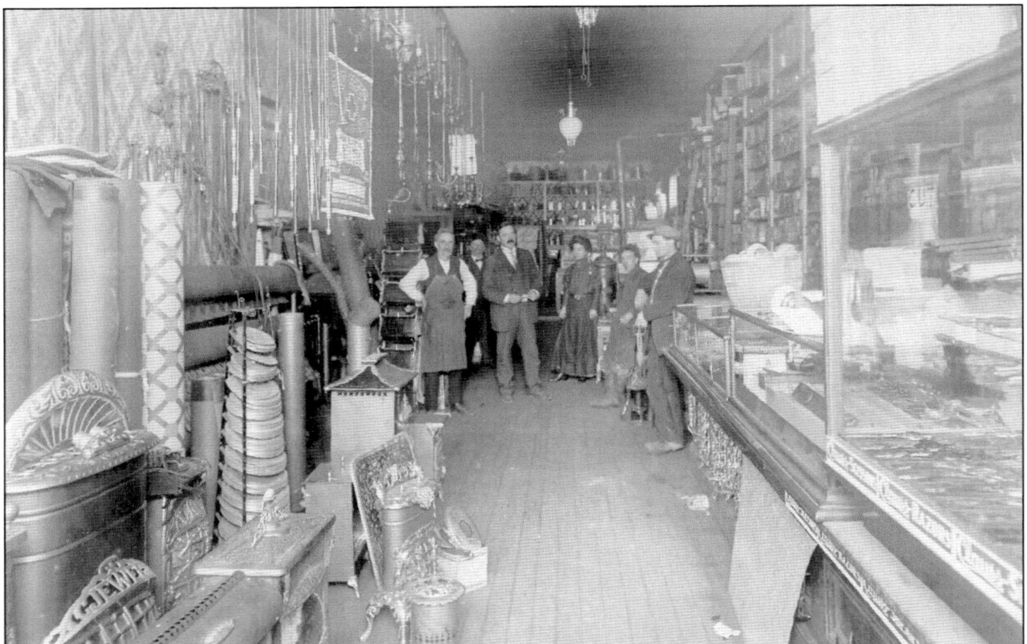

Louis Stanton Store had a variety of hardware and heating supplies for the turn-of-the-century home. Coal burners and gas light fixtures were just some of the accessories available. Louis Stanton operated this hardware store and was involved in the heating and plumbing business. At one time, the Stanton Store operated out of the ground floor of the former Moat's Opera House (see page 53).

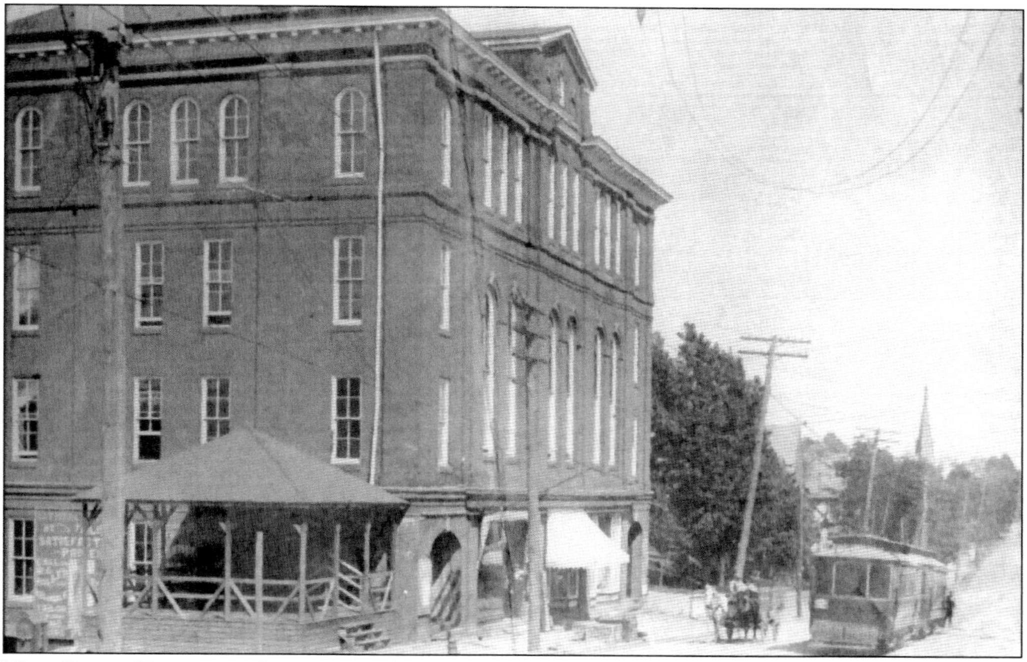

The Opera House, at the corner of Main Street and Depot Road, was erected in 1871 and 1872 and dominated the skyline along east Main Street for over 60 years. The opera house was the site of many theatrical and musical performances by local and nationally known performers, as well as motion pictures. The local Arion Band often performed in the bandstand in the foreground.

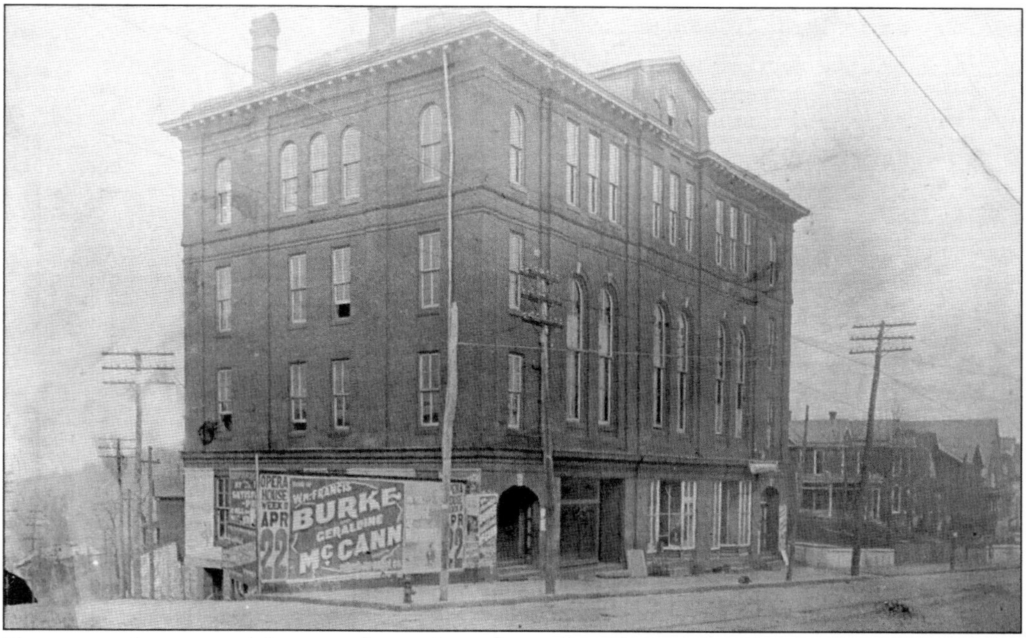

Here is another view of the opera house from the early 20th century. In April of 1894, the opera house was used for a unique "performance." The rag-tag Coxey's Army was passing through town on their protest journey to Washington, D.C. Town leaders, not wanting the rabble wandering the streets of Frostburg, "housed" the marchers for a night in a locked upstairs meeting room.

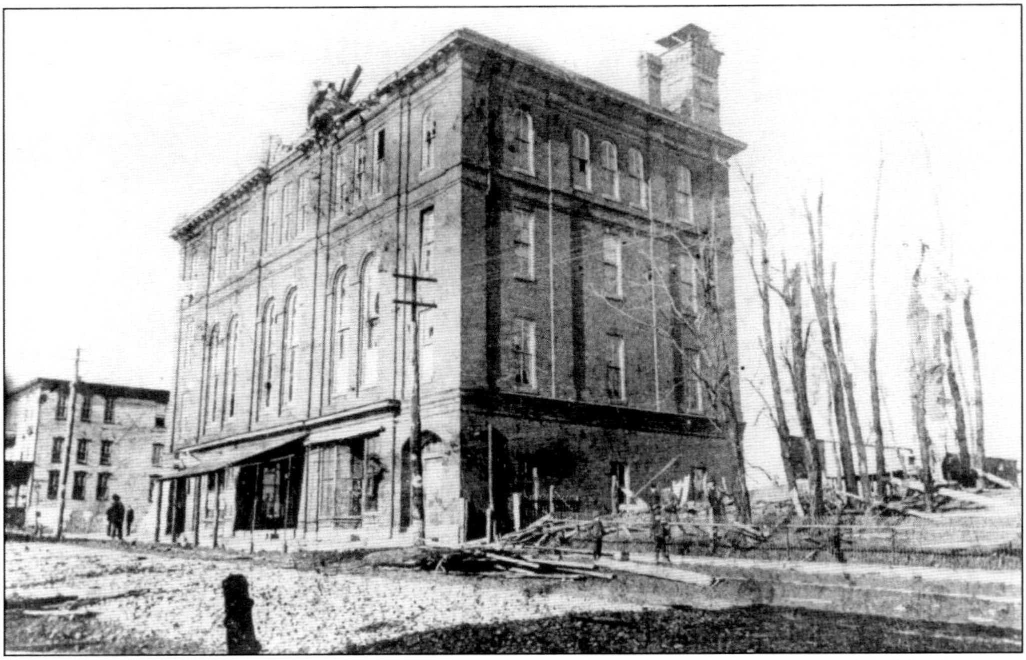

On November 23, 1891, a cyclone smashed through Frostburg causing considerable damage. Here the opera house is pictured with some damaged windows and a damaged roof, surrounded by downed trees and branches.

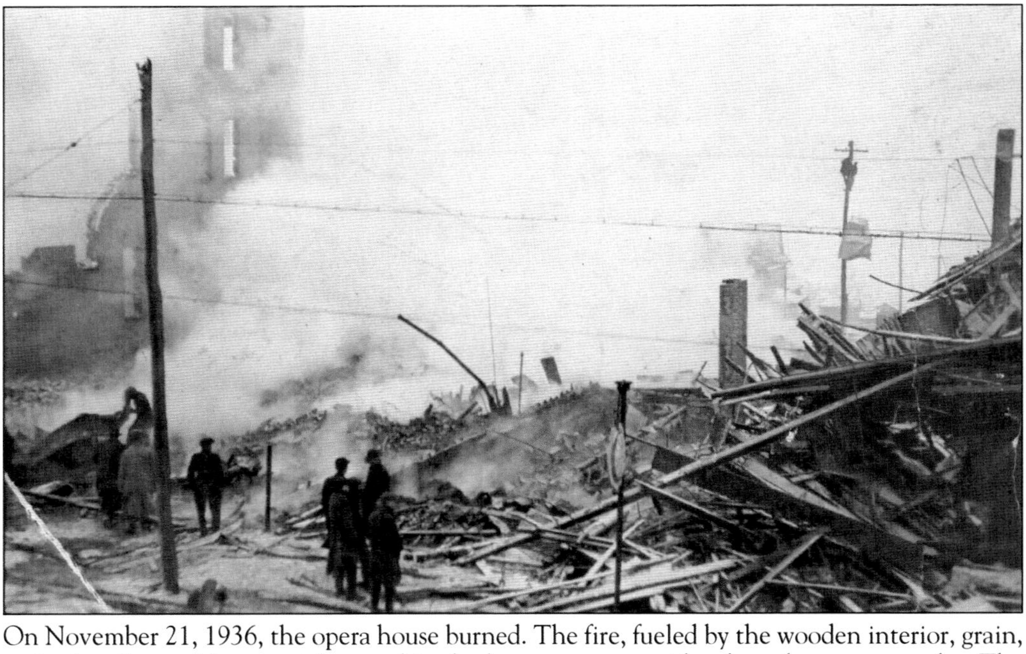

On November 21, 1936, the opera house burned. The fire, fueled by the wooden interior, grain, and other flammable materials stored in the basement, was said to have been spectacular. The heat was so intense that the copper roof melted, glowing and sparking through the night. While it was never proven, arson was suspected.

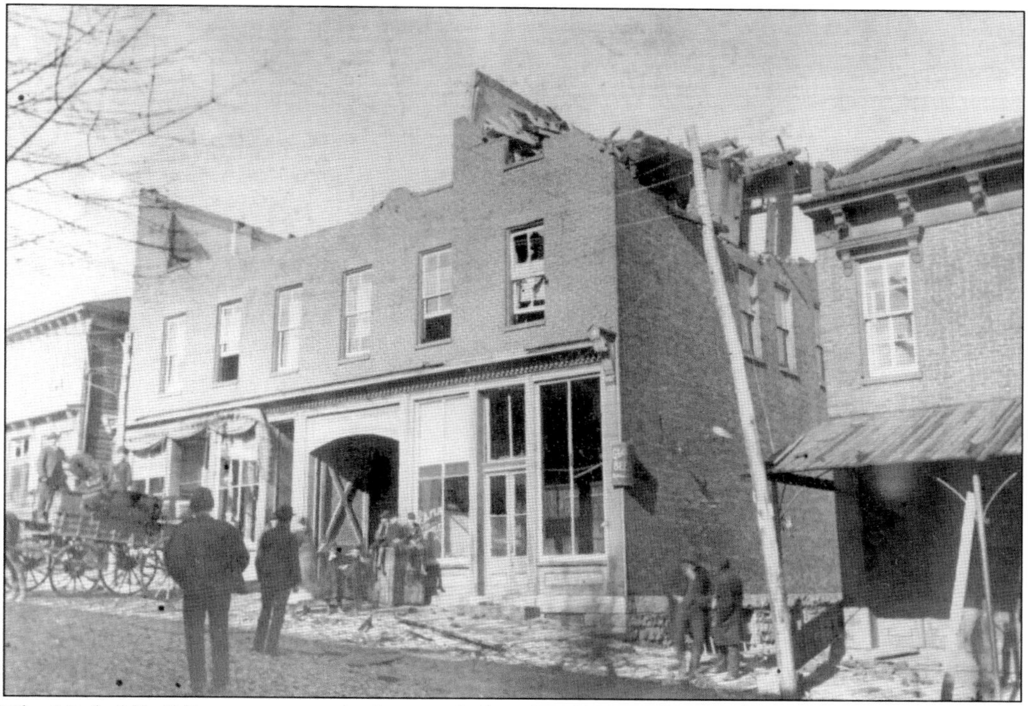

The Nickel Building was severely damaged after the 1891 cyclone. The Nickel Building, which was also the scene of several spectacular fires in the 1880s, housed a furniture shop and a print shop. The Au Petit Paris Restaurant now occupies the site.

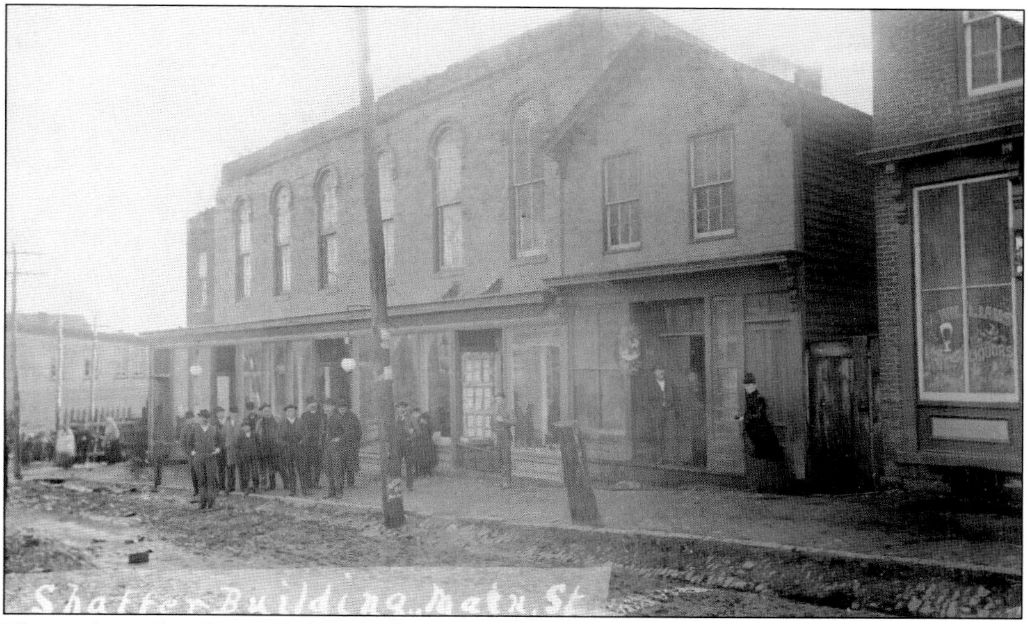

The cyclone also damaged the Shaffer Building that stood at what is now the corner of Main and Center Streets. The Shaffer Store on Main Street was a general merchandise store that sold everything from tobacco to groceries to harness and leather goods. There was a beauty shop for women and even a gristmill in the rear that produced flour and animal feeds. This photograph is from the Towles Studio (see page 54) series taken in the aftermath of the cyclone.

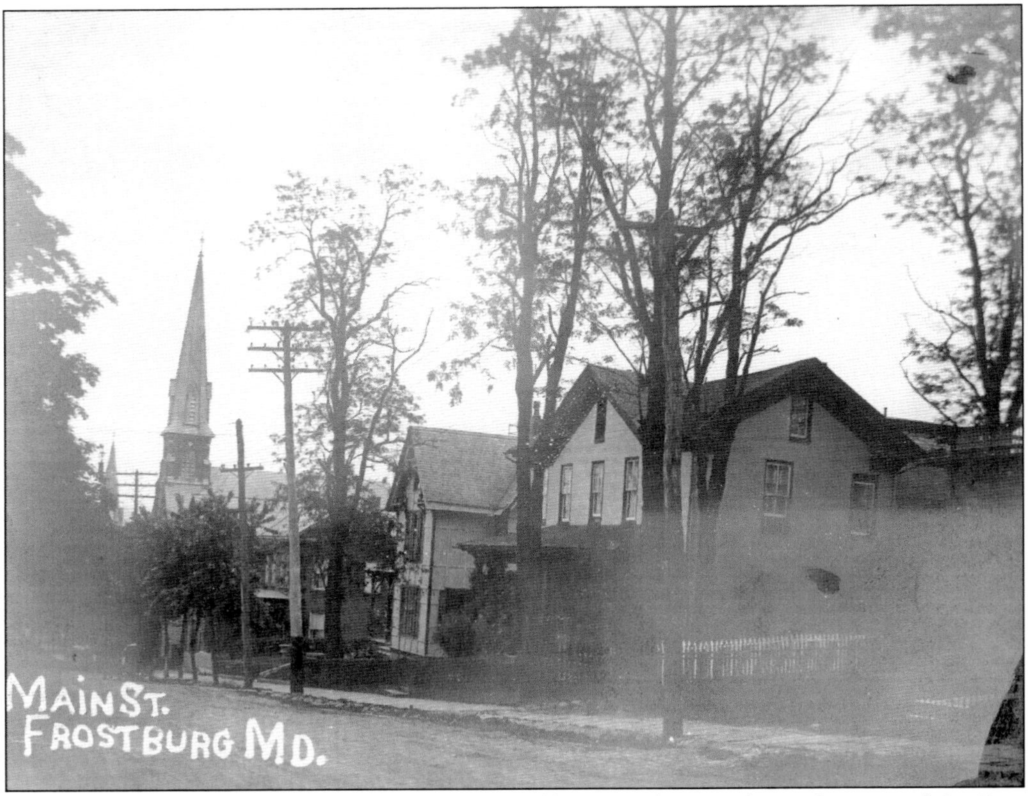

West Main Street, looking east toward the central business district, shows the spire of the First Methodist Church, one of the more recognizable sites on the town's skyline. The partially hidden spire of St. Paul's Lutheran church is visible just behind.

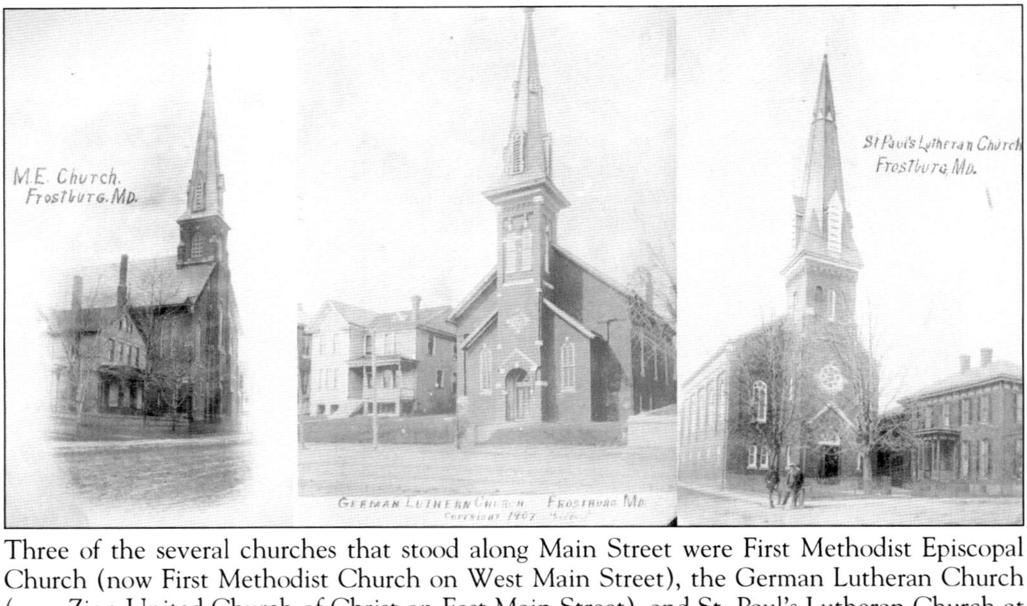

Three of the several churches that stood along Main Street were First Methodist Episcopal Church (now First Methodist Church on West Main Street), the German Lutheran Church (now Zion United Church of Christ on East Main Street), and St. Paul's Lutheran Church at the corner of Main and Water Streets.

St. Michael's Catholic Church stands on the site of Meshach Frost's Highland Hall, the hotel and former stage coach stop whose prosperity was in decline by 1850. Originally meeting in a wing of Highland Hall, St. Michael's Parish was formally established in 1852. Engineers for many of the coal companies often used the spire, which was removed in the 1960s, as a surveying point.

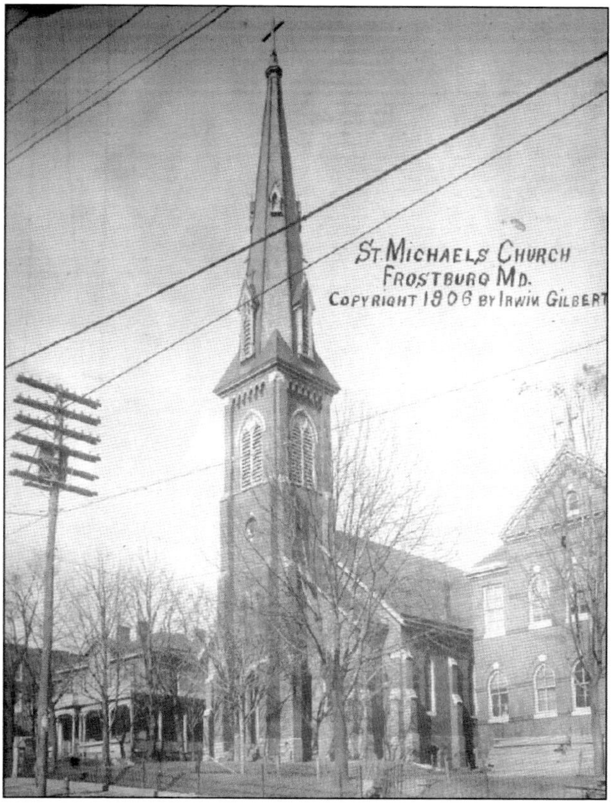

In 1891, a group of Ursuline nuns came to Frostburg to help establish the St. Michael's School. Here is the original convent for the St. Michael's parish. This building stood next to the church until it was razed to make way for a newer convent and school building.

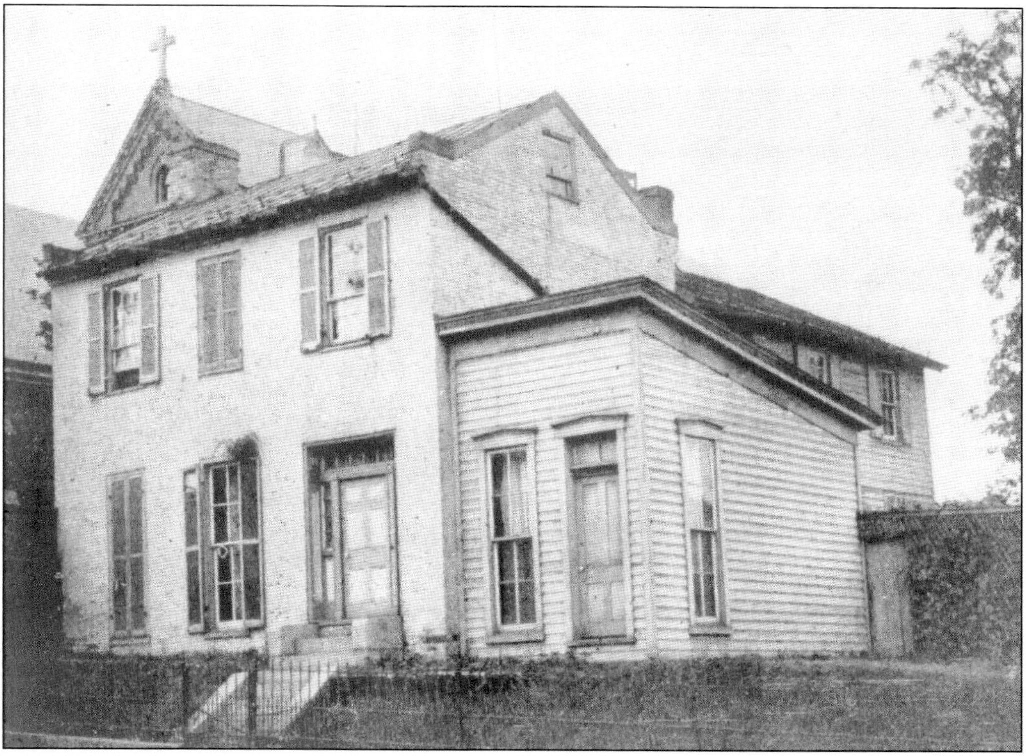

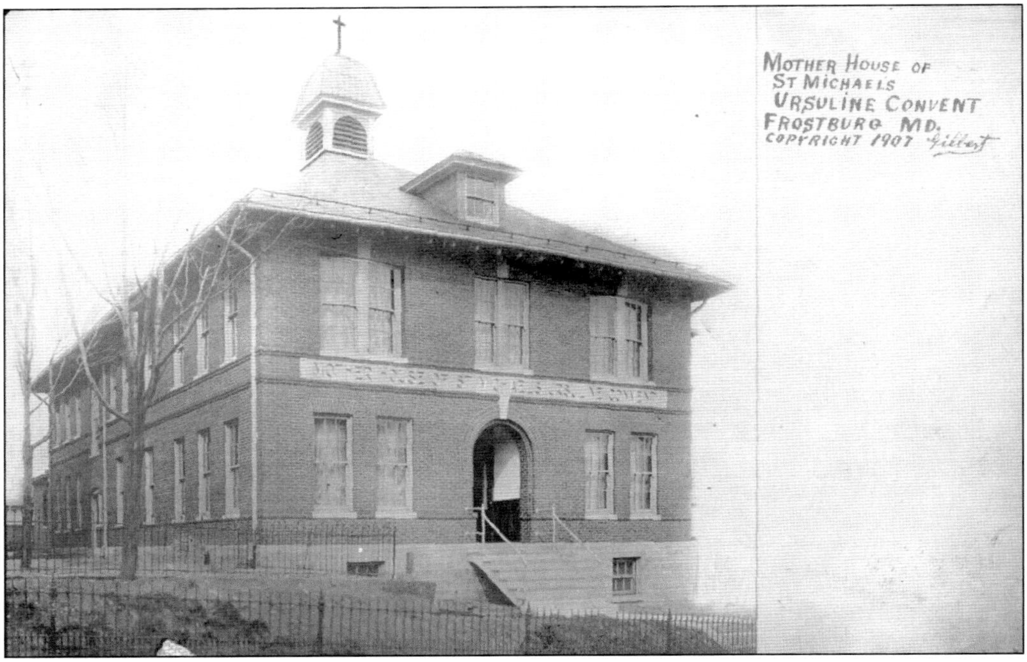

The original convent gave way to this structure in the early 1900s. Once the mother house for the St. Michael's Ursuline Convent, it is currently part of the St. Michael School classroom buildings.

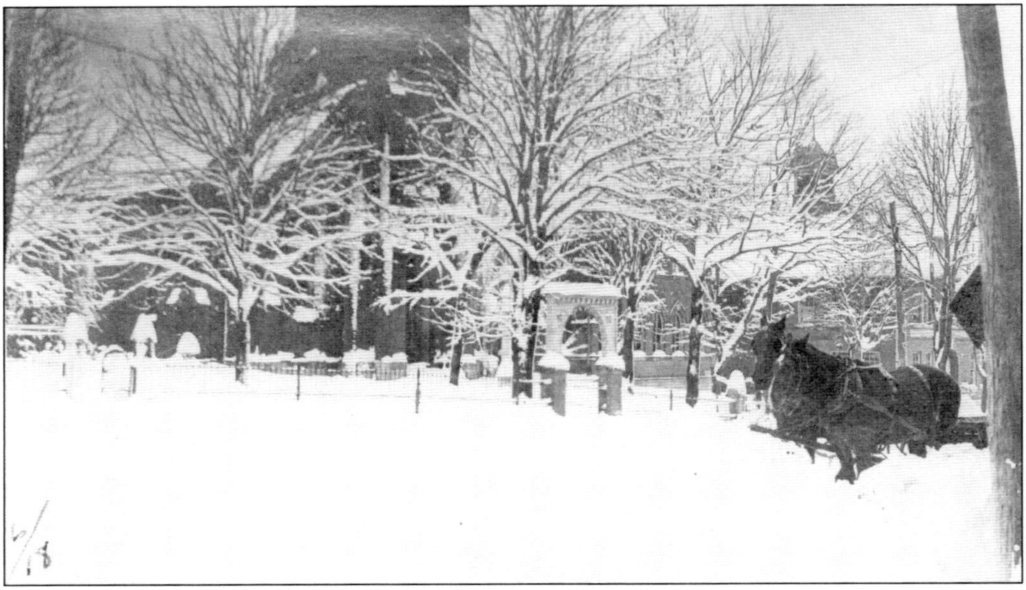

No portrait of Frostburg would be complete without a few views of the "frosty" winters. Here is St. Michael's Catholic Church courtyard under a blanket of heavy snow. The monument over the graves of Meshach and Catherine Frost is visible just to the left of the arched gate.

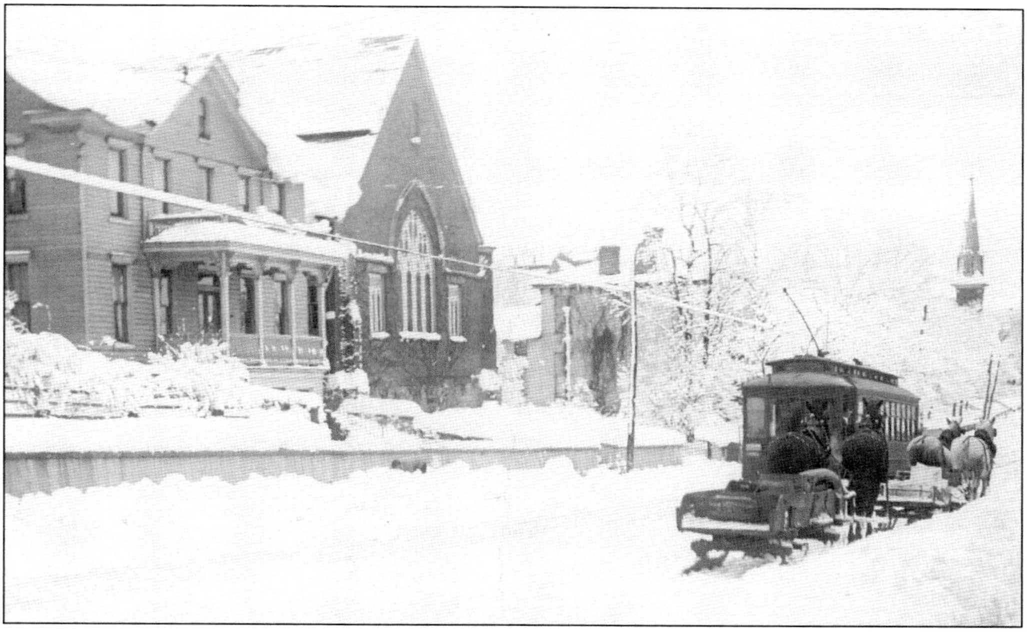

While the trolley struggles through the snow in front of the English Baptist Church, two horse-drawn sleds seem to be the way to travel. The First English Baptist church was formally organized on July 7, 1871, with 30 members who had broken from the Welsh Baptist Church because they wished the sermons to be conducted in English rather than Welsh.

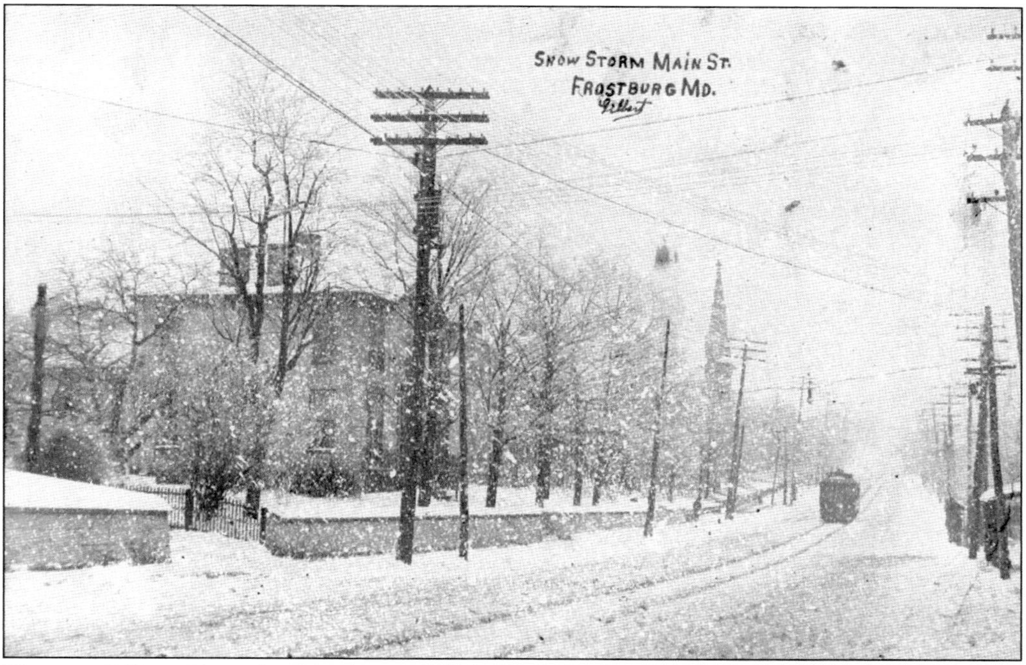

This is a Gilbert Photo Studio photograph from the early 20th century, showing the trolley car making tracks in a heavy snow storm on the lower end of East Main Street. The spire of the German Lutheran Church (now Zion United Church of Christ) can just be made out through the snow.

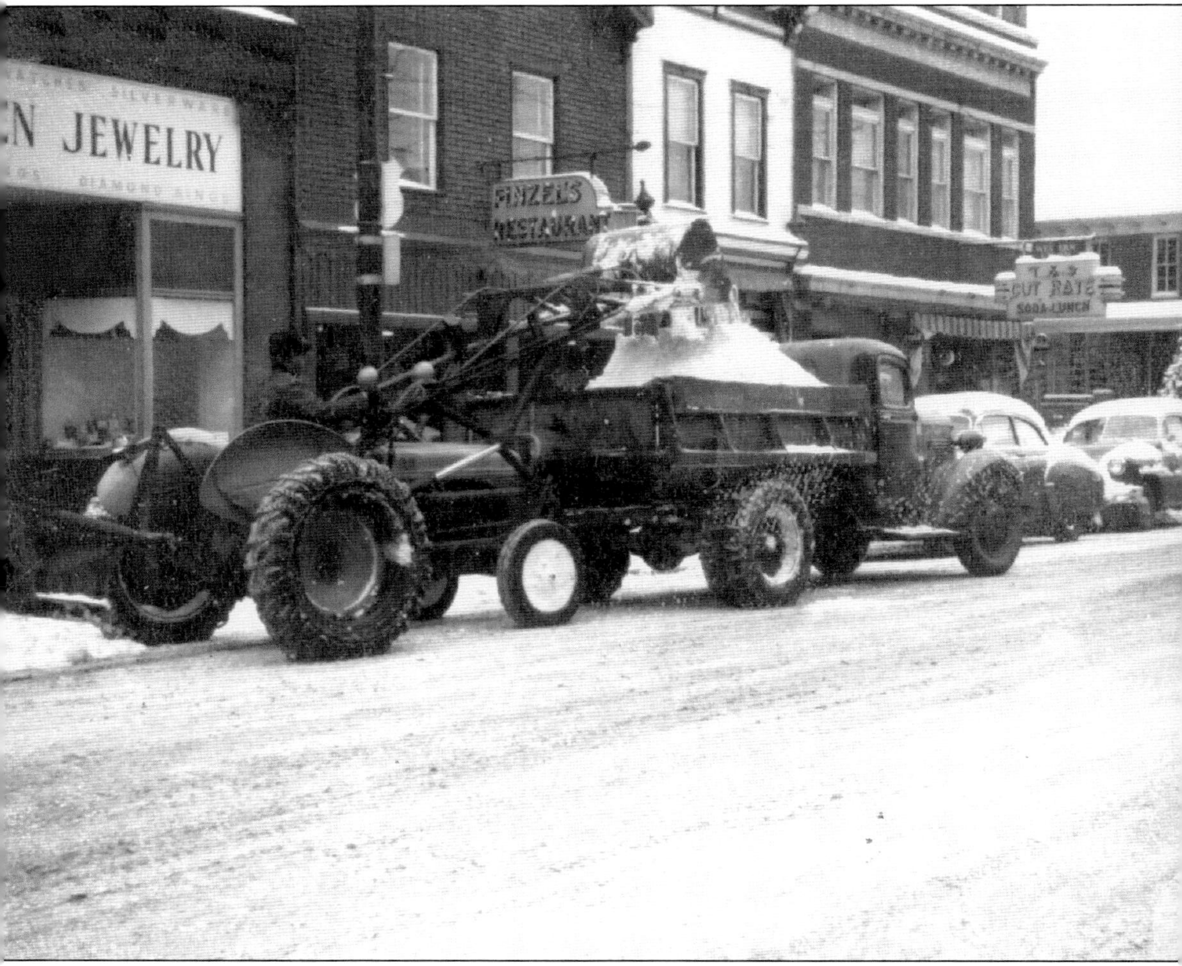

Snow is being removed on Main Street near Water Street after the war. Hosken Jewelry, Finzel Restaurant, Charlie Hill's Newsstand, and the T&S Cut-Rate are located behind the front-end loader and dump truck clearing more parking spaces along Main Street.

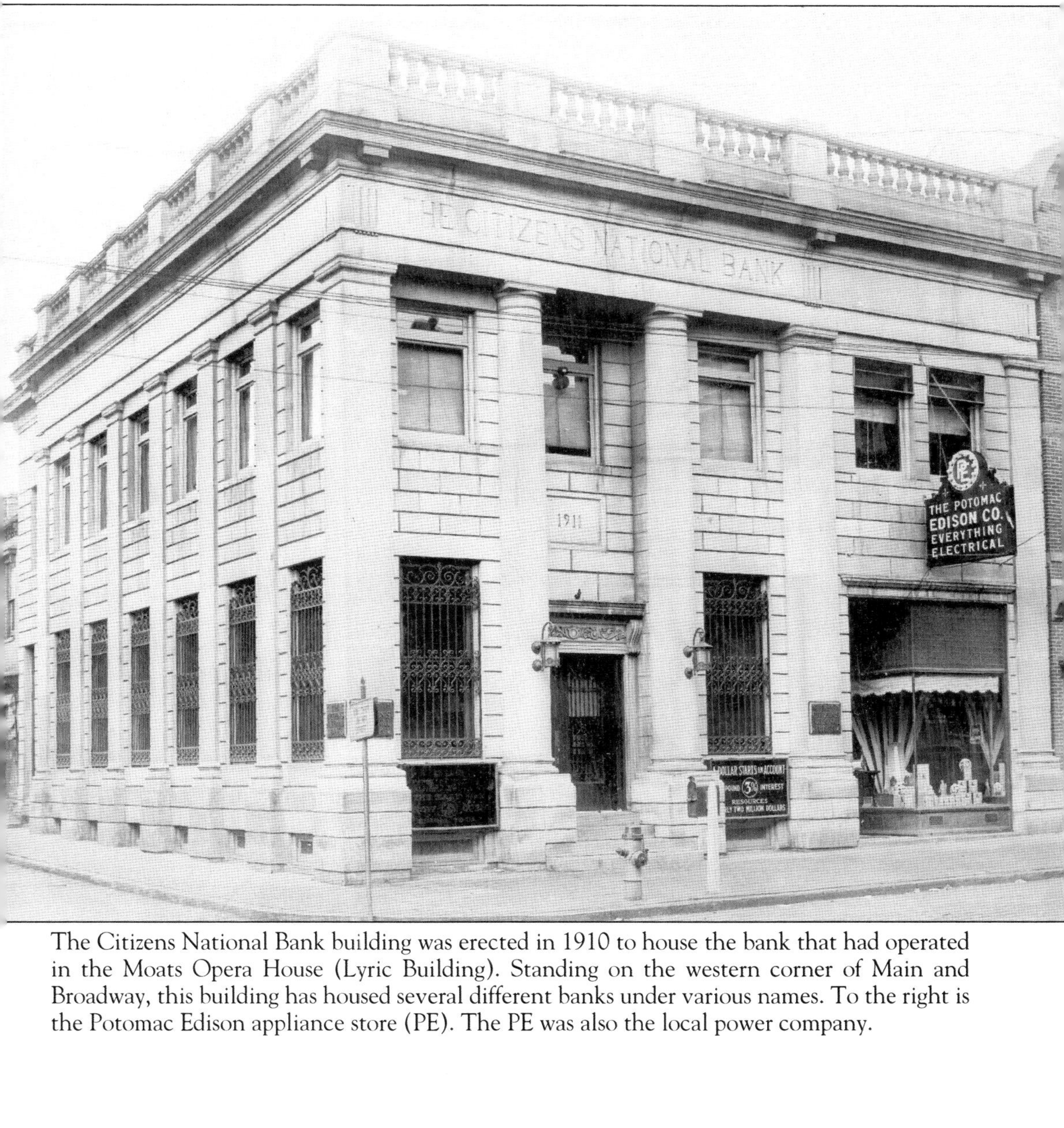

The Citizens National Bank building was erected in 1910 to house the bank that had operated in the Moats Opera House (Lyric Building). Standing on the western corner of Main and Broadway, this building has housed several different banks under various names. To the right is the Potomac Edison appliance store (PE). The PE was also the local power company.

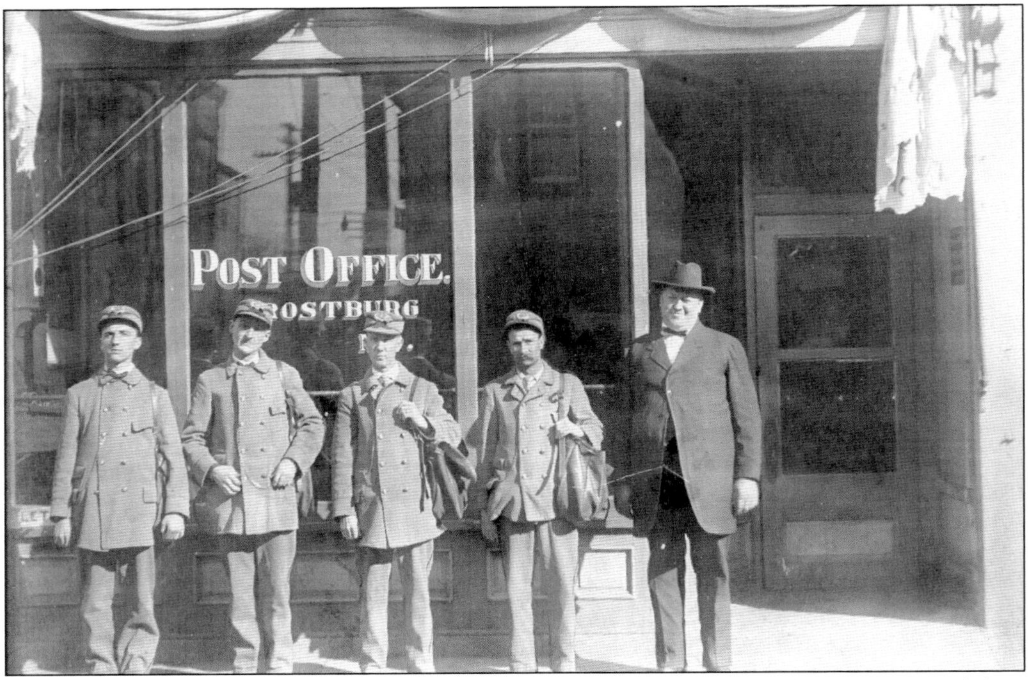

Postmaster Ulysses Hanna (right) is pictured here with several of his mail carriers. From left to right are Tom Pople, John Timmone, Bill Daily, and Tomm Jeffries in front the old Frostburg Post Office in the early 20th century. This post office was located on Main Street, just across Water Street from the current post office (where the American Legion now stands). Hanna served as postmaster of Frostburg from his appointment by President Theodore Roosevelt in 1903 until 1915.

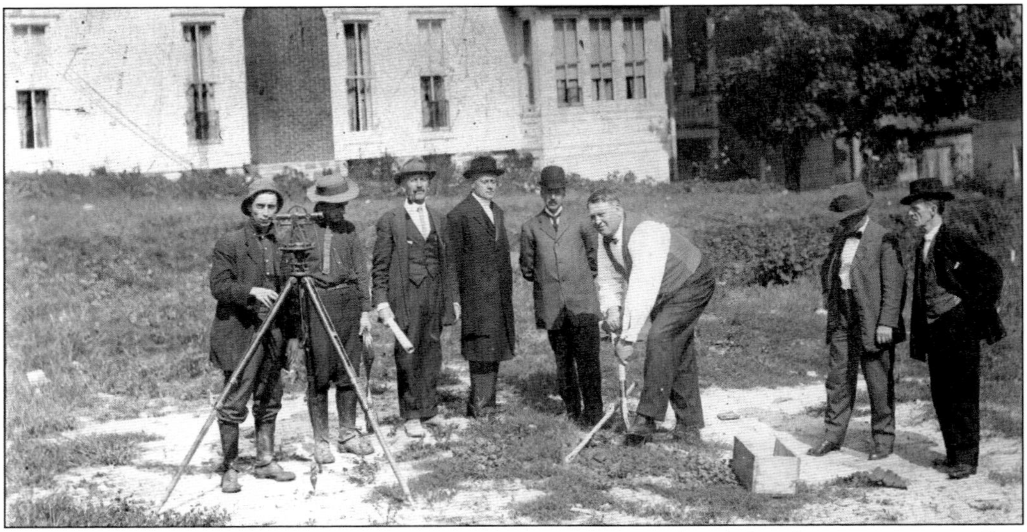

With shovel in hand, Postmaster Hanna turns the first spade of dirt for a new post office building on the northwest corner of Main Water Streets in September, 1912. In attendance are several notable Frostburg citizens. The third man from left is James H. Fuller of Fuller Brothers, Contractors. The Fuller Brothers would be the builders of the new post office. Fourth from the left is Frank Watts of Citizens National Bank and the gentleman in the bowler hat is Roberdeau Annan, president of the First National Bank of Frostburg.

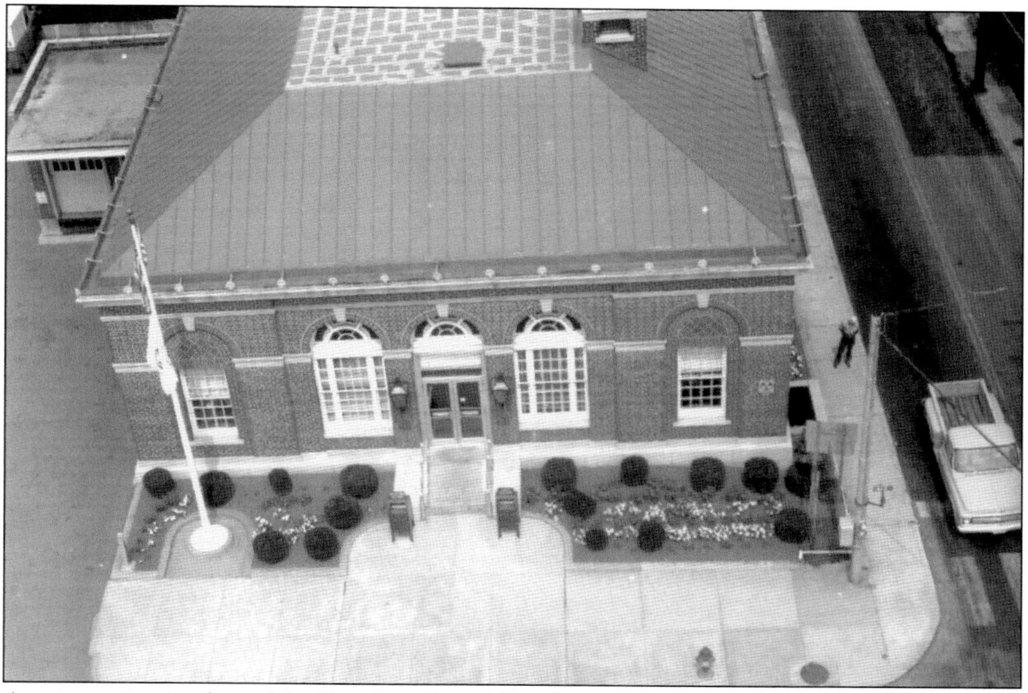

A unique view is taken of the Frostburg Post Office from just across Main Street from the steeple of St. Paul's Lutheran Church. Completed in 1913, this post office building would undergo several renovations, including expansion on the left side of the building and the addition of parking spaces.

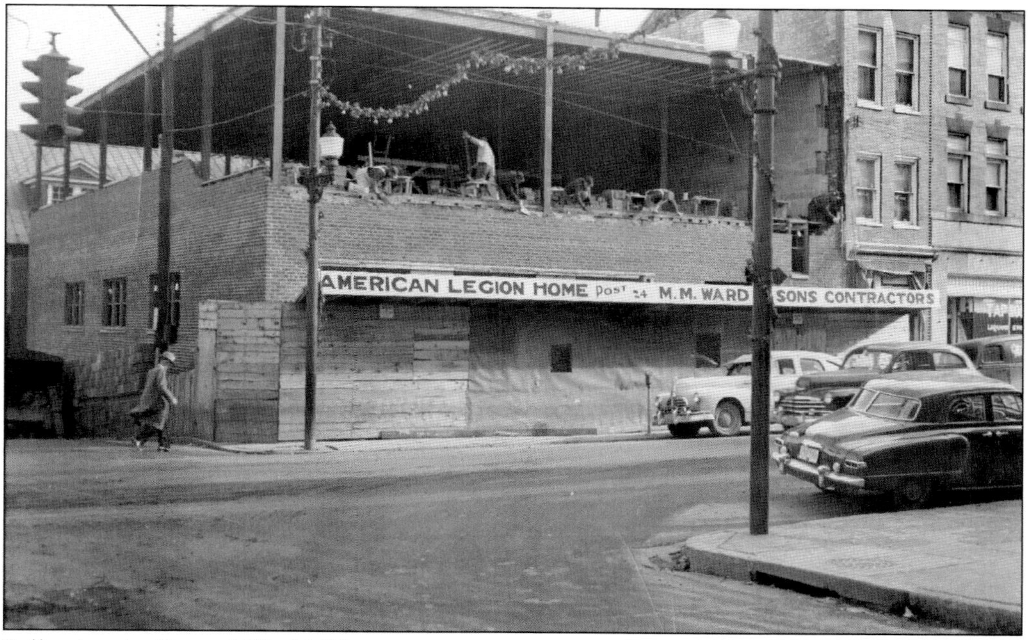

Following the Second World War, construction was stated on a new American Legion Post just across Water Street from the post office and next to the Gunter Hotel. Farrady Post No. 24 was charted in 1919, named for the two Farrady brothers, Hugh and John, who were killed in action in France during World War I.

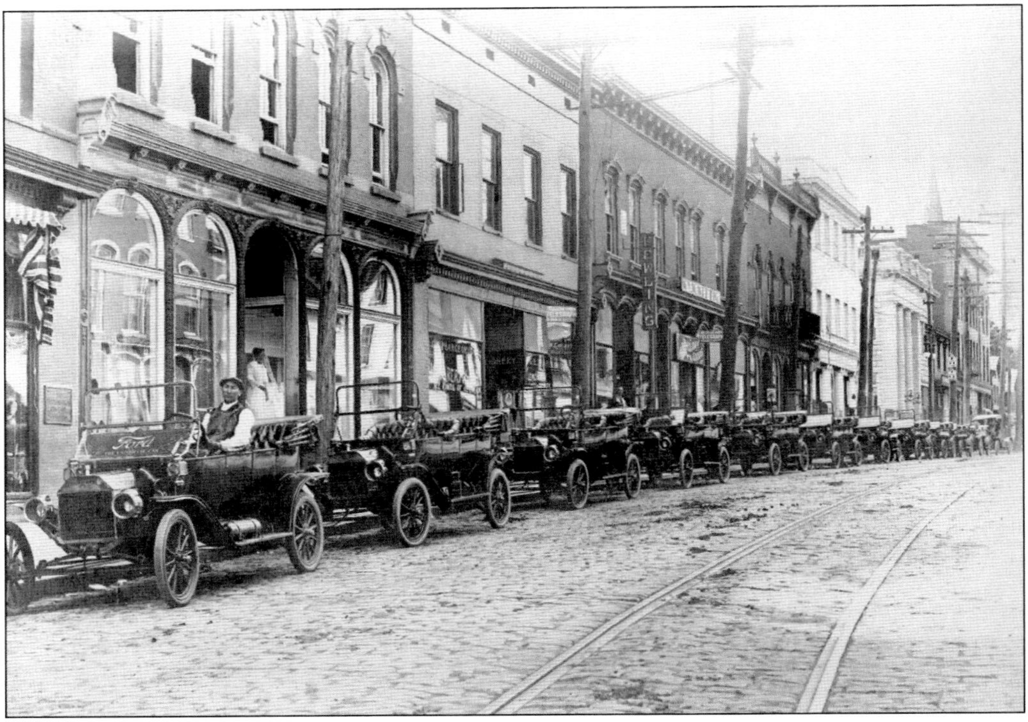

The Ford Model-T's lined up along Main Street are possibly being delivered to a dealership or are on display. Main Street is still cobblestone and the trolley car tracks run up the middle of the thoroughfare in this 1920s photograph.

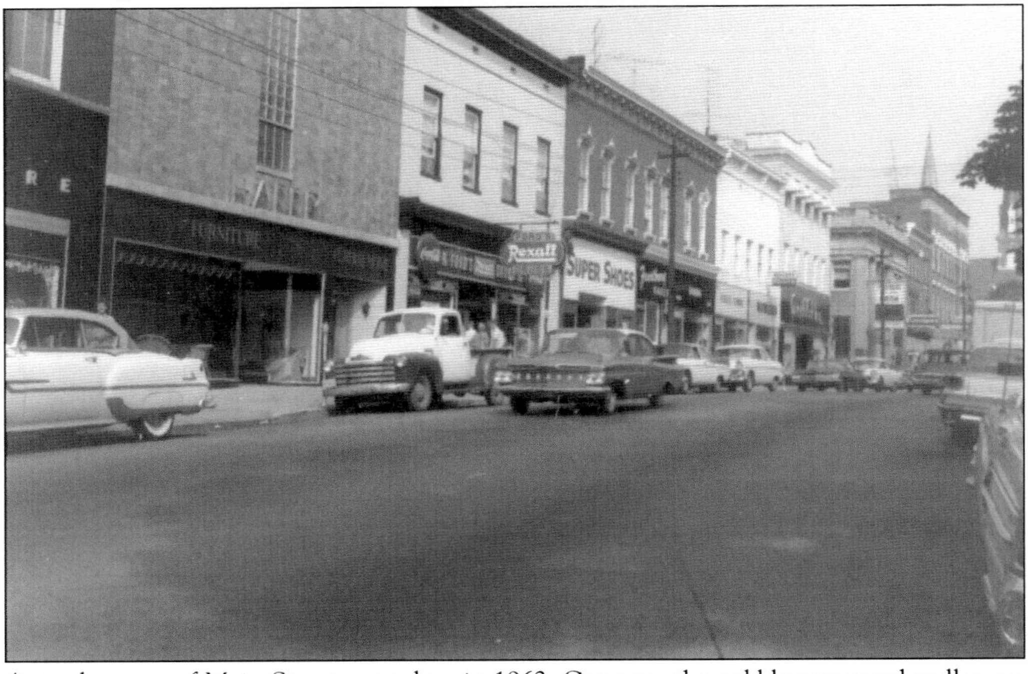

A similar view of Main Street was taken in 1962. Gone are the cobblestones and trolley car tracks. While a few of the buildings have changed, this section of Main Street would have been recognizable to the gentleman sitting in the Model-T.

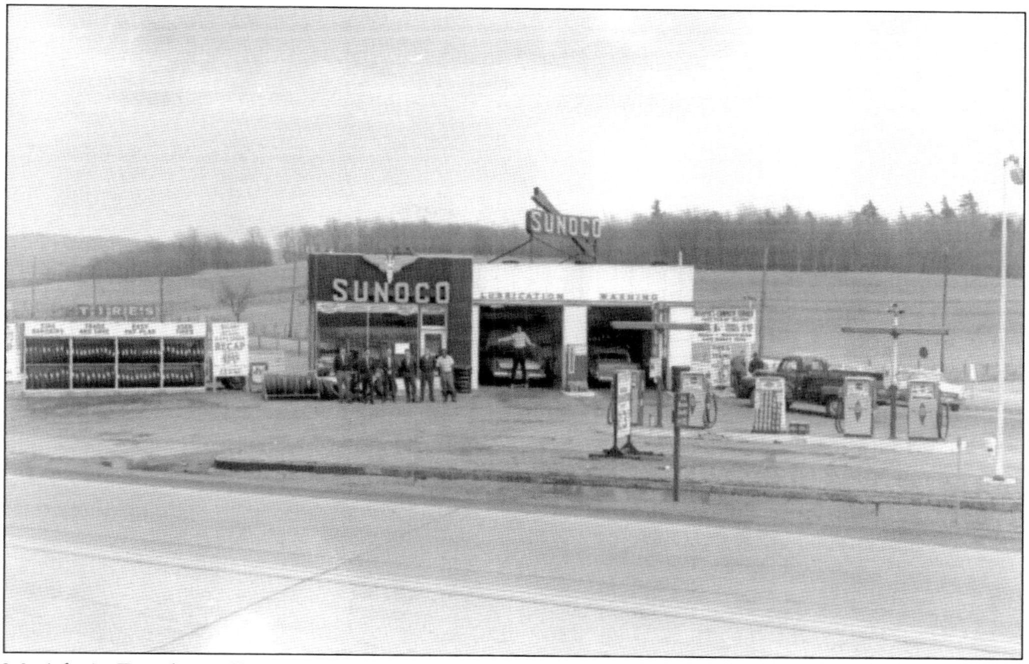

McAfee's Frostburg Sunoco Station was on the east end of town. When this photograph was taken in 1962, the land surrounding this station was largely undeveloped. In a photograph taken today, however, the hills in the background would show shopping centers and convenience stores, and the service station itself has been replaced by a used automobile dealership.

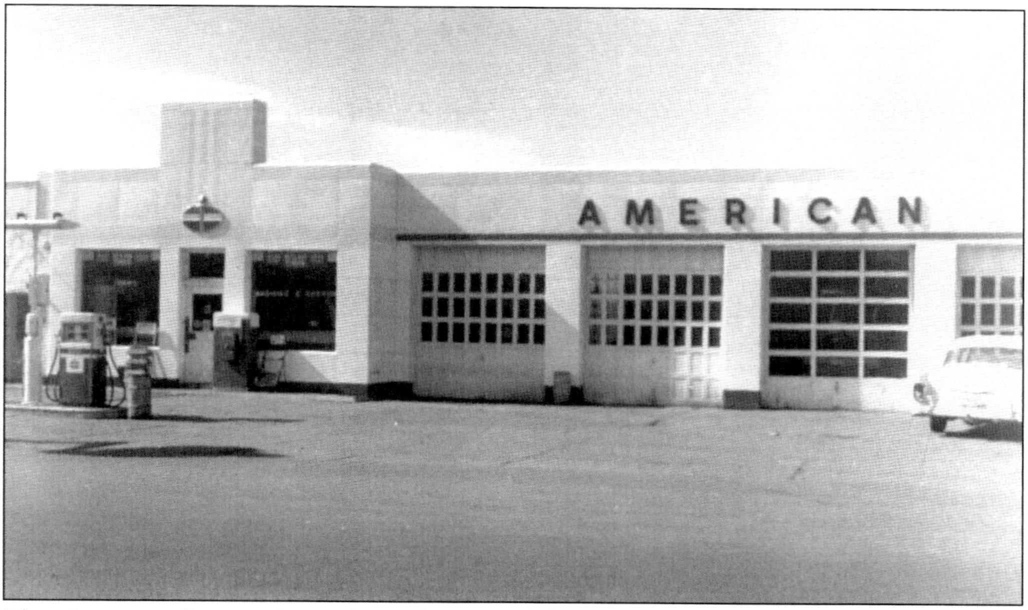

This American Station (now Amoco) is, as of this writing, the last remaining full-service gasoline station in Frostburg. What was unique about this particular station was the map of the routes from Frostburg to Baltimore and to Pittsburgh that used to adorn the wall just to the left of the windows. Not a scaled road map, to be sure, but it did give a good representation of the routes to travel east or west of town.

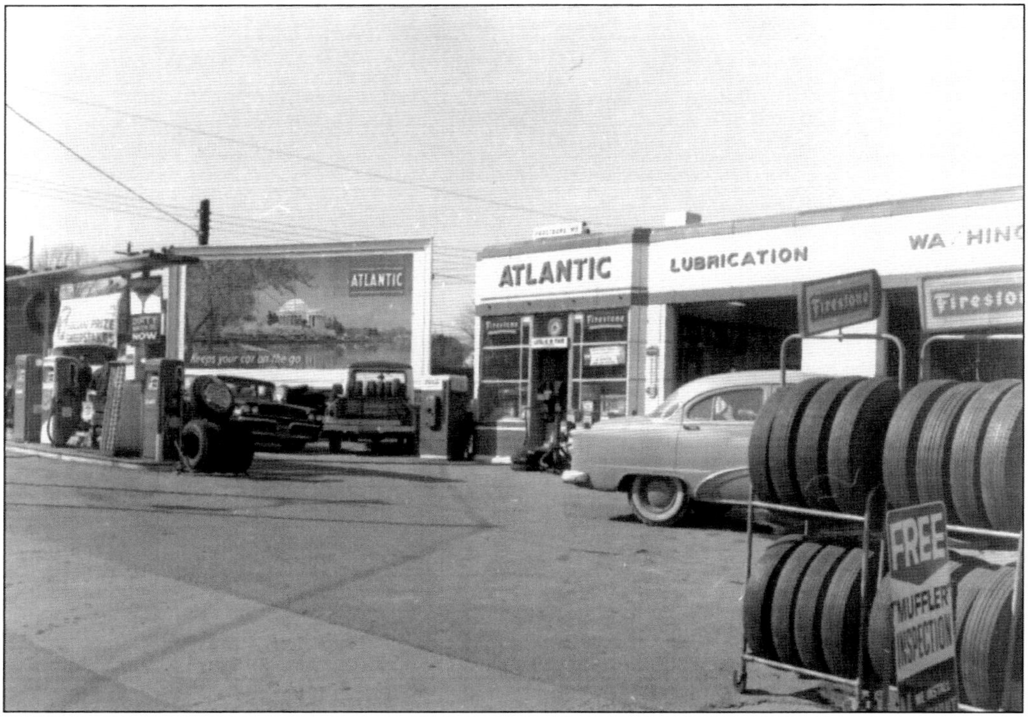

Another of the half-dozen service stations that were in Frostburg in 1962, this Atlantic Station sits on the northeast corner of Main Street and Depot Road, the site formerly occupied by the opera house (see page 61).

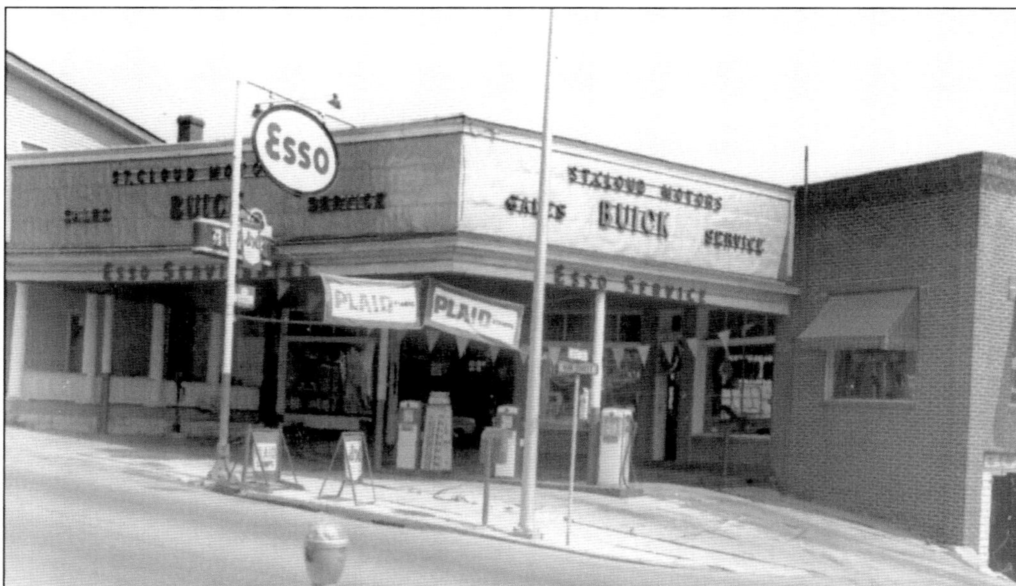

St. Cloud Motors, one of several car dealerships in town in the early 1960s, occupies the corner of Main Street and Depot Road, where the St. Cloud Hotel once stood (see page 51). In 1962, St. Cloud Motors was a Buick dealership. At one time, folks could actually purchase a DeSoto from an earlier dealership. And, as the signs remind, don't forget your plaid stamps!

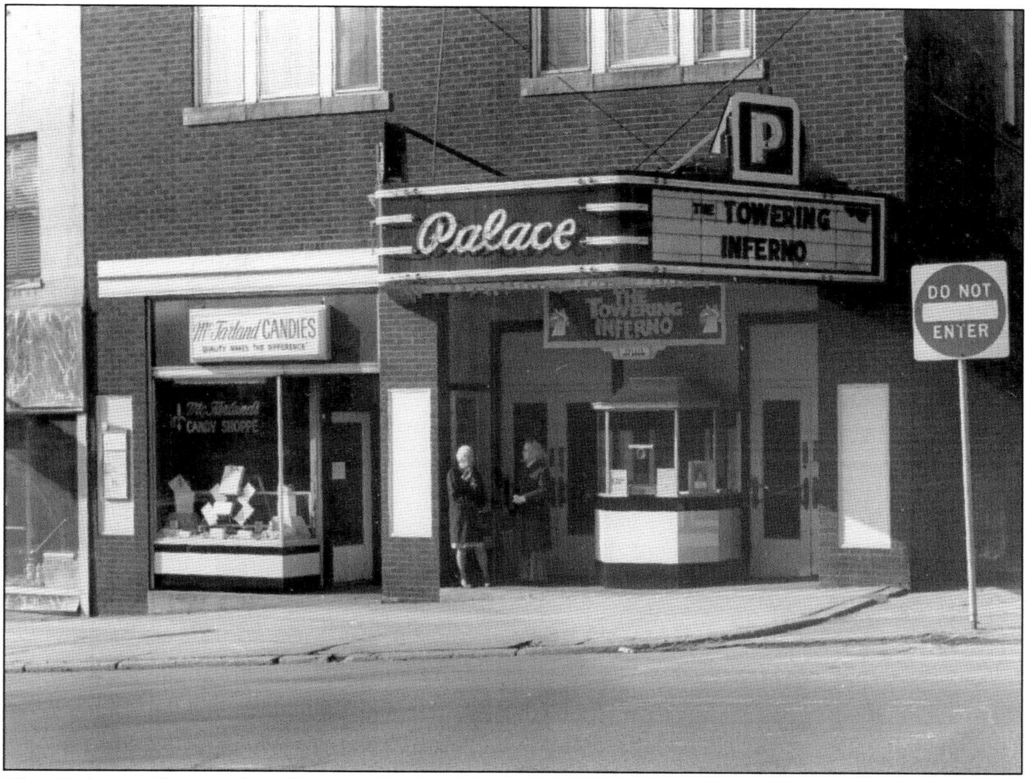

The Palace Theater has been a landmark in town since the Spates Brothers turned the nickelodeon, Dreamland, into a "moving picture" theater in 1913. A fixture on Main Street for decades, the Palace, unable to compete with multiplex theaters and video rentals, has been transformed from a motion picture theater to a multipurpose community theater.

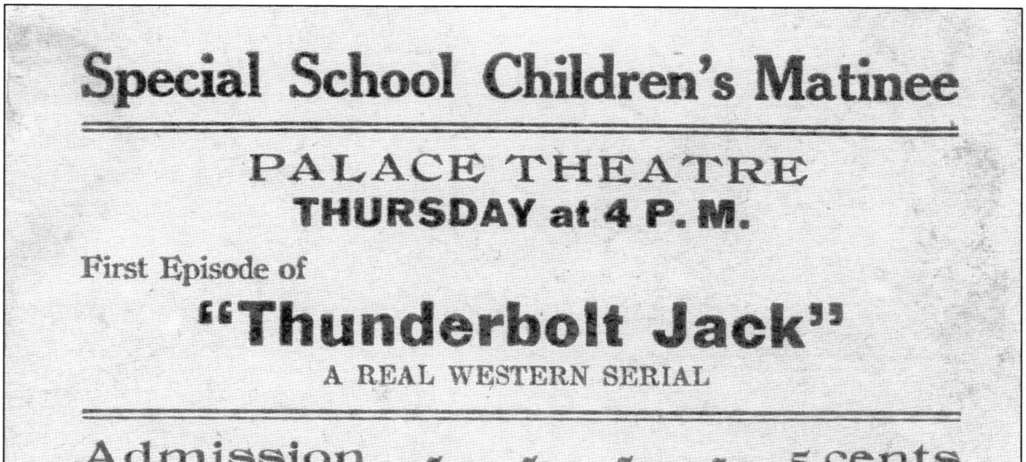

Generations of young people clutched tickets like this one anxious to see the flickering images on the silver screen of the Palace. Matinees and after-school specials attracted the young people, while giveaways (such as "Dish Night" during the Depression, where patrons were given a different piece of dinnerware each week with paid admission) and other special events enticed an older crowd.

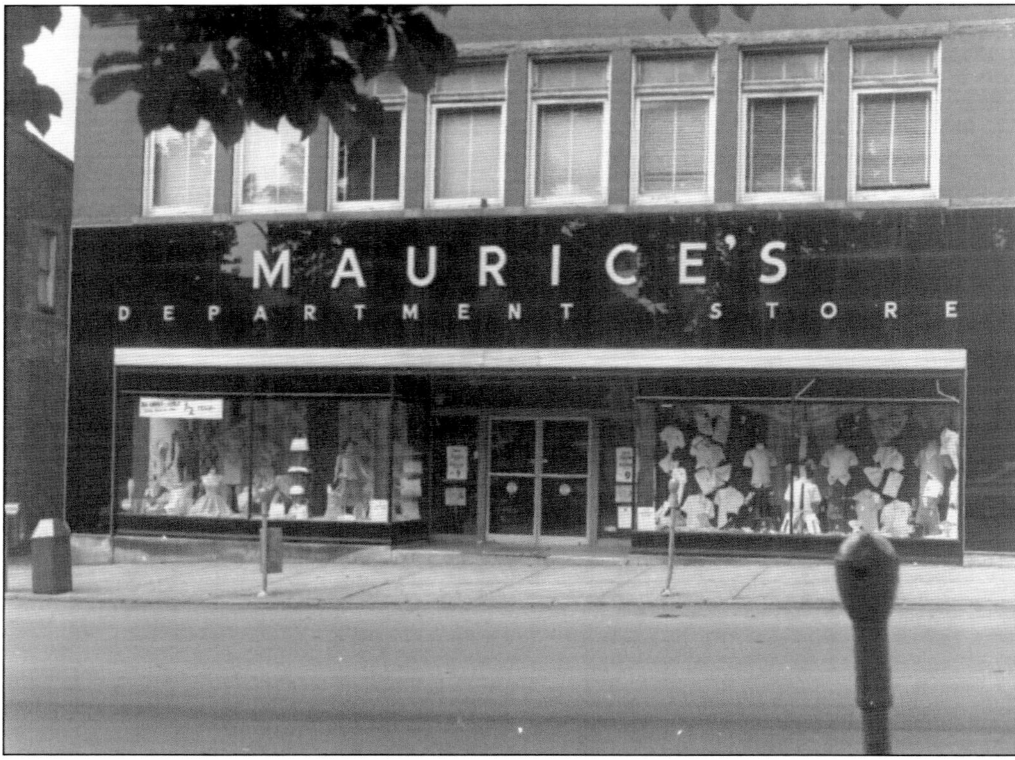

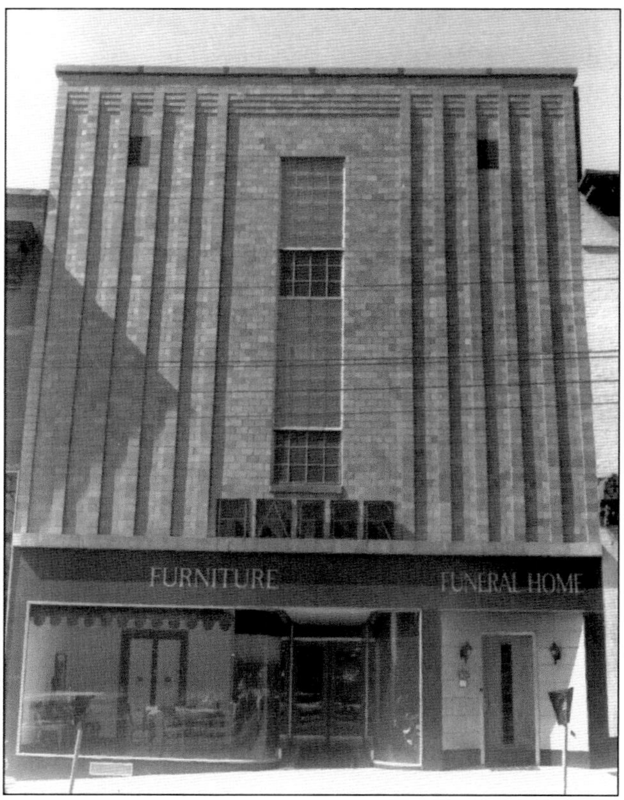

In 1962, as Frostburg was preparing for the sesquicentennial celebration, local photographer Howard Ward took photographs for the celebration souvenir book. His photographs give an excellent view of Main Street in the early 1960s. Here is Maurice's Department Store, offering "two complete floors of Quality Merchandise." Maurice's is located in the building that once housed the Hitchins Brothers store (see p. 55).

The unique Hafer Building was home to the Hafer furniture store and funeral home. The Hafer family first started in the furniture and undertaking business in 1907, when Jacob Hafer succeeded to the business previously run by Gehauf & Mayer. The Hafer family continues to operate funeral homes in the area.

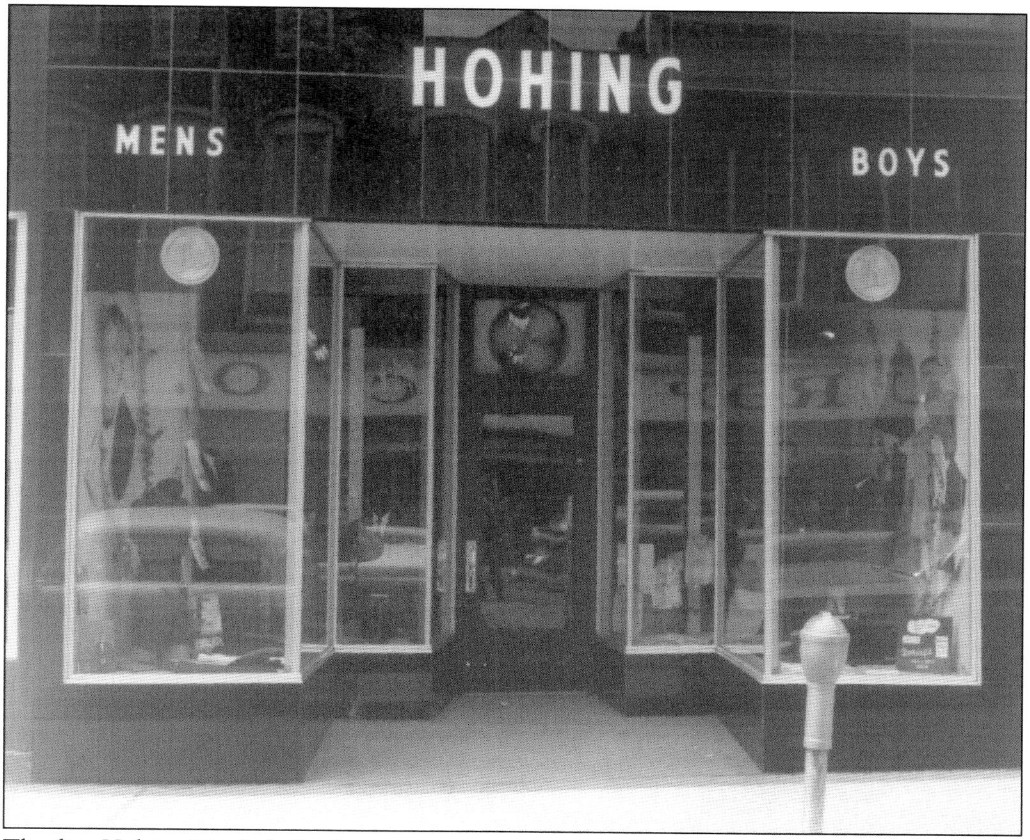

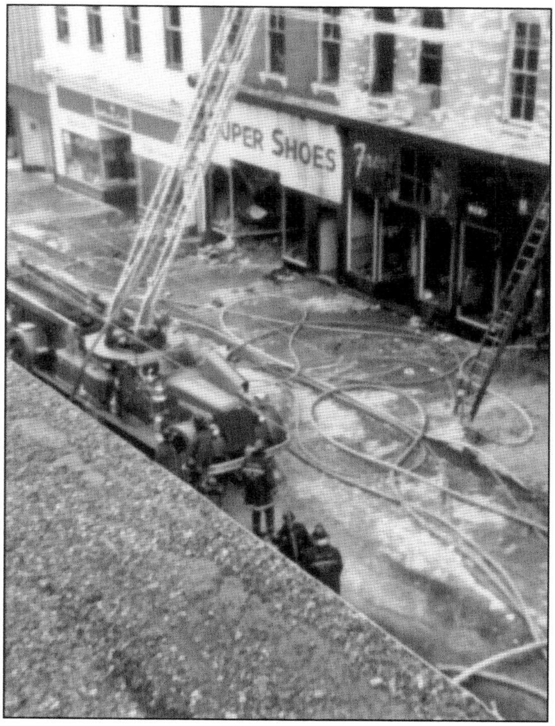

The first Hohing Men's & Boy's store was established on Main Street by Otto Hohing Sr. in 1905 as Otto Hohing & Sons. The store claimed to be "sole agents for Kuppenheinmer Clothes." The Hohing family was active in many community organizations, including the Cumberland Committee for the Relief of the Johnstown Suffers following the Johnstown Flood of 1889. By 1962, the Hohing shop was being run by Bob and Ruth Hohing.

On January 13, 1973, the Hohing Men's & Boy's store was one of eight businesses gutted or damaged by a fire that began in the rear of the Frostburg Bakery. The bakery is in the center of the photograph, with the Hohing shop to the right. These photographs taken from the roof of the G.C Murphy Store show Frostburg Fire Department's ladder truck, Truck 1, standing by as cleanup begins.

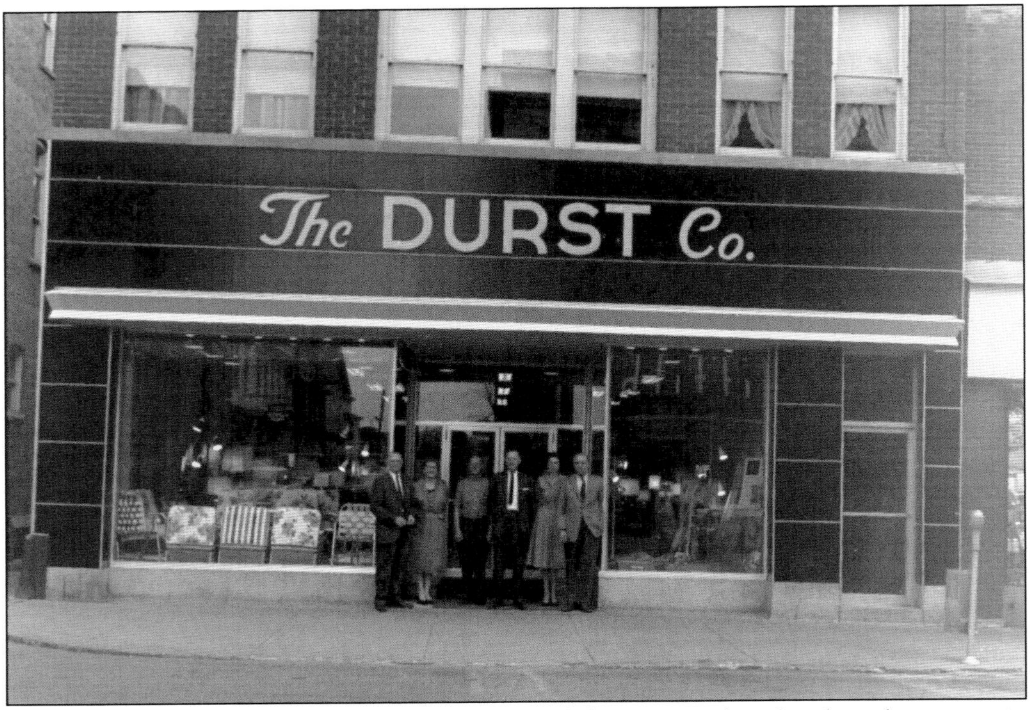

The Durst family, like the Hafer family, operated furniture and undertaking businesses in town for several generations. Established in 1904, The Durst Company proclaimed itself, "Frostburg's Second Oldest Establishment completing 58 years of continuous service to the community" in 1962. Both Durst and Hafer operated ambulance service to Frostburg for nearly 50 years until the creation of the Frostburg Area Ambulance Service in 1975. The Durst Building, erected in 1919, stands at the corner of Main Street and north Broadway and is now home to Main Street Books.

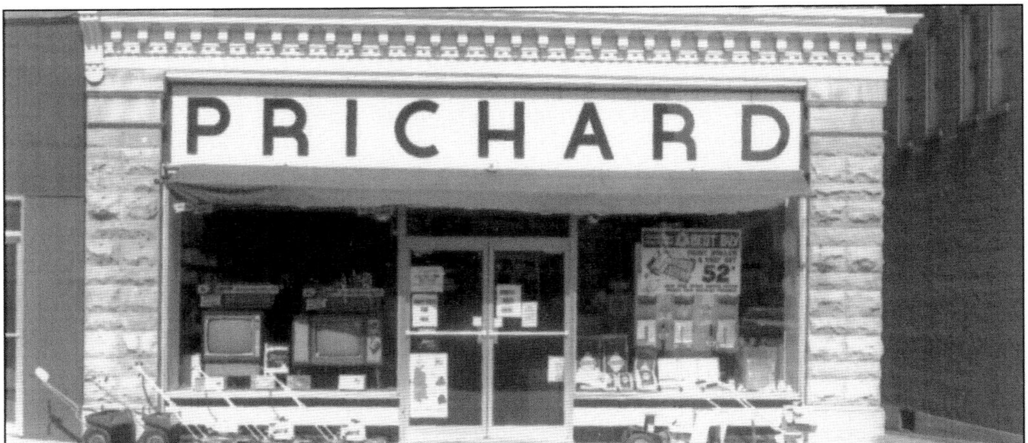

Pritchard's, "the hardware department store," boasted 55 years of continuous service in 1962. The large brick building, built in 1919 from the ashes of the Shea building, was an anchor along Main Street until competition from large discount lumber and hardware stores forced Pritchard's to close in the late 1990s.

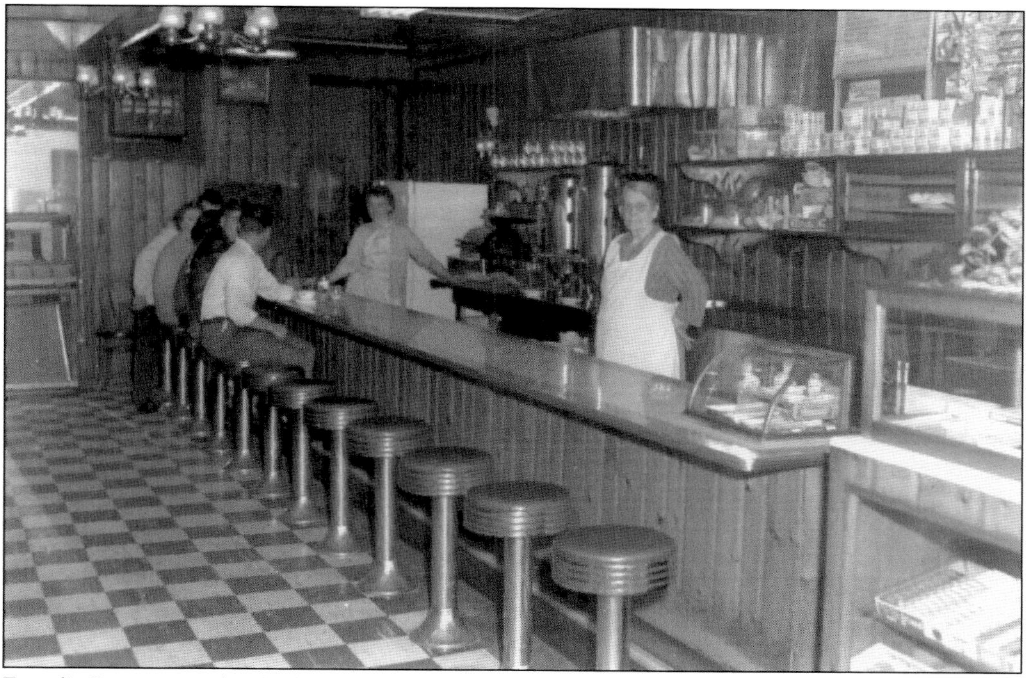

Finzel's Restaurant (with the slogan "Meet & Eat at Finzel's Restaurant") was one of several restaurants on Main Street in 1962. Over a dozen eating establishments lined Main Street, from soda fountains, like Parise's, to restaurant/bars like Stoop's and Al's, to "Frostburg's most exclusive" Au Petit Paris French Restaurant.

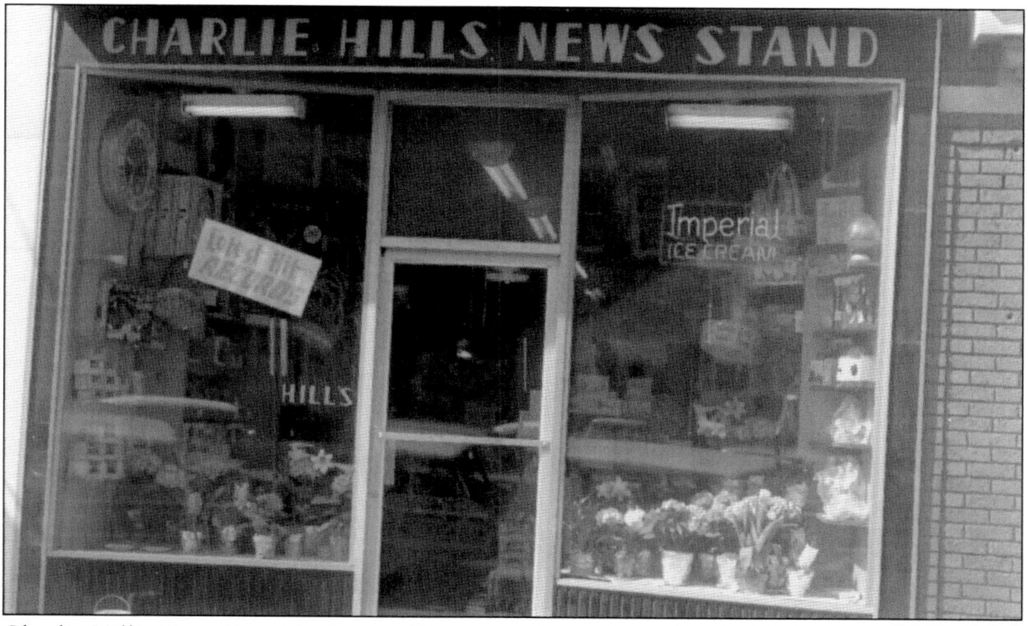

Charlie Hill's News Stand had spent 23 years on Main Street by 1962. The shop claimed that it was "built on service and variety" and that "whatever season it is—Charlie has it." Charlie Hill's was also home to another fixture on Main Street, Minnehaha. Minnehaha was a wooden cigar store Indian who made her first appearance in town in the early 19th century in front of what was the Davis Brothers' Tobacco Store.

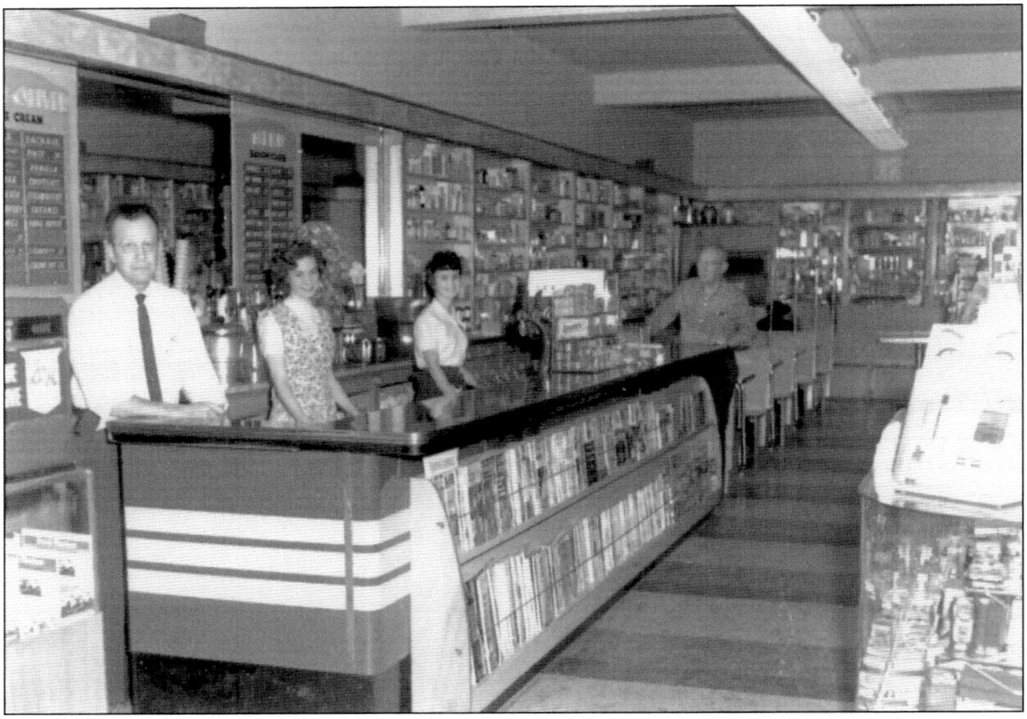
The T&S Cut-Rate, a longtime fixture at the corner of Main and Water Streets, offered a variety of goods and services from film development to a luncheon counter with cheerful waitresses. Established in 1938, Bill and Madeline Thomas owned and operated the shop into the 1970s.

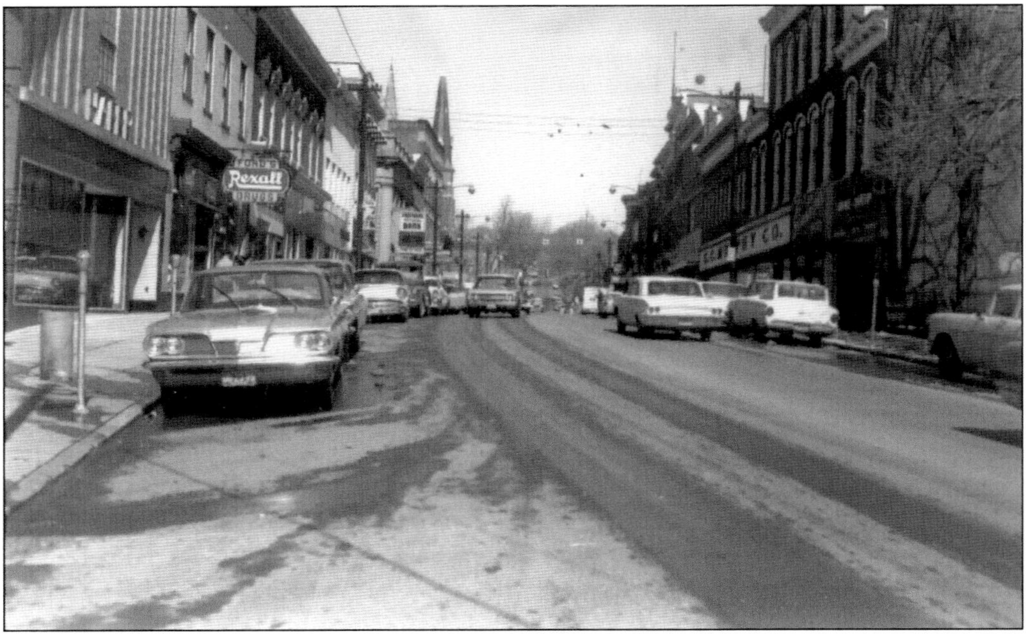

This is Main Street in 1962. While the road is now paved, trolley car tracks are long gone, and a different type of vehicle lines the street, the skyline is still remarkably similar to the photograph opening this chapter.

Five

From the Town's Attic

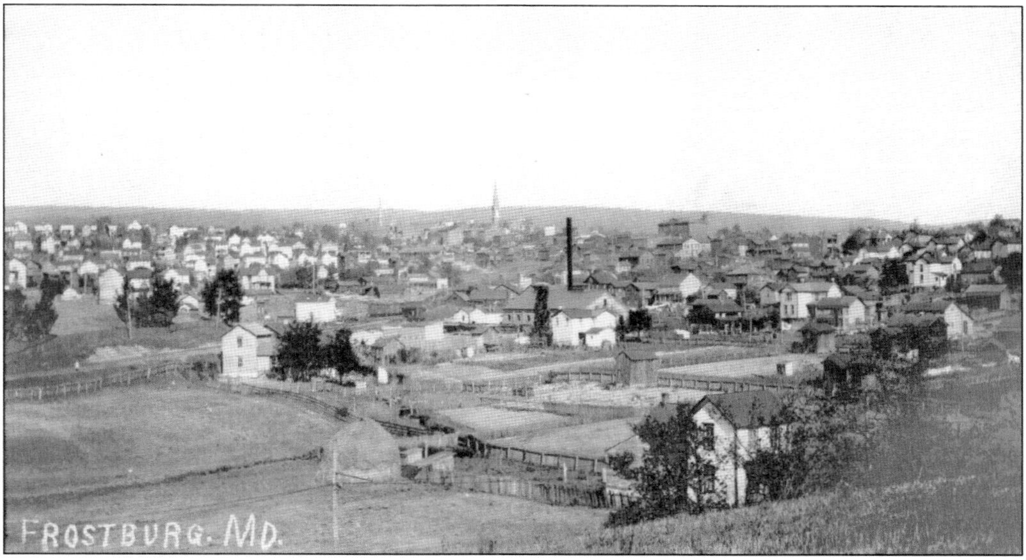

A late 19th-century view of Frostburg from what is now Frostburg Memorial Gardens cemetery shows a sprawling community of rather substantial houses. The opera house and the spire of St. Michael's Church can be seen in the distance. The C&P railroad branch to the George's Creek mining area can be seen to the left.

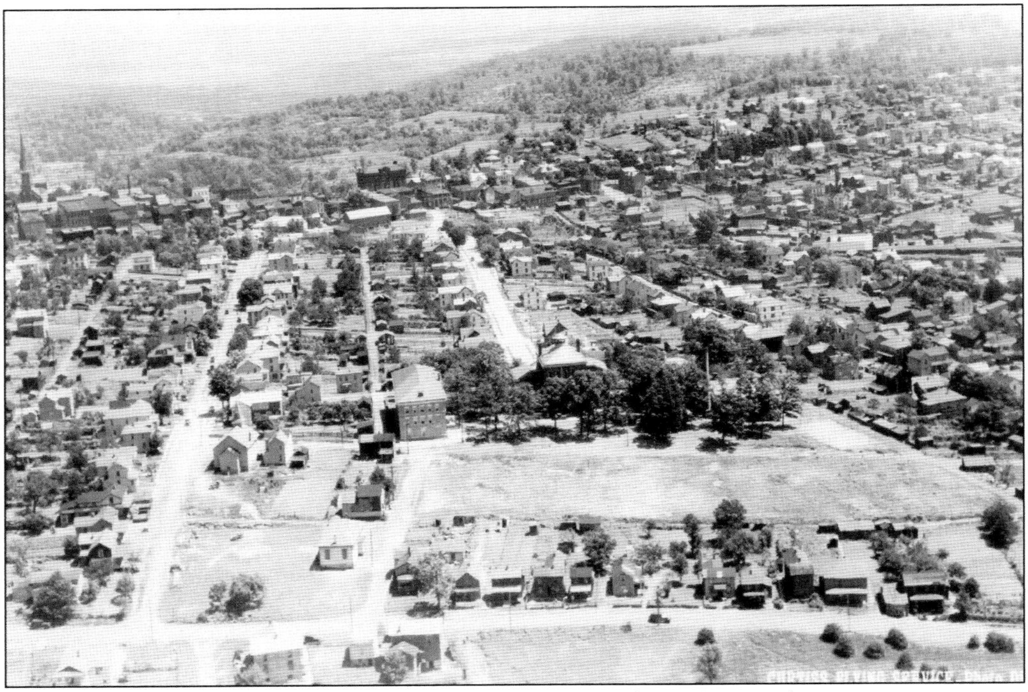

An aerial photograph of Frostburg taken by the Curtiss Flying Service (an aviation company that traveled from town to town taking aerial photos and offering airplane rides) shows a birds-eye view of the town before 1936. The cluster of buildings of Frostburg State Teachers College is in the center foreground, while the opera house stills stands on Main Street in the center of the photo.

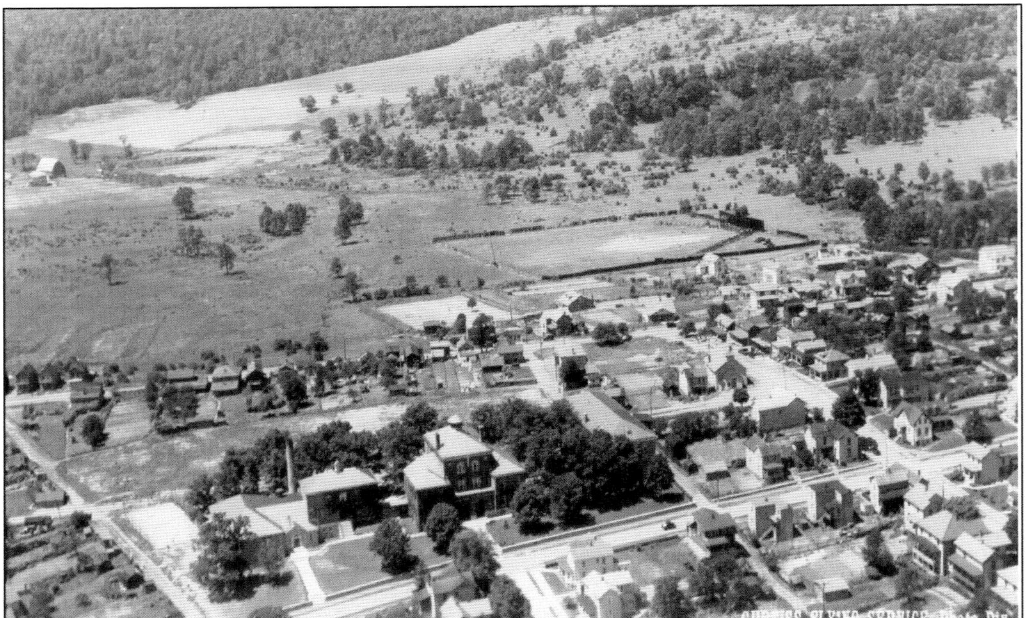

Another of the Curtiss Flying Service shots, this photo shows the view from the college towards the southwest. In the background is the baseball park where the many teams of the area played. That area is now the site of several of the Frostburg State University's dormitories.

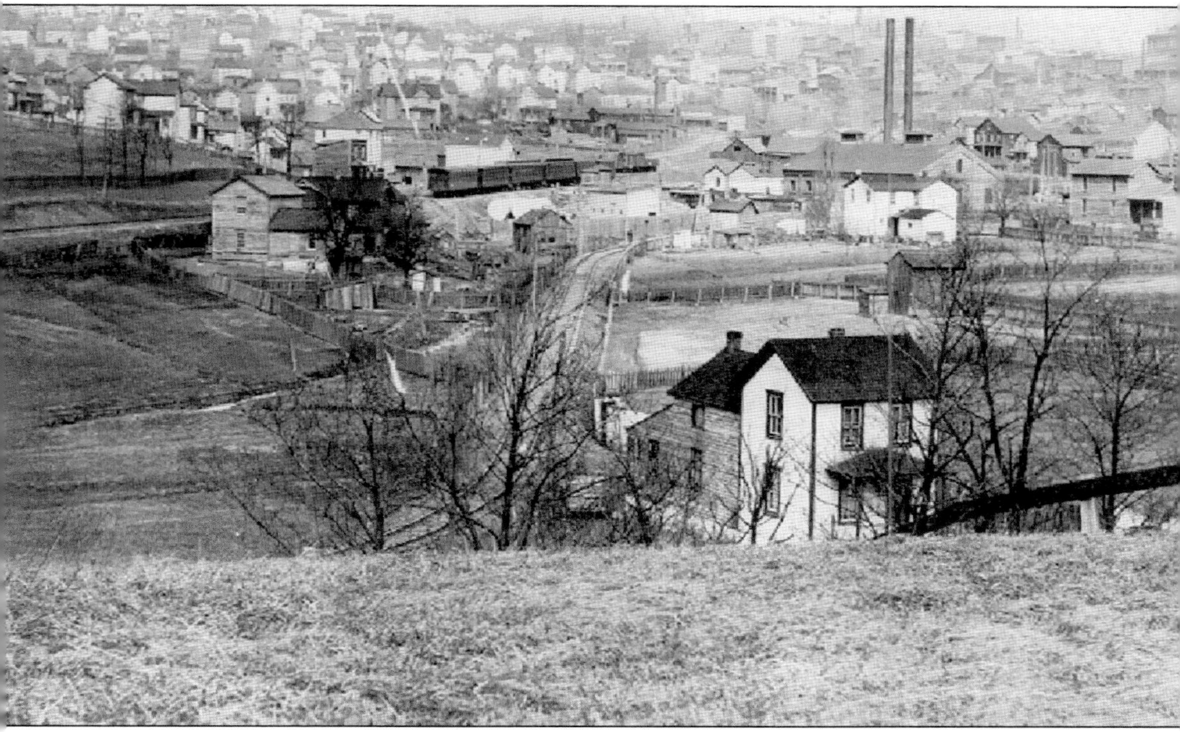

This view is similar to the one on page 81, but was taken several years later. The Cumberland & Westernport Electric Railway tracks can be seen in the foreground and the electrical power plant for the line has added a second smokestack (in the center of the photo). A local C&P train can be seen on the C&P track just to the right of the power plant.

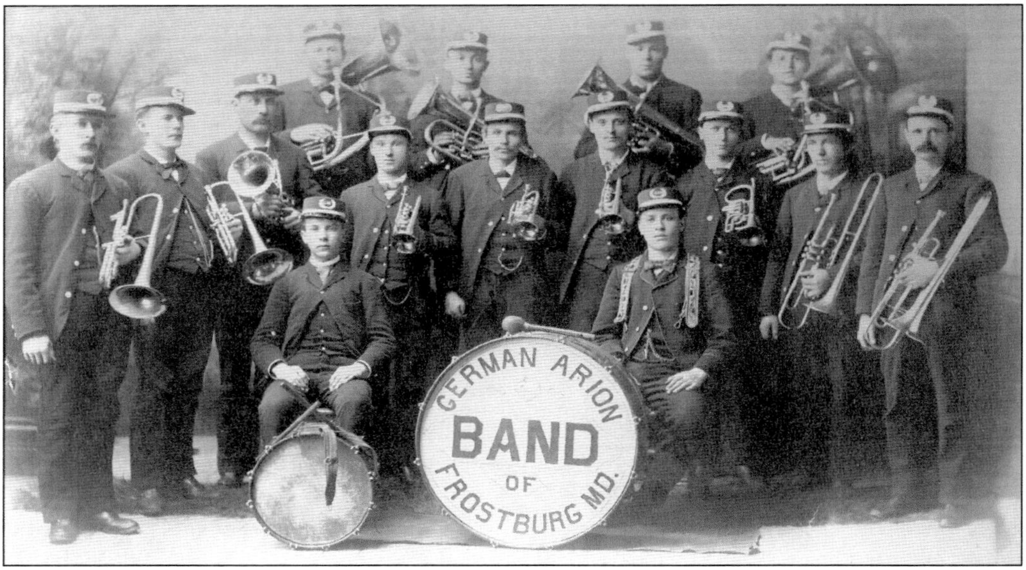

The German Arion Band of Frostburg was established in 1877 by Conrad Nickel, and has continued to perform to the present day. A fixture during celebrations and ceremonies in town, the Arion Band also had a marching unit as well as a dance band for programs at the Opera House. The term "Arion" comes from a mythological musician who when tossed into the sea by bandits, was saved by dolphins because of the beautiful music he played.

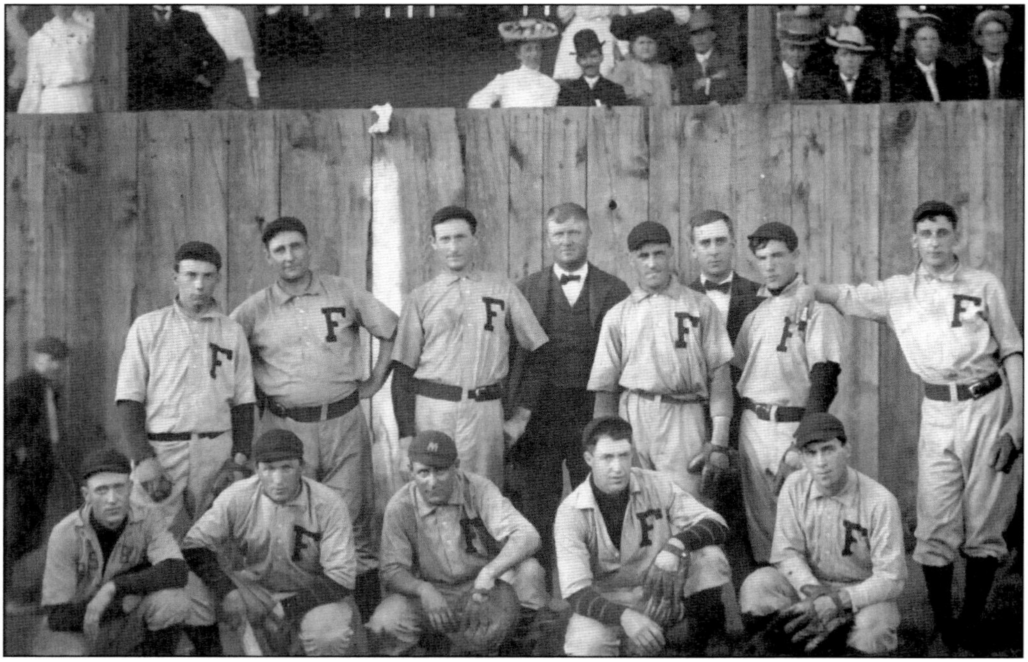

Baseball was a favorite pasttime of many in the area. By 1871, teams sporting names such as the Frostburg Haymakers, the Grahamtown Big Feet, and the Dolly Vardens were playing regularly in the area. In 1921, the Frostburg Demons hosted the then-minor league Baltimore Orioles and their star pitcher Lefty Grove. (Grove, who was from nearby Lonaconing, is buried in Frostburg). Many of these very popular games were played on the ball diamond seen in the photograph on page 82.

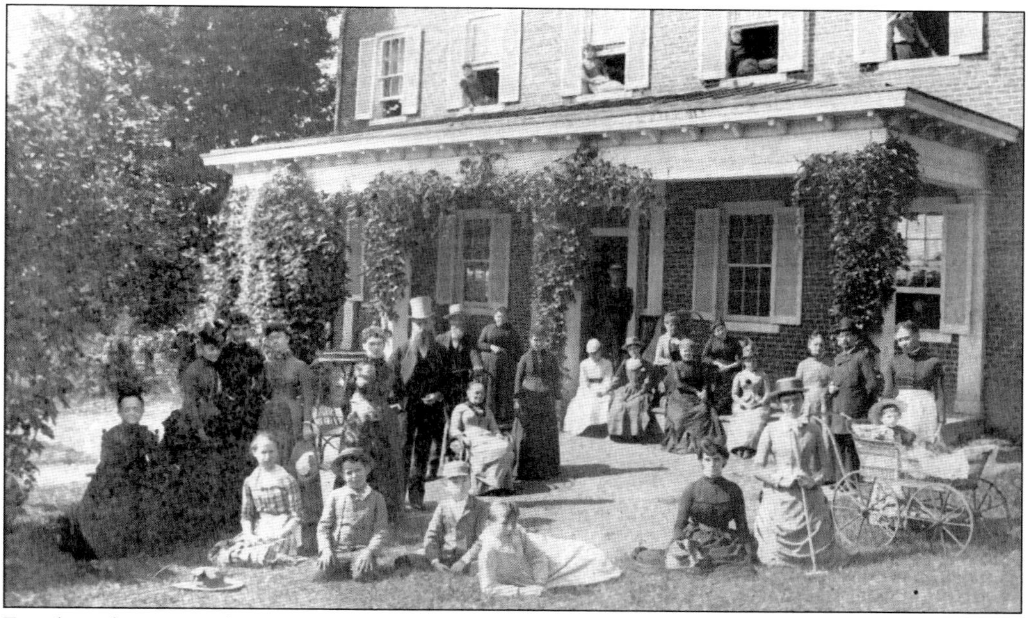

Frostburg became a favorite destination for folks trying to beat the heat and noise of summers in the city. Others came for the medicinal qualities of the mountain air! In 1883, Nathan Frost, son of Meshach Frost, turned what was the old Frost farmhouse into a summer hotel, offering running water in the rooms and an indoor privy. Here is a group of folks posing in front of the Frost Mansion, located on Frost Avenue.

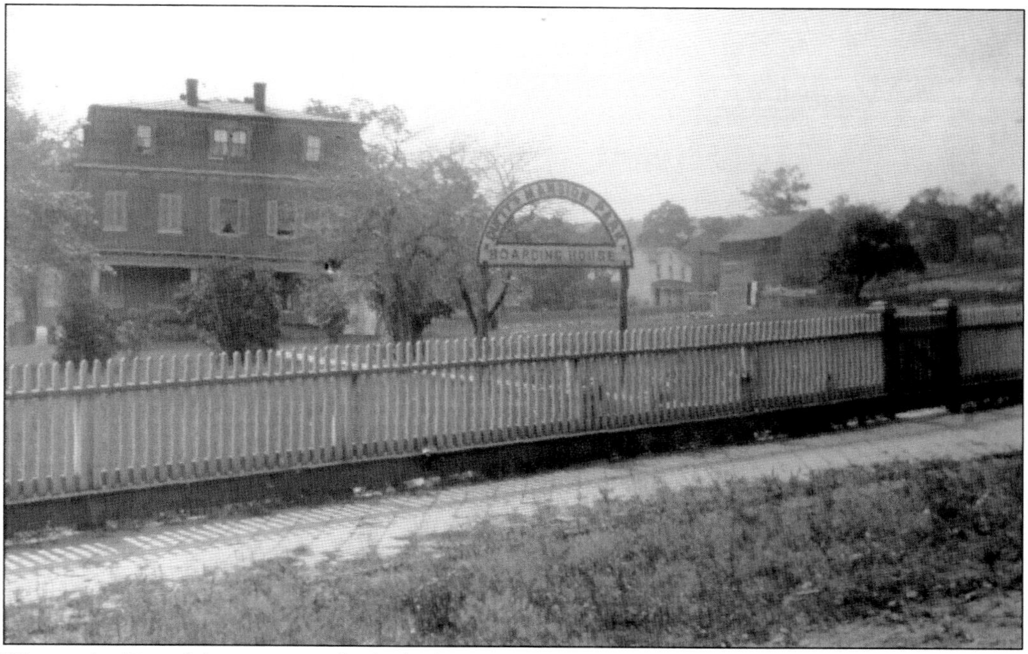

This is the Frost Mansion as it looked when it was Dufty's Mansion Park Boarding House from 1893 to1903. Nathan Frost, wishing to add more rooms to the original two-story building, added a third floor and mansard roof in the 1880s. Many notables from society and government spent time at the Frost Mansion and at several other homes and hotels in town. Today, the mansion is the John J. Hafer Frost Mansion Funeral Home.

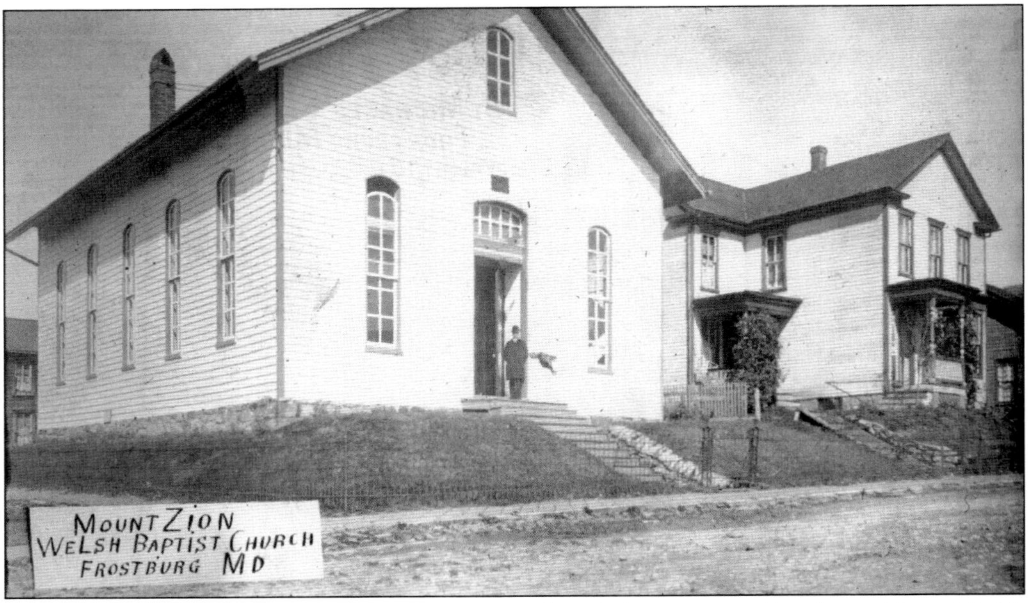

During the coal boom years, many immigrants found their way to Frostburg. Many Welsh miners, stone masons, and bricklayers came to Frostburg to raise their families and work in the mines and building trades. Bringing a bit of Wales with them, the Welsh Baptist Church was established. Services were often conducted in Welsh. This frame building was later covered in stone.

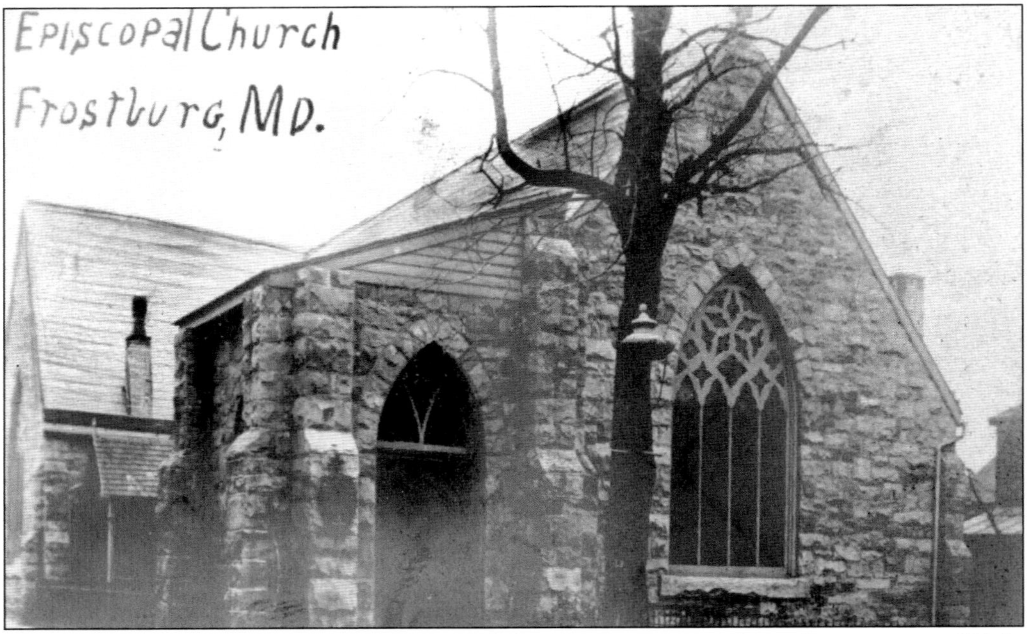

St. John's Episcopal on Broadway is one of the unique houses of worship in town. While the Episcopal Church first came to Frostburg in 1840, it wasn't until the 1850s that the congregation began to grow. The present church was built in 1890 and 1891, with stone walls two-feet thick and built by local stonemasons. Several additions have been made since the above photograph was taken, such as the tower erected in 1926, the side chapel, and the high altar.

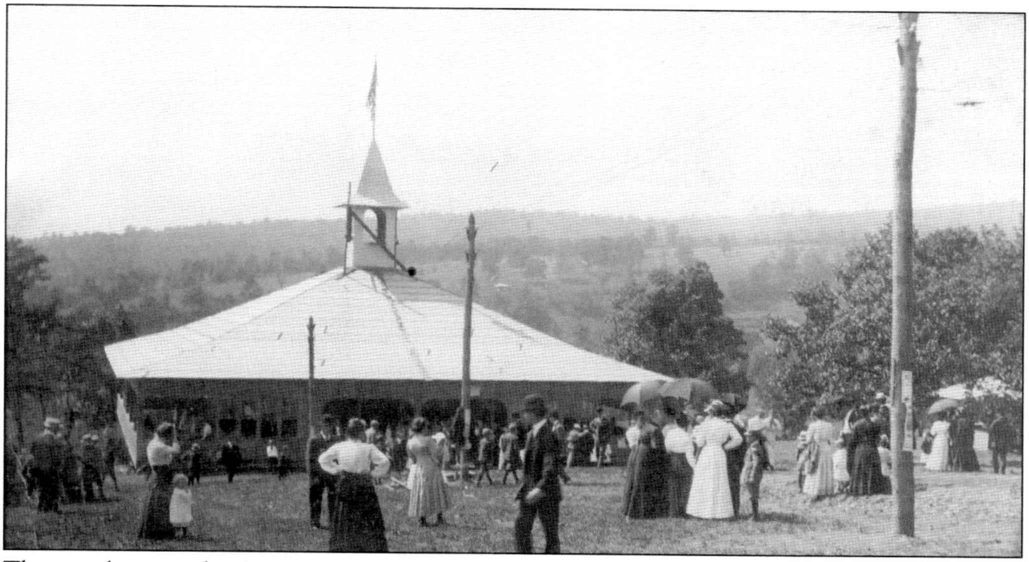

The pavilion at the Junior Order Park was an 80-foot square structure that served as an entertainment center in town for over 50 years. The Junior Order Park hosted many picnics, carnivals, and other activities, and while the park was intended for all in the community, visitors were expected to observe proper rules of behavior. These rules even dictated what types of dance steps were appropriate, with the Turkey Trot, Banana Glide, and Boston Dip unacceptable! The pavilion, a favorite rolling-skating rink for several generations, was torn down in the early 1960s and the park turned into the Meshach Frost Village.

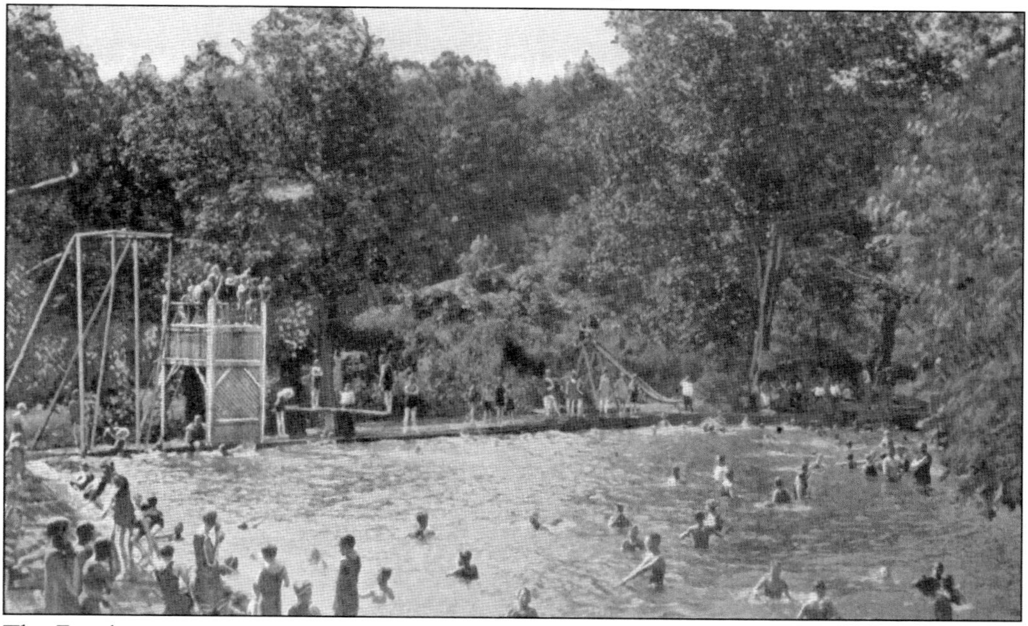

The Frostburg swimming pool is one of many examples of residents pitching in to better the community. In 1921, the Commercial Club of Frostburg convinced the Consolidation Coal Company to donate nine acres of land near a small-dammed stream that the company used to water livestock. This had always been a favorite place for young people to cool off during the summer. Volunteers from town showed up at the end of June with picks and shovels, even working shifts to complete the project that summer. On August 24, the pool was dedicated.

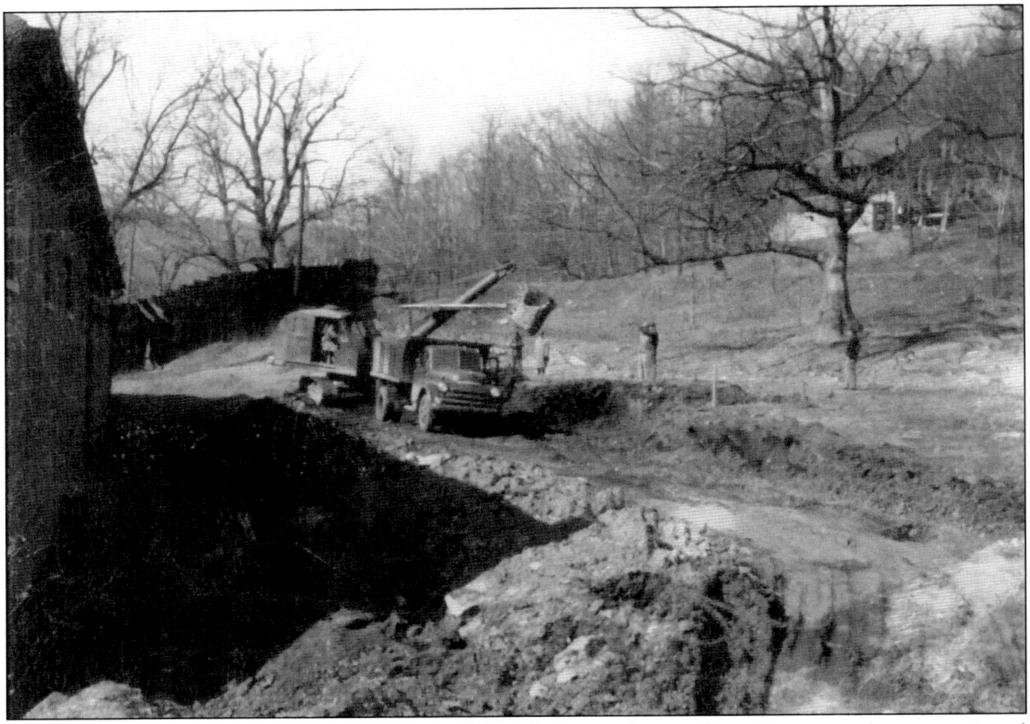

While the original swimming pool was a useful and extremely popular addition to the recreational life of the community, by the early 1950s a newer, modern pool was needed. In 1954, a filtration system was installed and bathhouses and a concession stand were added.

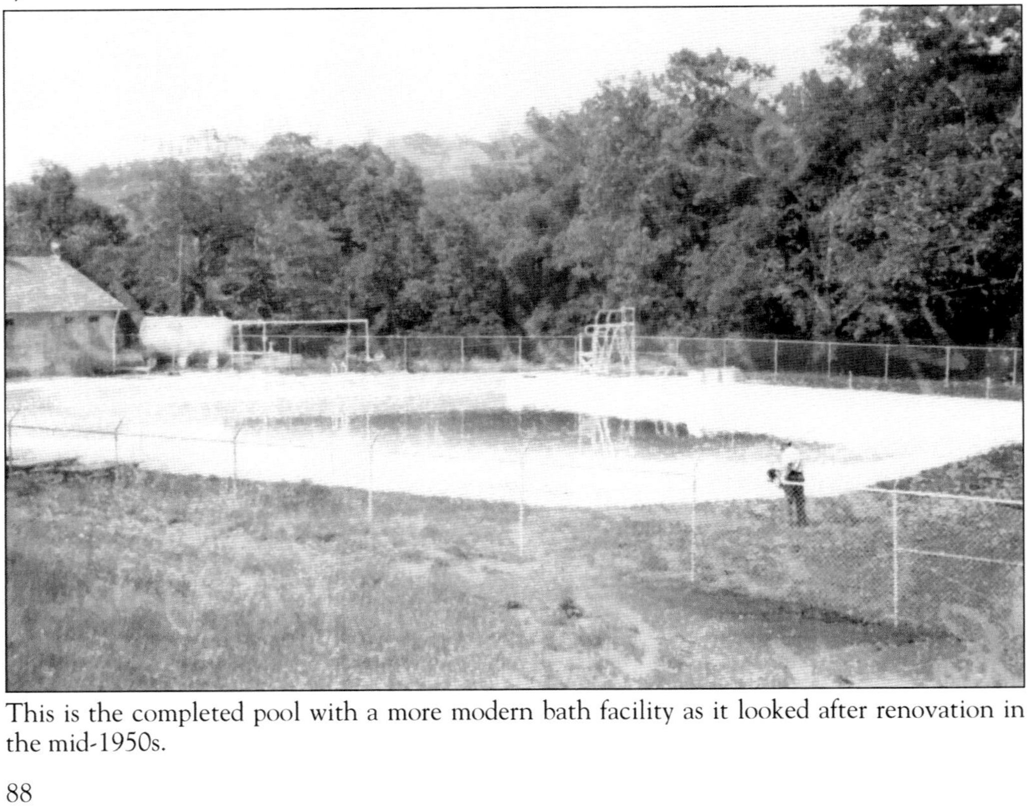

This is the completed pool with a more modern bath facility as it looked after renovation in the mid-1950s.

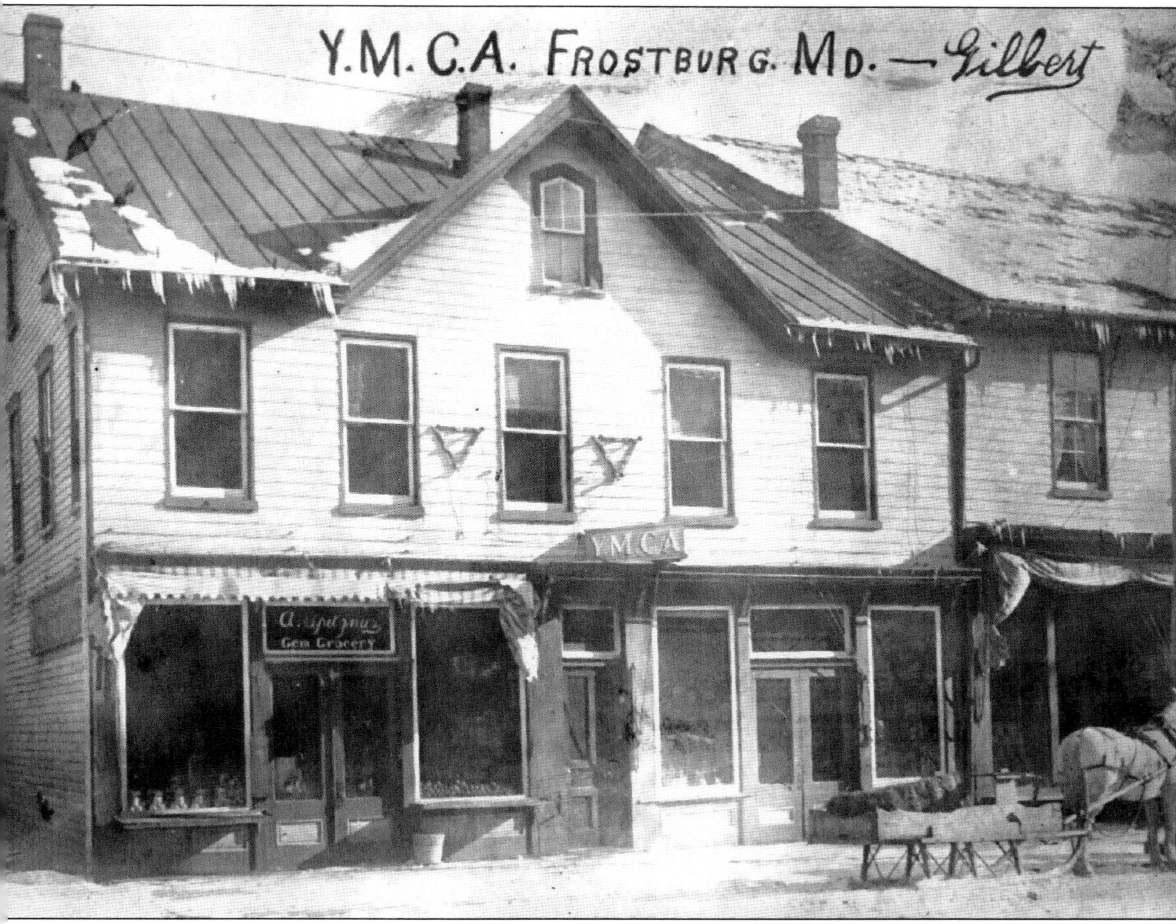

While its presence in other towns may have been more noticeable and lasting, the YMCA did play a significant role in the community in the late 19th and early 20th centuries. Housed in different buildings at different times, this version of the YMCA was located on Main Street on the second floor above the Albert Spitznas' grocery, next to the original Betz building, where Main Street Books is located today.

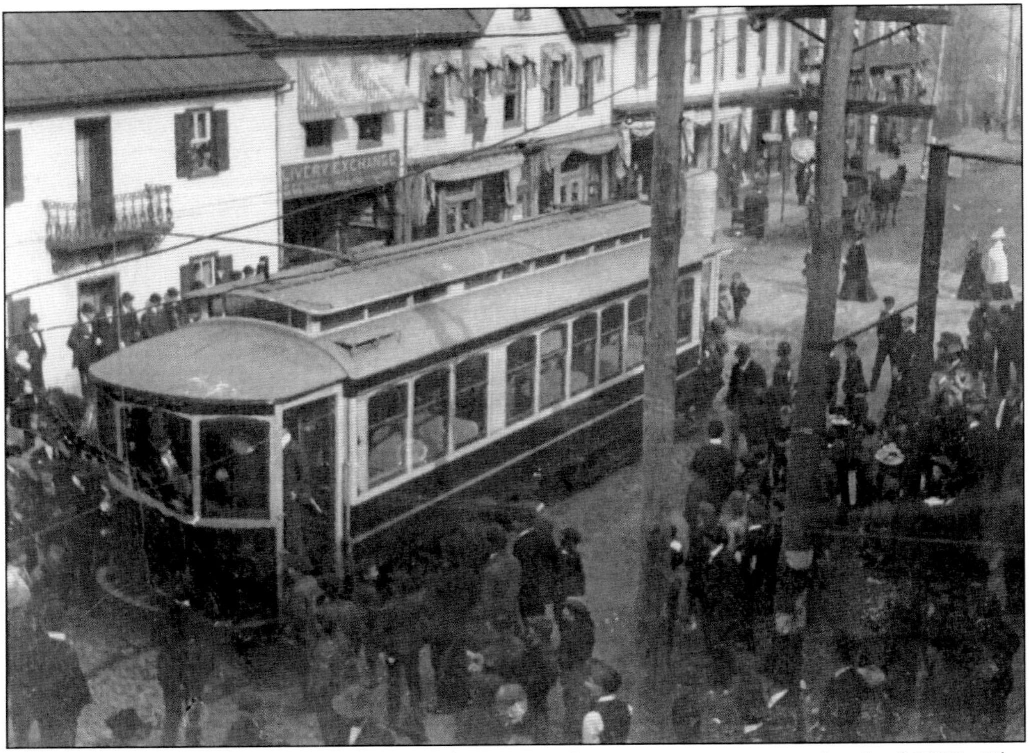

The arrival of the first streetcar in Frostburg caused quite a sensation in April of 1902. The Cumberland and Westernport Electric Railroad ran the electric-powered cars from Cumberland to Frostburg and on down George's Creek to Westernport. They were in business from 1902 until the company fell on hard times in the 1920s and turned to busses in 1925. The company ran regular cars for passengers, shift-cars for coal miners, freight cars for perishable goods, and a variety of special occasion cars.

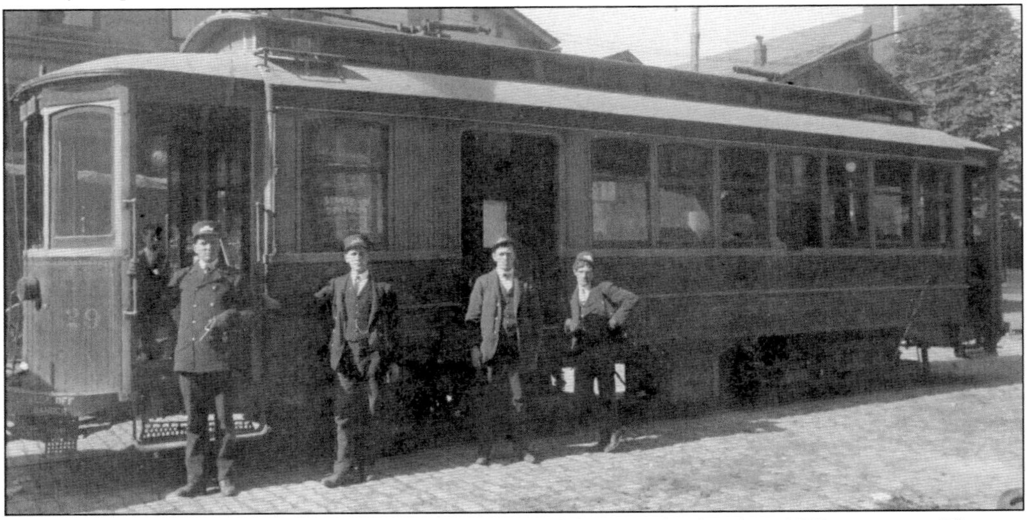

Motormen and conductors for the #29 trolley car of the Cumberland and Westernport Electric Railroad pose in front of the Eleanor Building in Frostburg. The cars were double-ended so they did not have to turn around at the end of the line. The motorman would use the other set of controls at the opposite end of the car, and the conductor would reverse the seats.

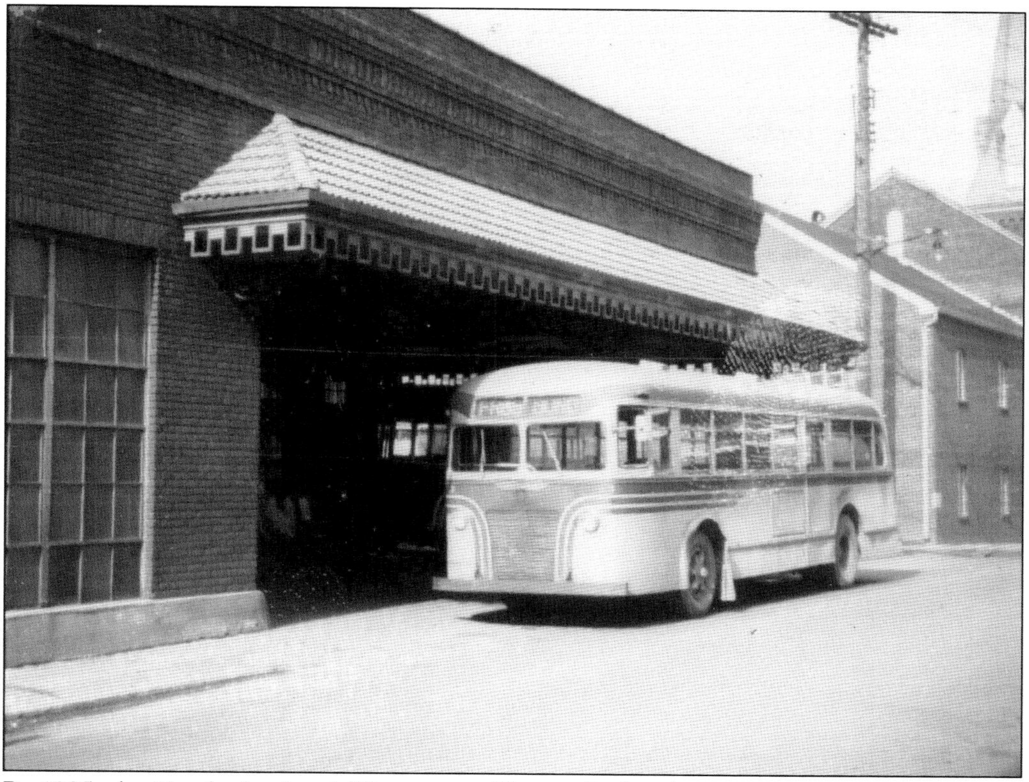

By 1925, the Cumberland and Westernport Electric Railroad gave way to busses. In 1928, a weekly pass to ride between Cumberland and Frostburg and to the Kelly Springfield plant and/or Celanese plant cost $3. By 1952, 23 drivers kept the busses moving around the clock. The Frostburg Terminal still stands at the southwest corner of Water and Mechanic Streets.

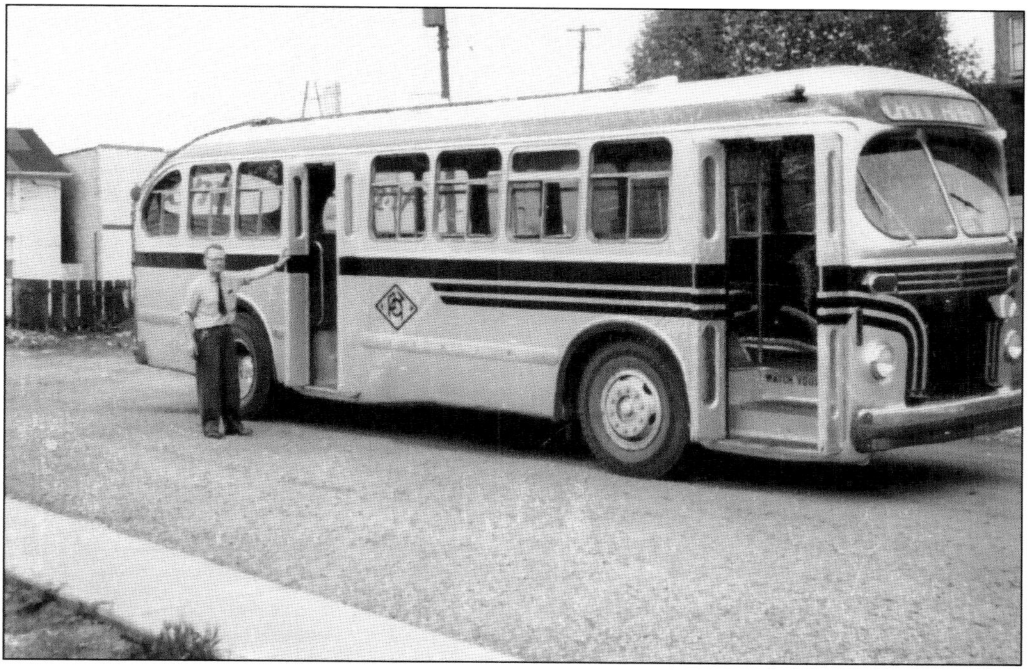

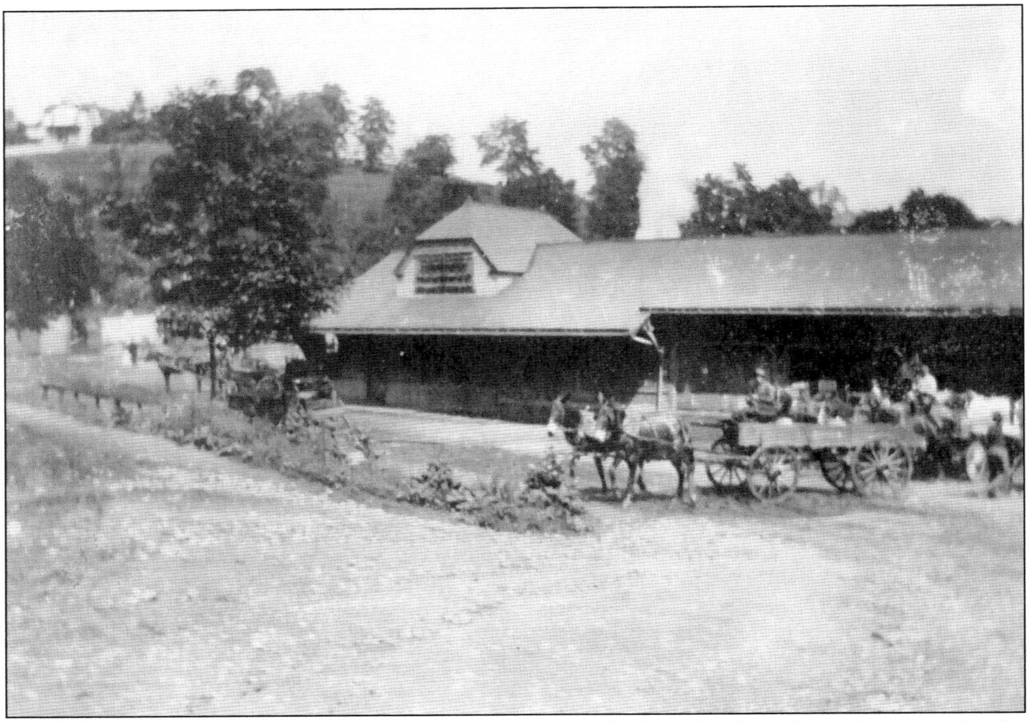

The C&P depot, just over the hill from Main Street, was built in 1891, and was the major freight depot in Frostburg on the Cumberland and Pennsylvania Railroad line. Here some teamsters with their loads prepare for the long, steep haul up Depot Road and into town.

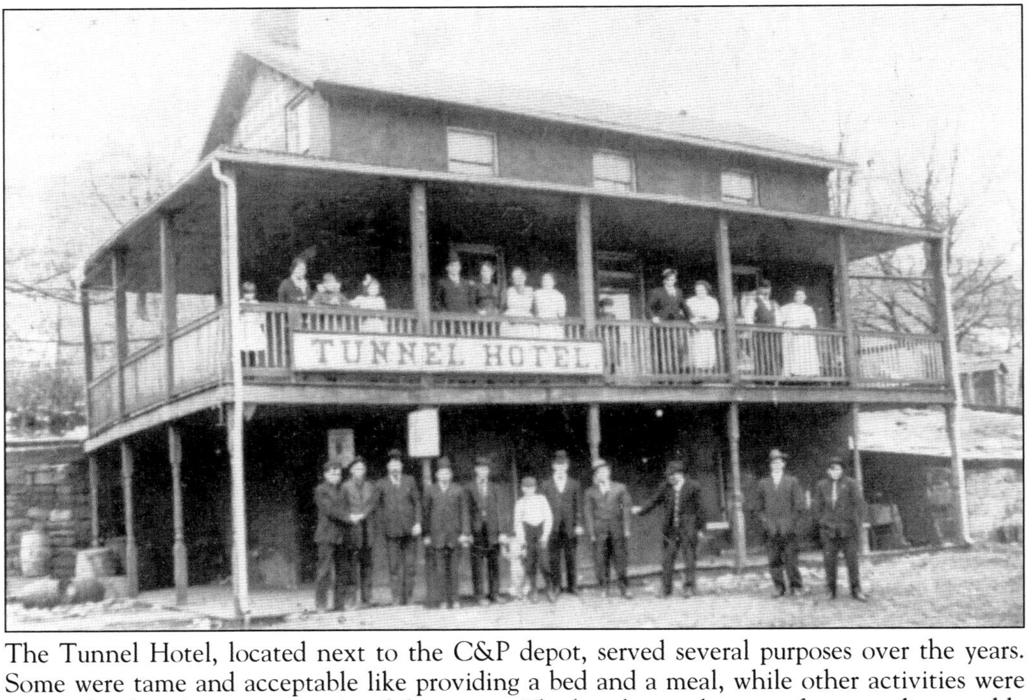

The Tunnel Hotel, located next to the C&P depot, served several purposes over the years. Some were tame and acceptable like providing a bed and a meal, while other activities were rumored to be a bit more risqué and dangerous. The hotel was a hangout for some disreputable characters, both male and female!

These are two views of train crews of the C&P Railroad during a layover at the depot in Frostburg. The C&P evolved out of the consolidation of several smaller rail lines, and gave Frostburg a through railroad. It ran from Cumberland to the east (with connections to the C&O Canal and other railroads) and Piedmont, West Virginia to the south (with a link with the B&O Railroad). In addition to freight and coal trains, the C&P ran passenger service along its lines. Between 1929 and 1942, the company found that it was not feasible to run a steam locomotive for passenger service. A gasoline-driven electric engine serviced the passenger trains until wartime necessities and a low number of passengers caused the cancellation of passenger service.

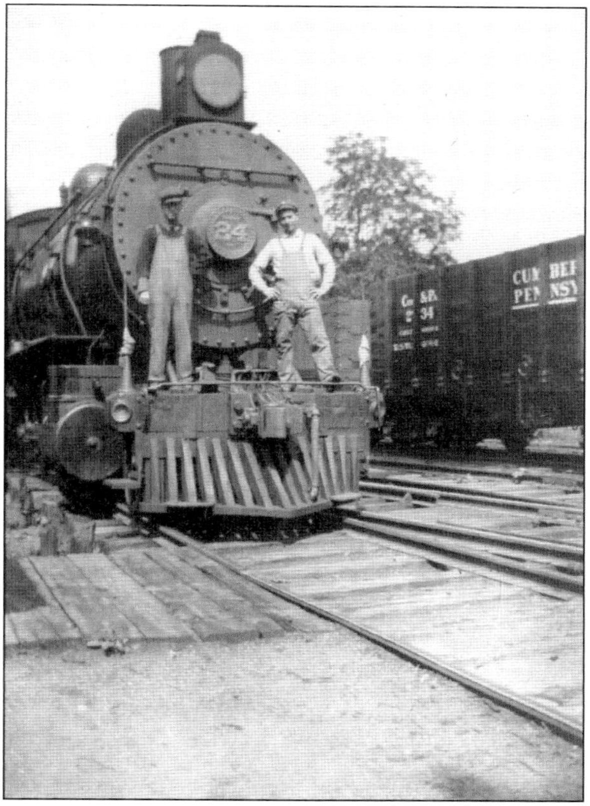

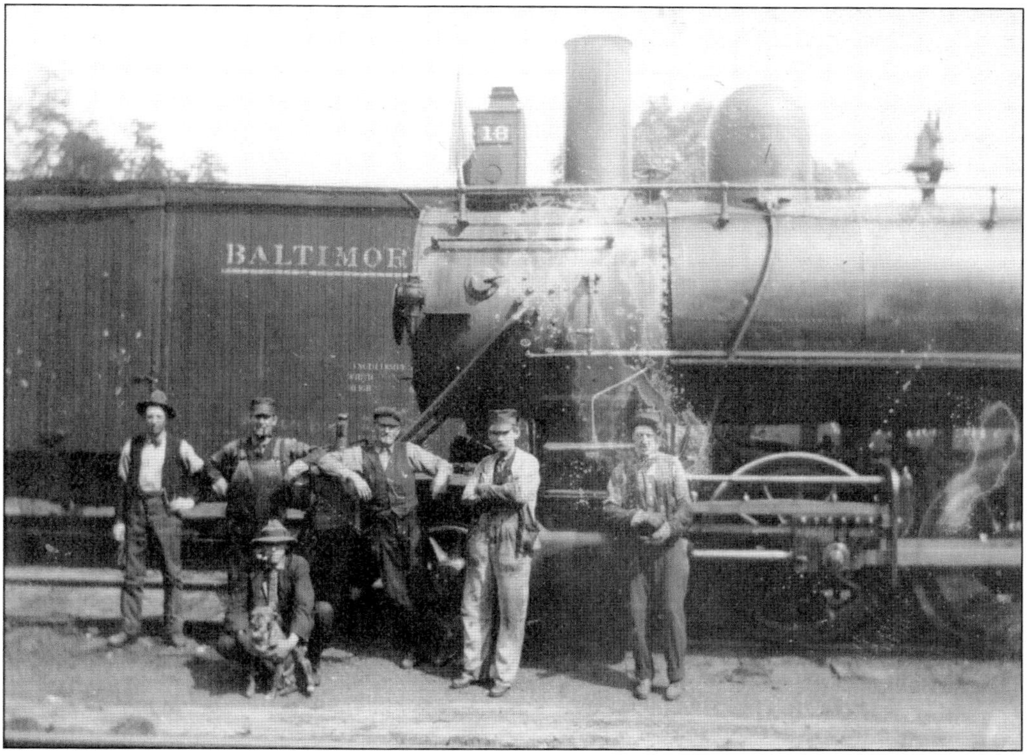

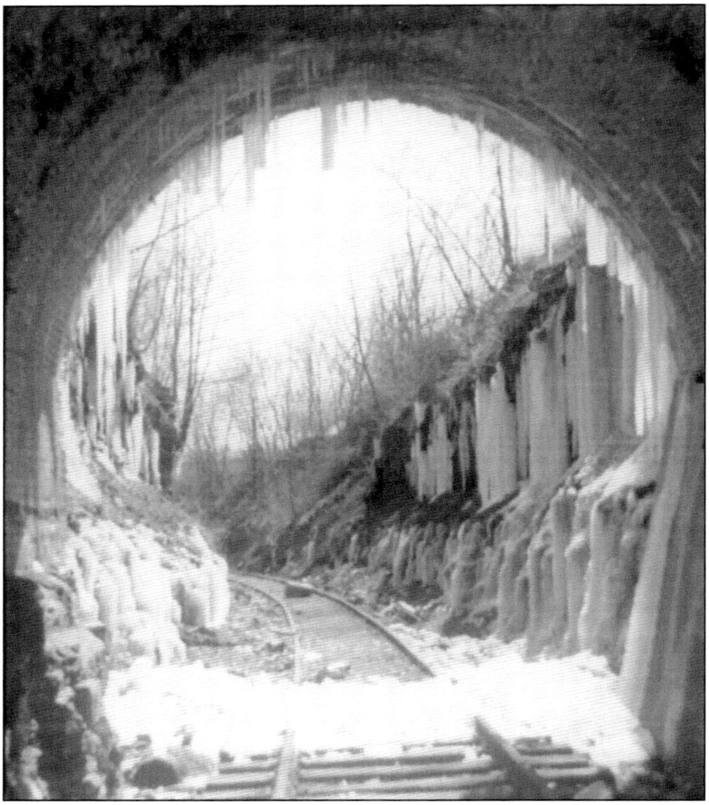

The tunnel under Frostburg that linked the C&P to the George's Creek mining region was dug under Main Street in 1857, and is 500 feet of long curved tunnel. This 1972 photo shows the ice and snow that often greeted train crews as they passed out of the tunnel on their journey to and from the coal fields.

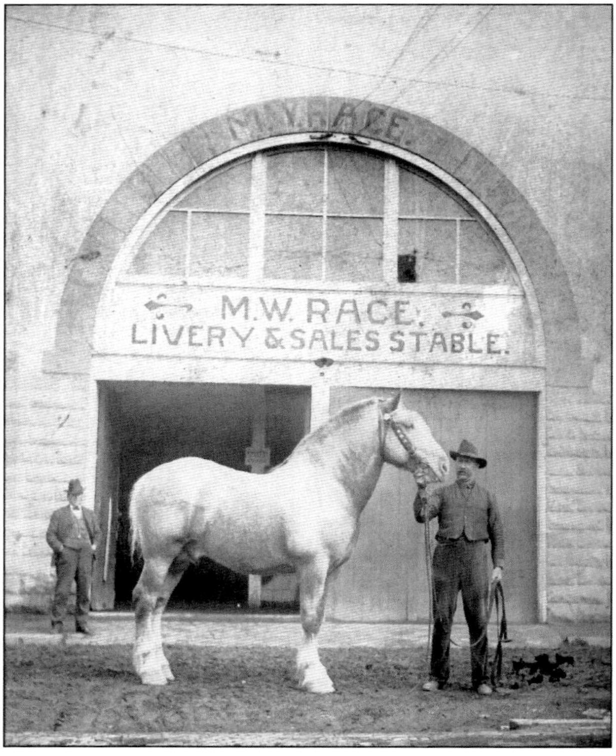

While railroads, trolleys, and buses moved people around the area, the use of horses and mules was a mainstay in business and pleasure. One of the leading livery men in the area was Milton Race, who is pictured here in the background behind a prize-winning Percheron. Race was born near Frostburg in 1874 and, in 1902, established his livery business that, by 1912, was reported to be one of the largest in Western Maryland.

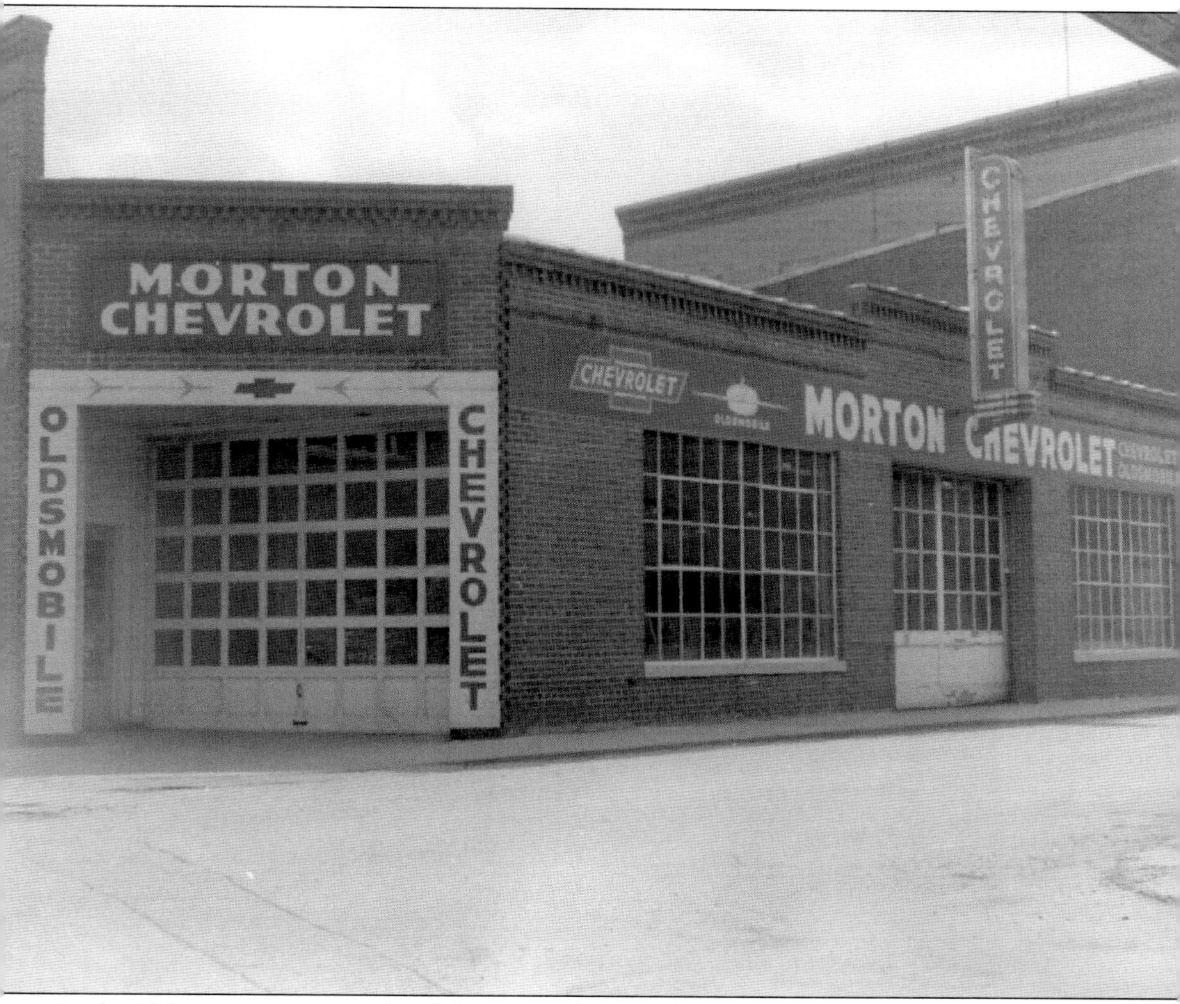

As the 20th century progressed and the personal automobile became the more common mode of transportation, automobile dealerships sprang up around town. Pictured here in a 1962 photograph is the Morton Chevrolet dealership, which was located at the corner of Water and Mechanic Streets in town.

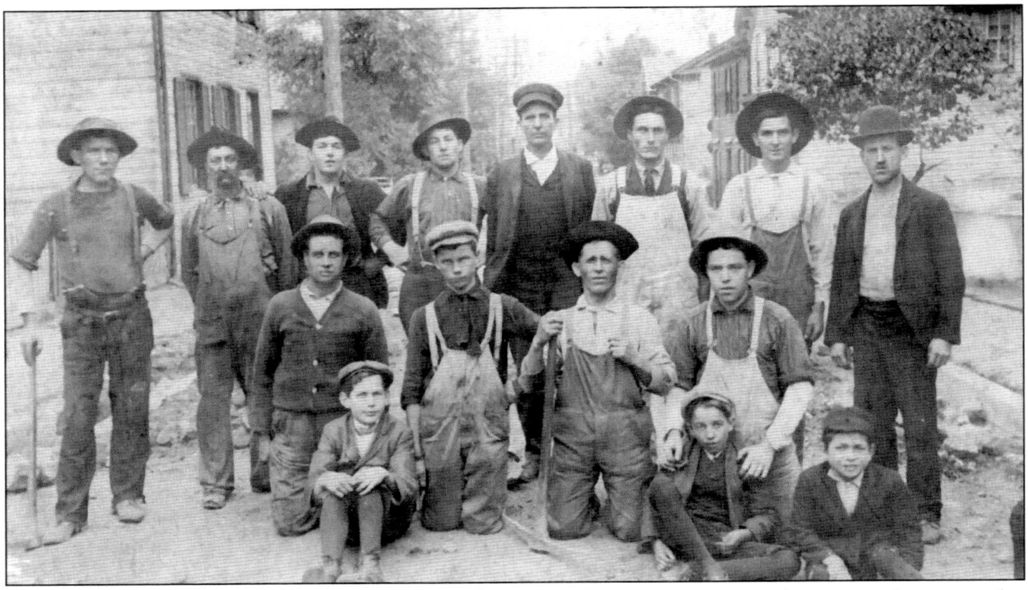

Not all of the workmen in town were coal miners! Here is a group of men working on the cobblestone streets in a residential section of town. Many of Frostburg's major streets were made of cobblestones in the late 19th and early 20th centuries. The Fuller Brothers were often contracted lay or repair the cobblestones, some of which were yellow brick. Folks in town could truly follow the "yellow brick road!"

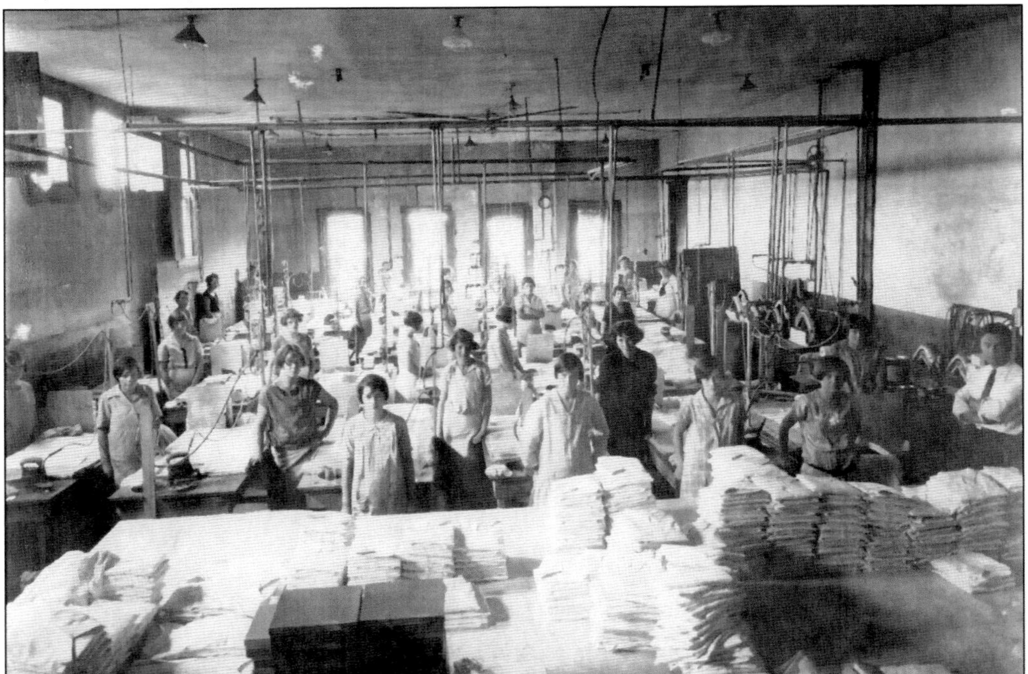

The Frostburg Shirt Factory of the Michael Berkowitz Company was established in 1917. Early factories were located on Main Street (where the Diamond Apartments are located today) and, appropriately, on Mechanic Street, before relocating south of Frostburg in Grahamtown. The shirt factory provided employment for several generations of women and men from the area.

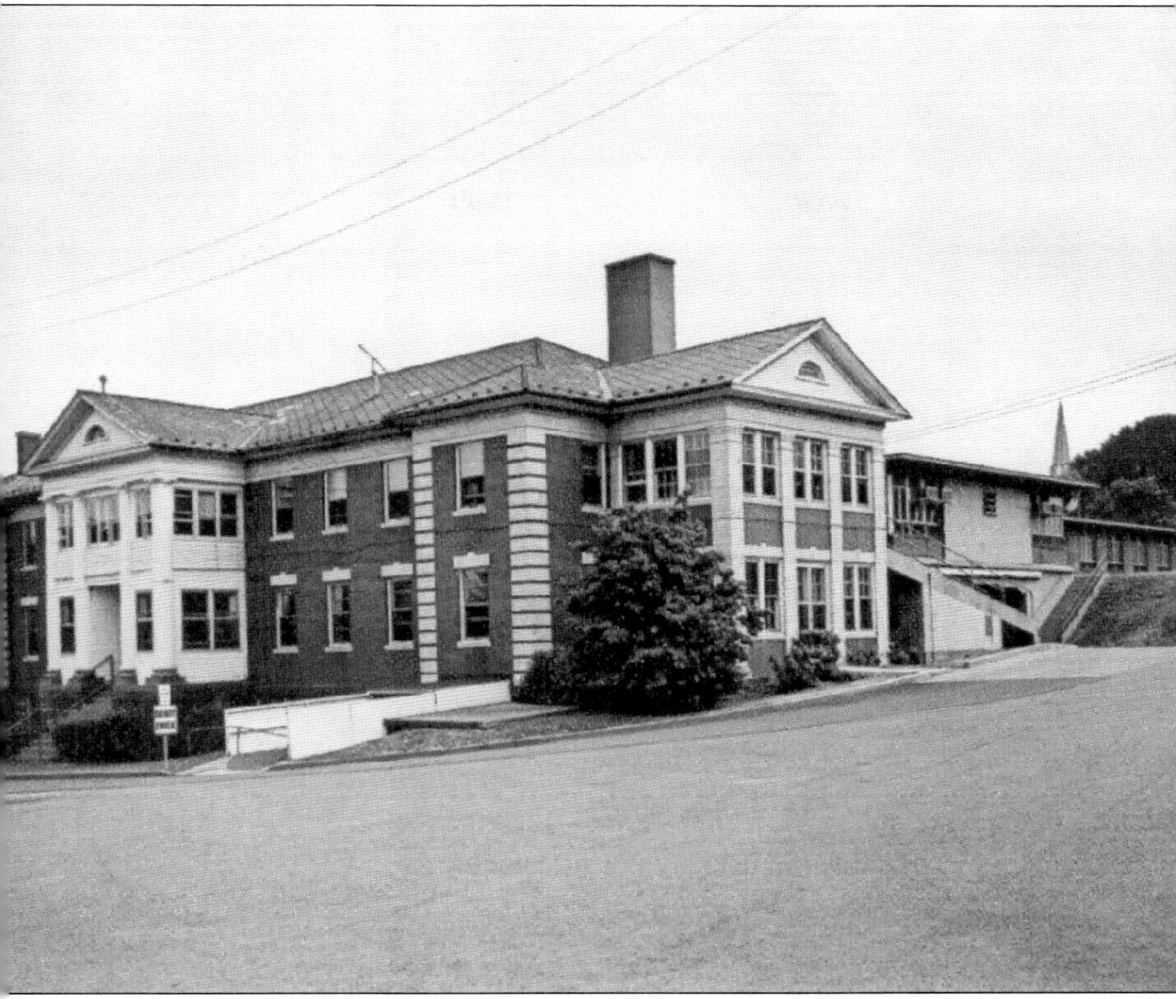

By 1912, the need for a hospital in Frostburg was apparent. Through an act of the Maryland General Assembly, $25,000 was given to establish a hospital. The unique stipulation was that the board of directors had to include a miner and a mine operator, in addition to two physicians and several town businessmen. Miners Hospital opened in December of 1913 with a woman, Dr. Helen Binnie, as the physician-director. Miners Hospital served the community until the late 1990s when it was turned into a nursing home facility.

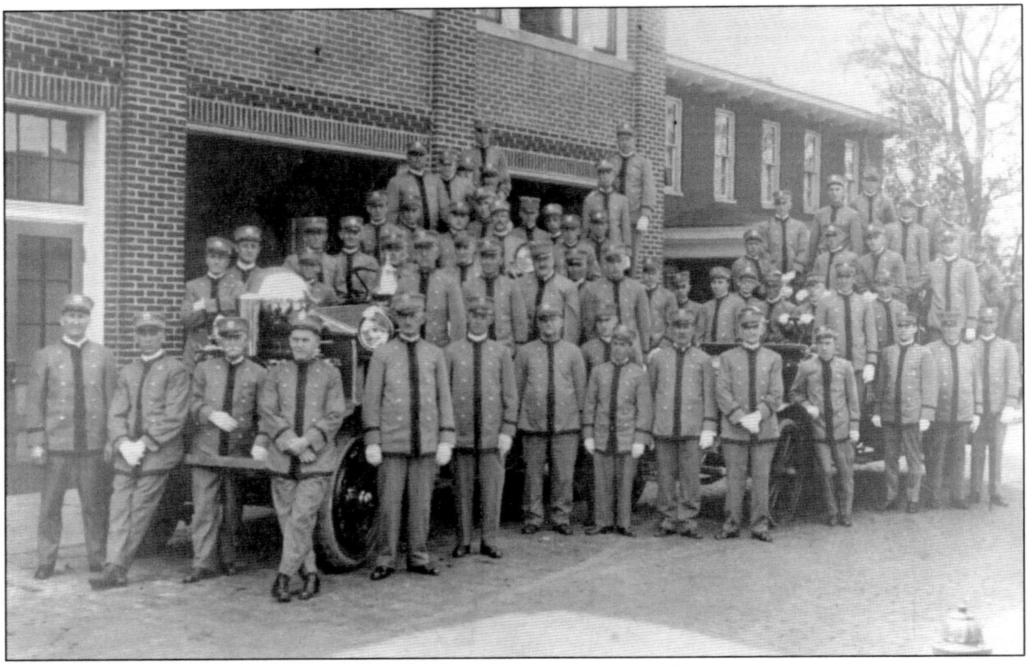

With the motto "Our Deeds, Our Reward," the Frostburg Fire Department has been protecting lives and property for almost 125 years. After several fires devastated the business district in 1874, the Frostburg Fire Department No. 1 was established on March 18, 1878 with over 50 members. Here, dressed in snappy uniforms, are members of the department in 1926, standing in front of the fire station on Water Street.

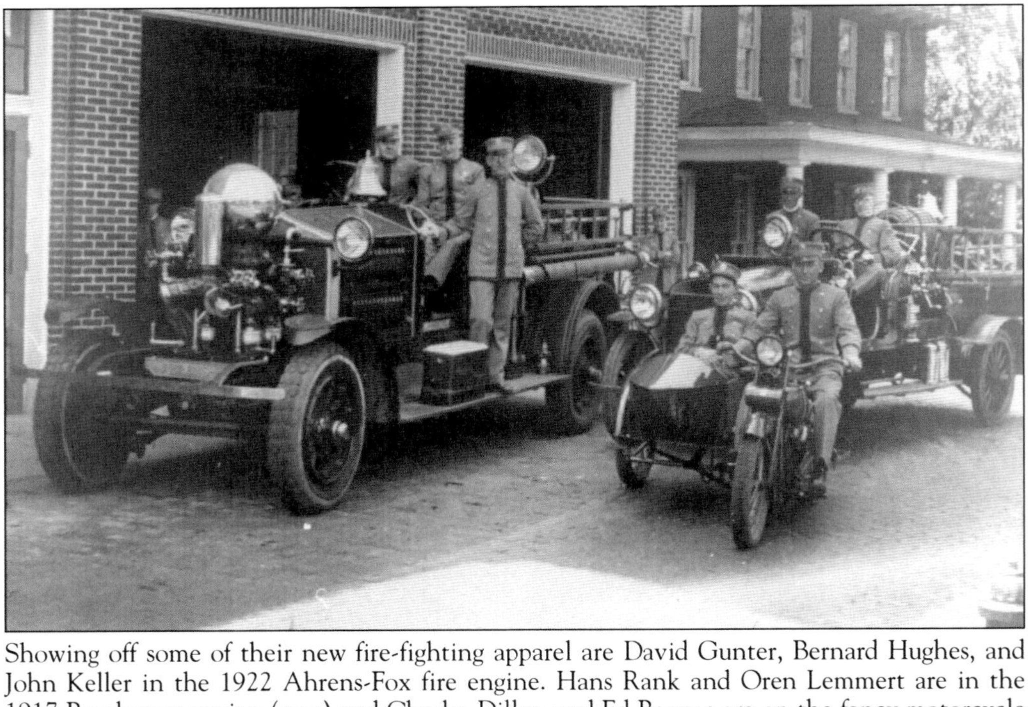

Showing off some of their new fire-fighting apparel are David Gunter, Bernard Hughes, and John Keller in the 1922 Ahrens-Fox fire engine. Hans Rank and Oren Lemmert are in the 1917 Brockaway engine (rear) and Charles Dillon and Ed Bevnas are on the fancy motorcycle and sidecar.

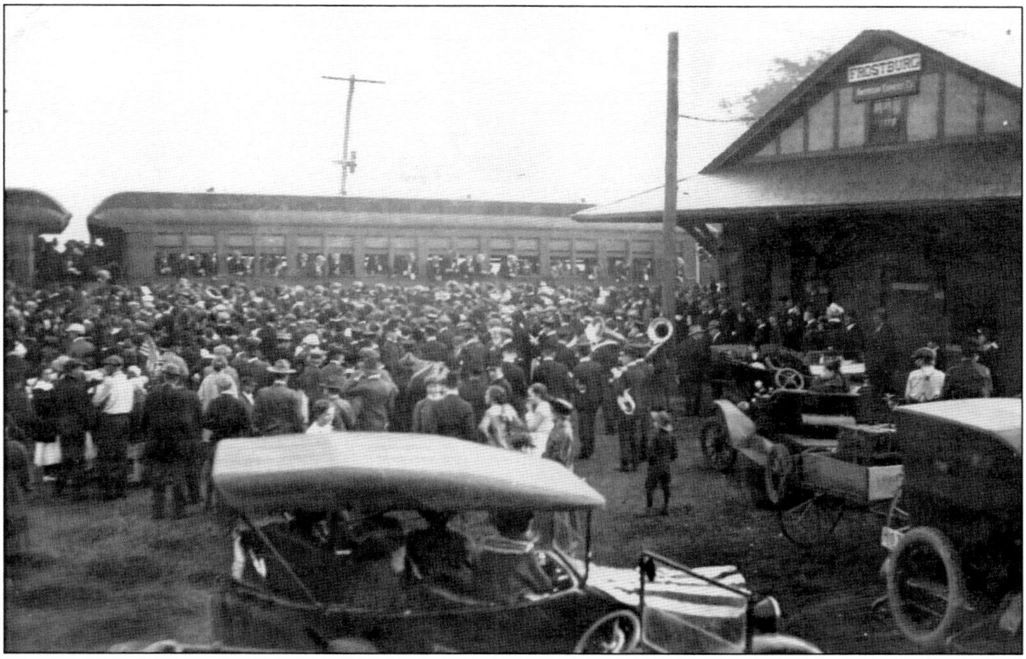

When the call to arms went out, the men of Frostburg always answered. Here is a special train at the C&P depot, taking some Frostburg men off to join the fight during World War I.

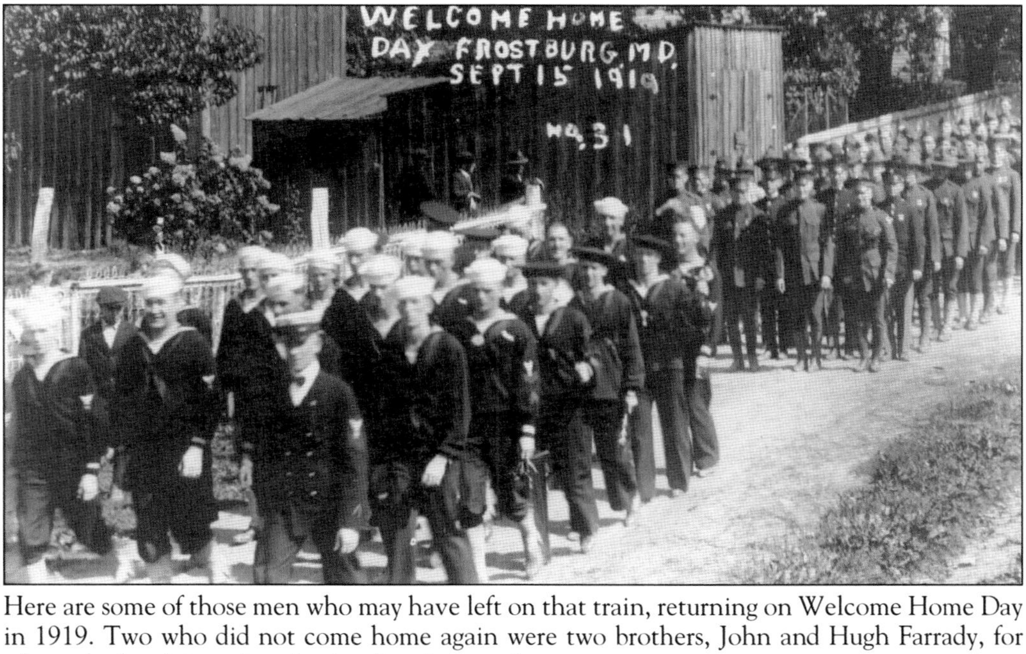

Here are some of those men who may have left on that train, returning on Welcome Home Day in 1919. Two who did not come home again were two brothers, John and Hugh Farrady, for whom the local American Legion Post is named.

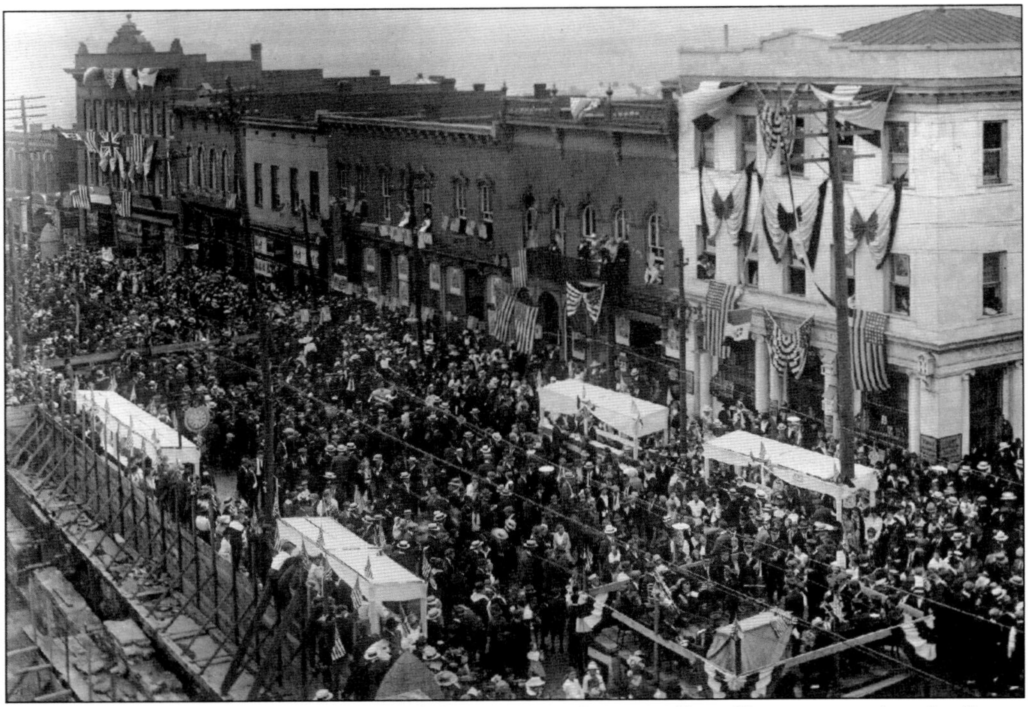

Those back on the home front also did their part in the war effort. Here is a war bond rally on Main Street in 1918. Flags of the allied countries hang from many of the shops and businesses. The Frostburg National Bank Building is to the right, while in the lower left work is being done on the foundation of the burned-out Shea Building.

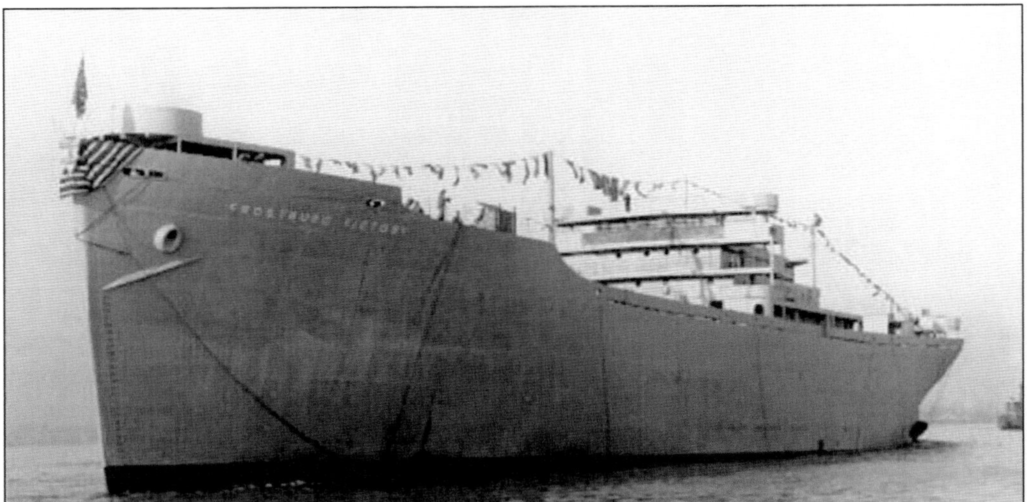

During World War II, many liberty cargo ships were constructed to carry material to soldiers and sailors around the world. One such ship was the SS *Frostburg Victory*, pictured here just before her outfitting for sea duty. The Frostburg Victory was 455 feet long and had three decks with 7,612 tons gross tonnage and capable of 15.5 knots. There was 8 miles of piping, 10 miles of cable, 60.5 miles of welding, and a crew of about 80. It was reported that the name was selected by the United States Maritime Commission, whose members considered Frostburg a typical main street American town.

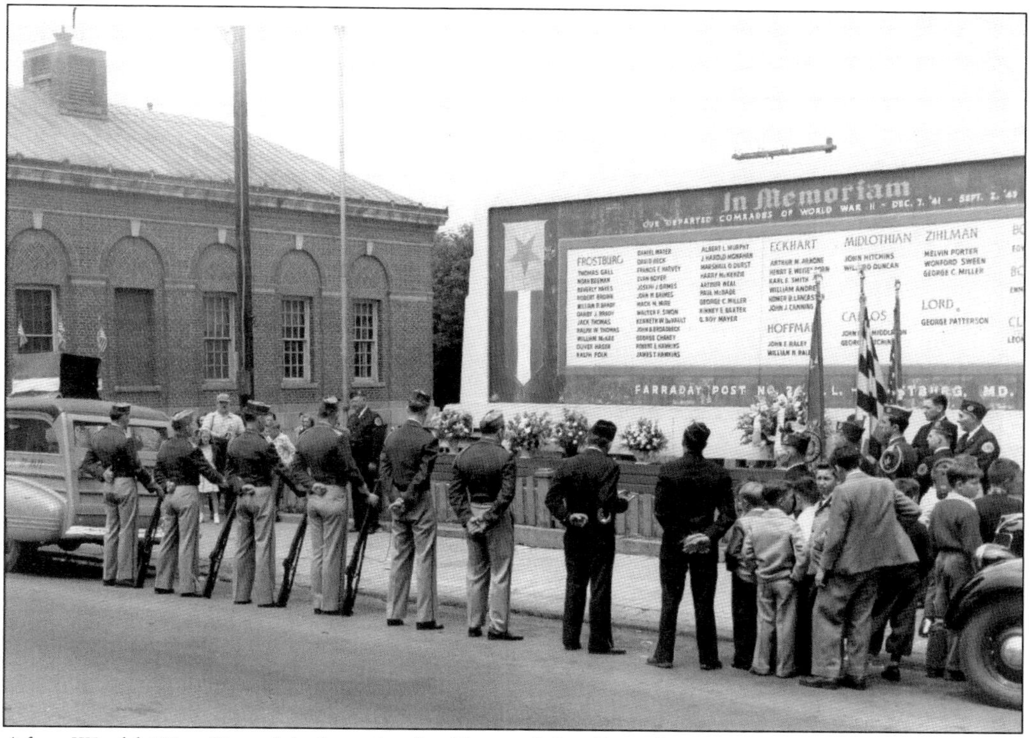

After World War II and before the building of the Farrady Post American Legion on the northeast corner of Main and Water Streets, a billboard was displayed. It listed the names of the men of the area who gave their lives between December 7, 1941 and September 2, 1945. Here an honor guard stands at-ease during the dedication ceremony.

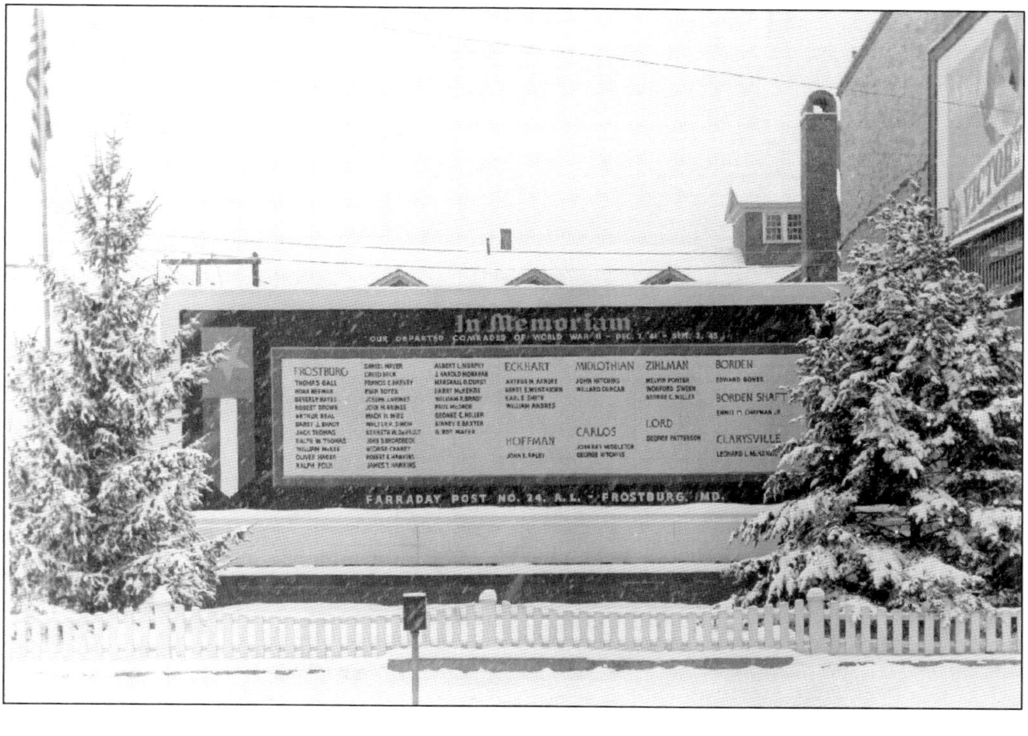

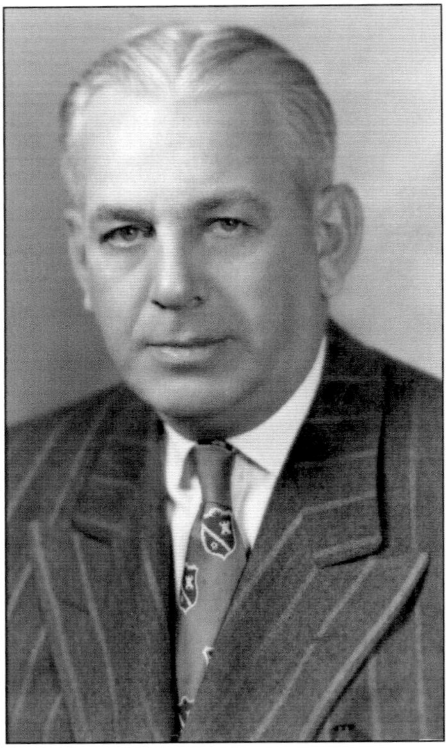

For a small, rural town, Frostburg has the distinction of having two of its residents being elected to the United States Senate. Sen. J. Glenn Beall, pictured here, served in both the House of Representatives and the Senate during the 1940s into the 1960s, as did his son J. Glenn Beall Jr. in the 1960s and 1970s (see page 122).

On Father's Day 1953, the Princess Restaurant on Main Street had a rather distinguished diner. On a trip back to Washington, D.C. from his home in Independence, Missouri, former President Harry Truman and his wife, Bess, stopped at the restaurant for lunch. Pictured with President and Mrs. Truman are George Pappas, owner of the Princess (center), and Bill Byrnes, a local businessman and politician. Visitors to the restaurant can still sit in the "Truman Booth" and enjoy a delightful meal.

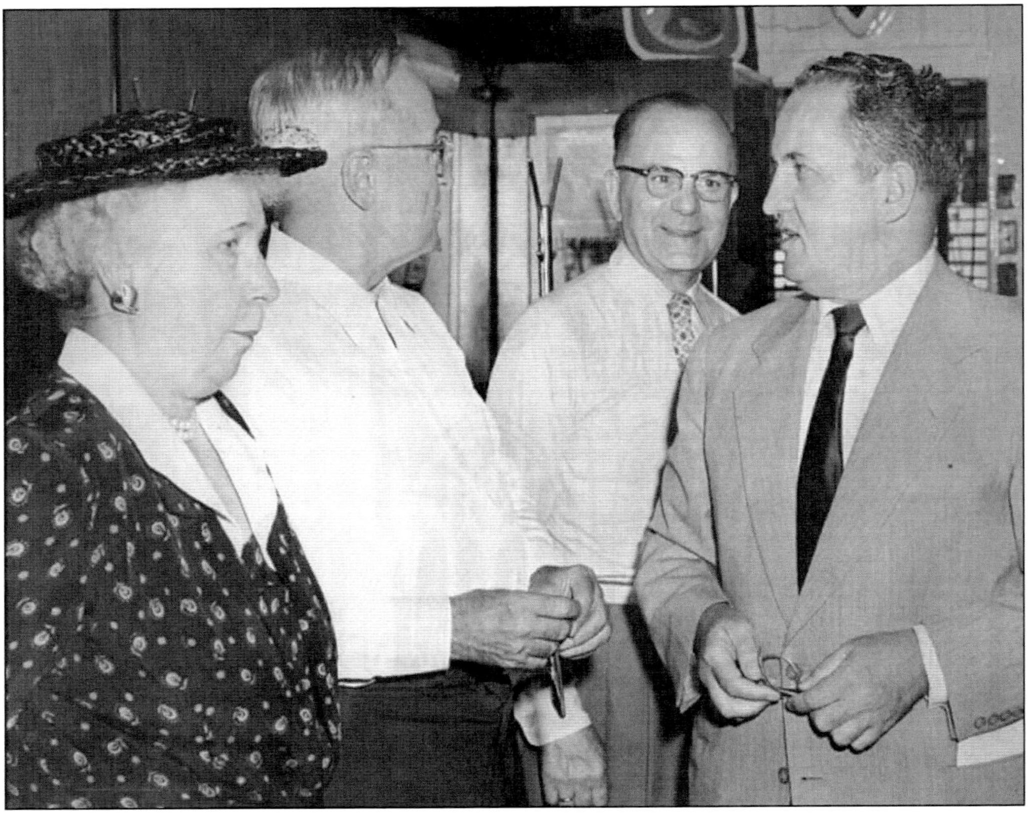

Frostburg had its share of characters. One such colorful resident was Bigga-da-lou Riley (second from right) who ran a "near-beer" bar and seafood restaurant on Mechanic Street that was also a speak-easy during Prohibition. Known for his eccentricities, Bigga-da-lou carried on conversations with his collie and, as one storyteller shared, Bigga-da-Lou even played checkers with the dog. One visitor, who observed a game, said that the dog must be pretty smart. Bigga-da-Lou reportedly responded that he didn't think the dog was smart because he had beaten him three out of the last four games!

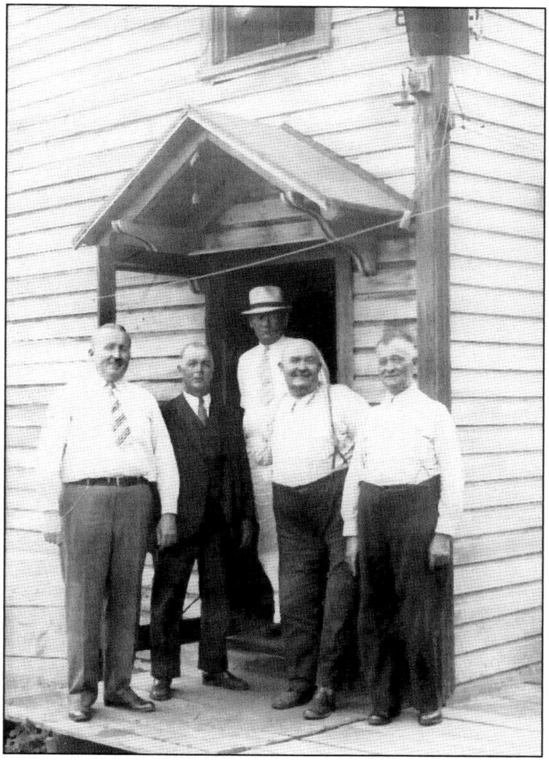

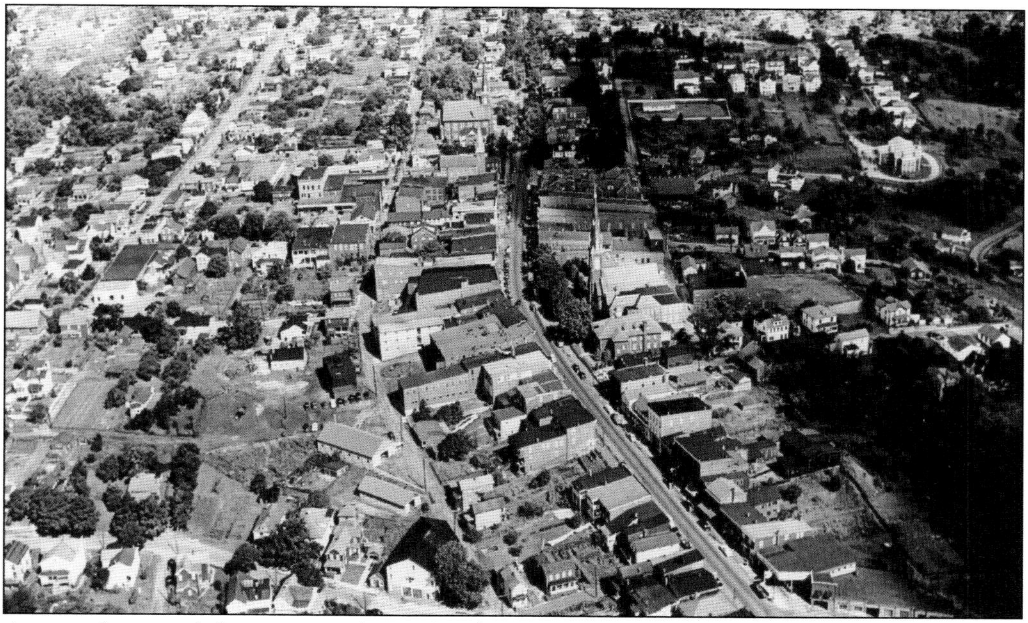

An aerial view of the town in the 1950s shows several major changes from the turn of the century. Gone are the opera house and the St. Cloud Hotel that stood at the intersection of Main Street and Depot Road (lower right corner). With more automobiles and new businesses such as gas stations and auto dealerships, Frostburg was making the change to a post–World War II college town. St. Michael's Church still had the spire, and Miners Hospital (upper right) had not expanded.

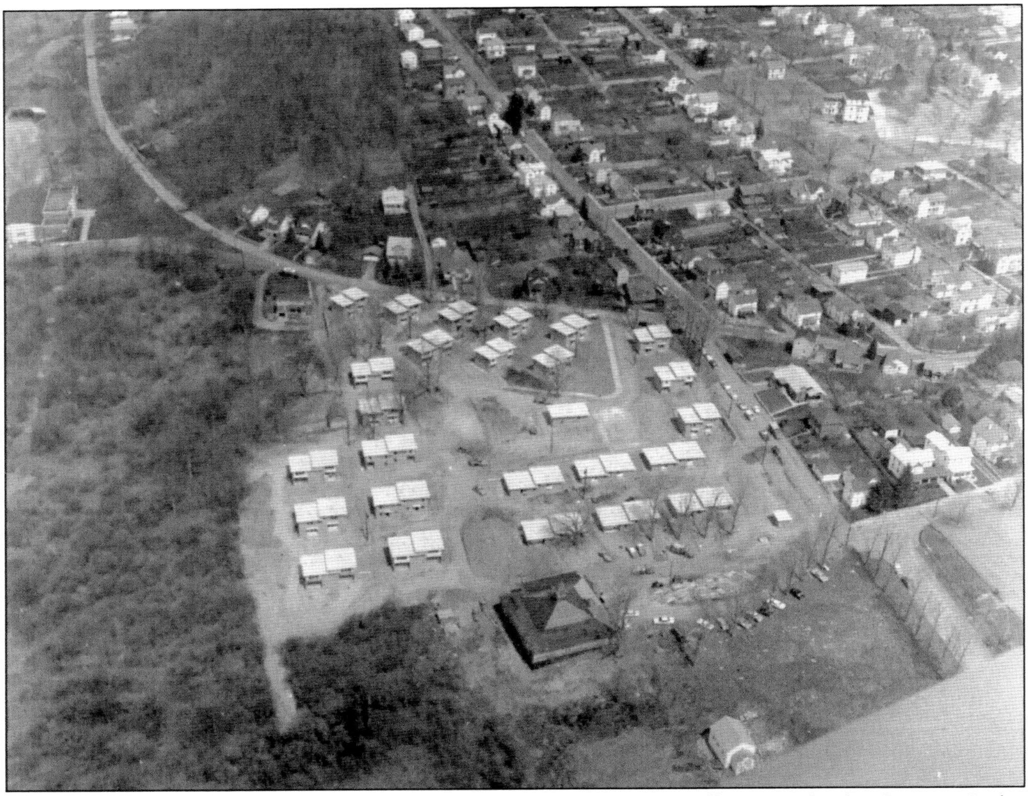

A 1962 view shows the newly constructed Meshach Frost Village, with the Junior Order Park Pavilion, which was soon to be demolished, in the foreground. In the upper left is the National Guard Armory, beyond which is the swimming pool. Meshach Frost Village was created as public housing units in part for the elderly and those displaced by the expansion of Frostburg State.

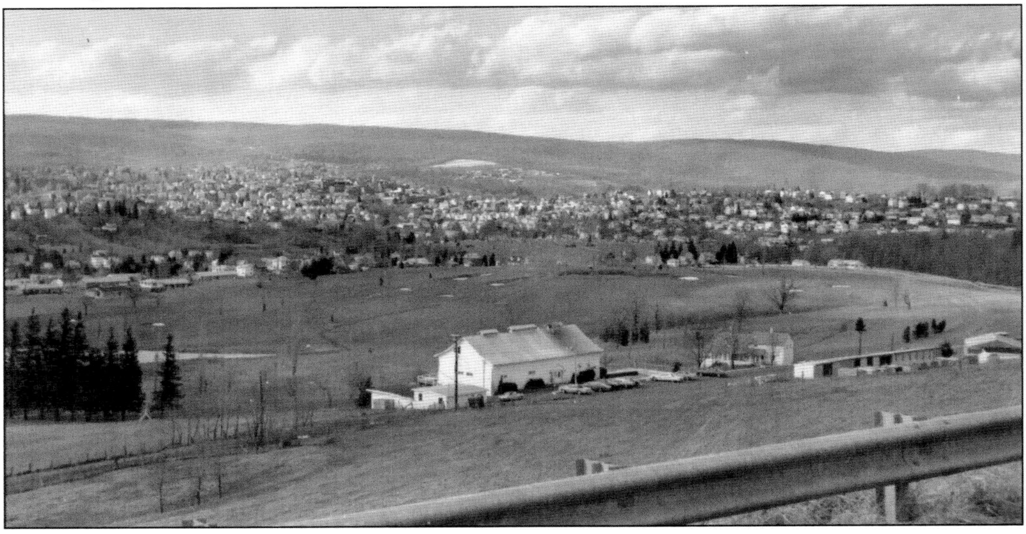

By the second half of the 20th century, Frostburg can still be seen nestled against Savage Mountain. From across the Maplehurst Country Club, the skyline of the town had changed quite a bit since the turn of the century.

Six

Eckhart Mines

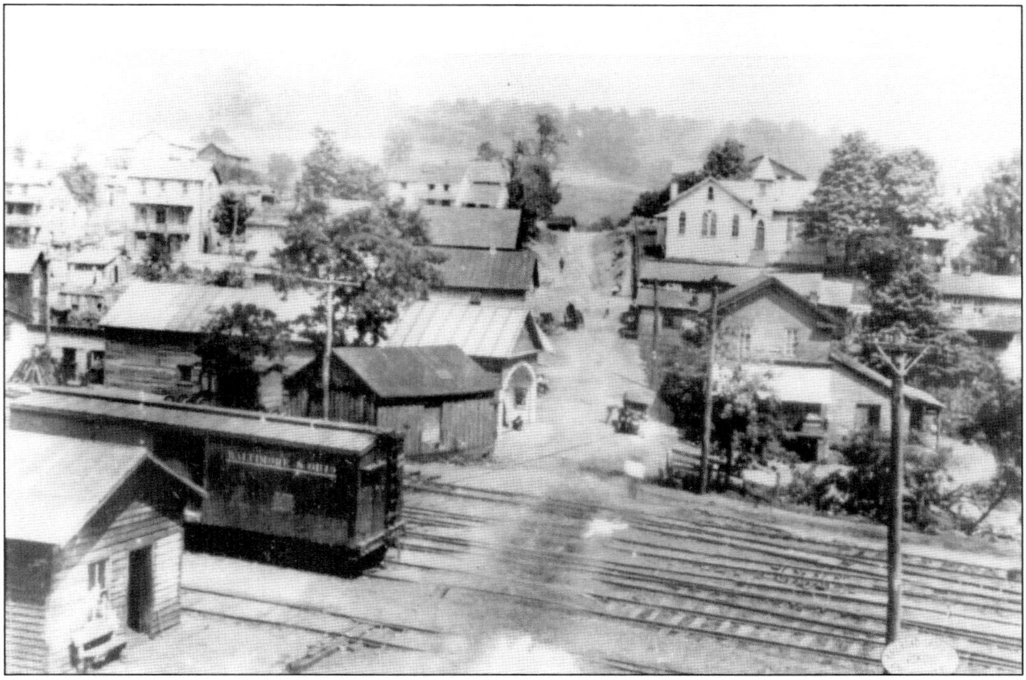

This is an early 20th-century view of Eckhart Mines, with the tracks of C&P railroad yards in the foreground and the stores and shops clustered on the hill towards the Methodist Church on the right. The building on the left with the arched front was once a movie theater.

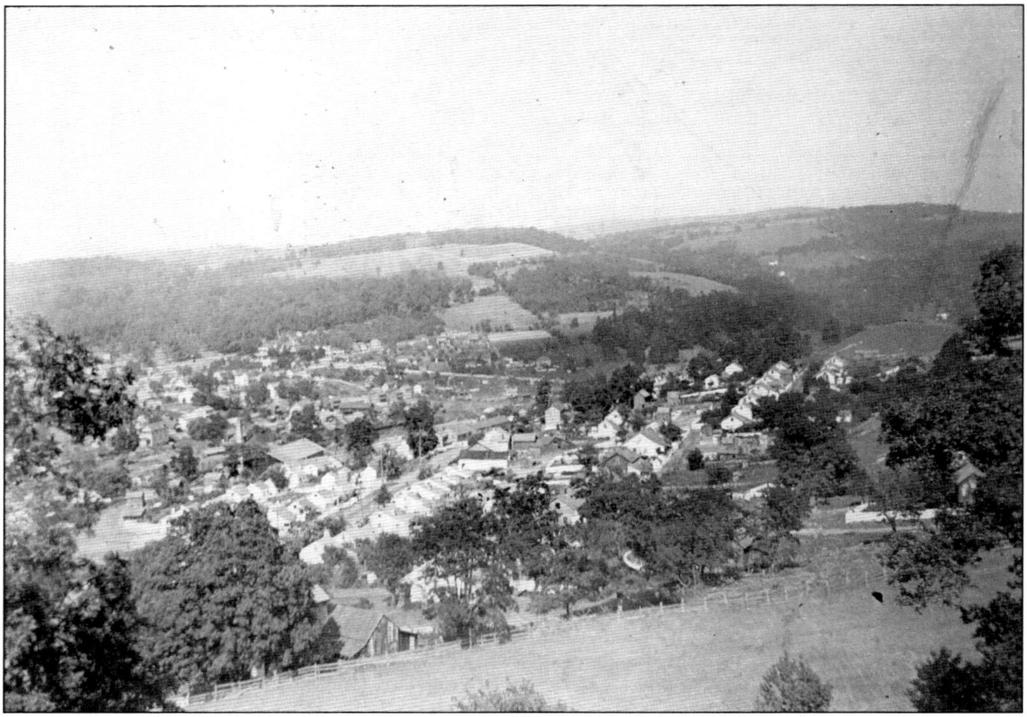

Eckhart Mines is nestled under Piney Mountain in the early 20th century. The uniformity of many of the homes shows Eckhart's heritage as a coal-mining town. The National Road creeps up the hill in the center of the photograph.

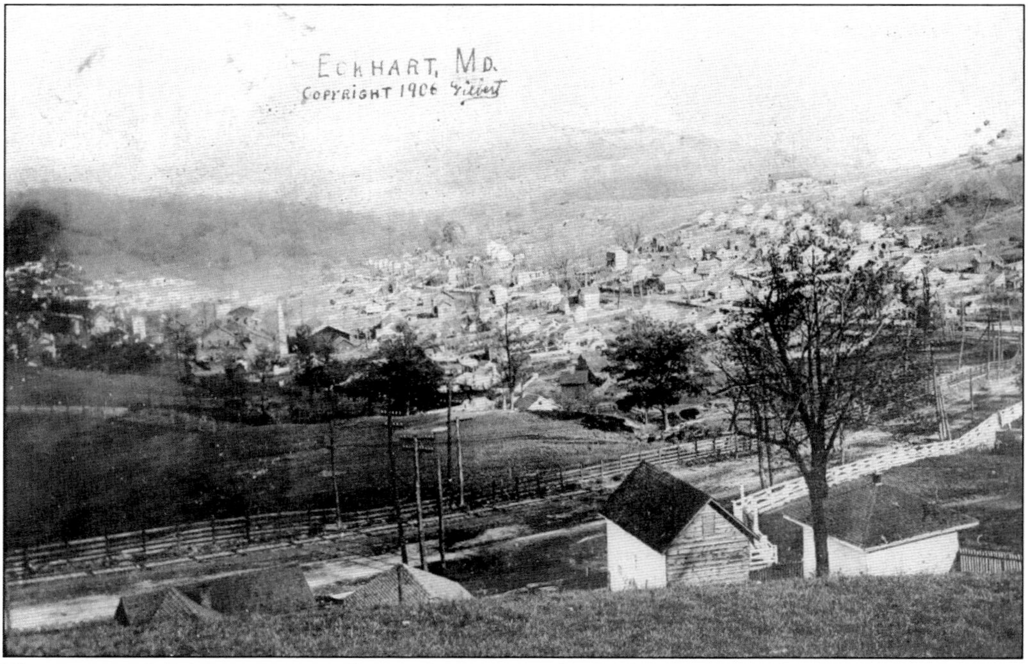

This view of Eckhart Mines shows the National Road easing up the hillside above the Consolidation Coal works in the center left. The cookie-cutter company houses are apparent along the hillsides.

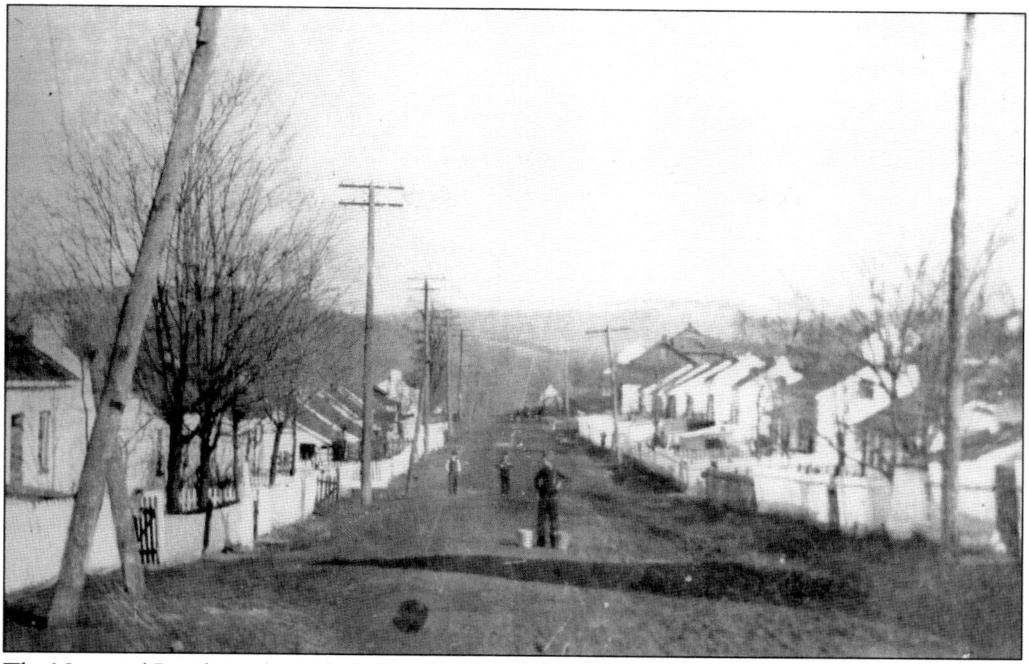

The National Road ran through Eckhart Mines in the early 20th century. The tidy miners homes with picket fences lined the thoroughfare on its way out of Cumberland towards Frostburg. This photograph was taken before the building of the Cumberland and Westernport Electric Railroad. The taller, darker building on the right of the Road is Byrnes' Store.

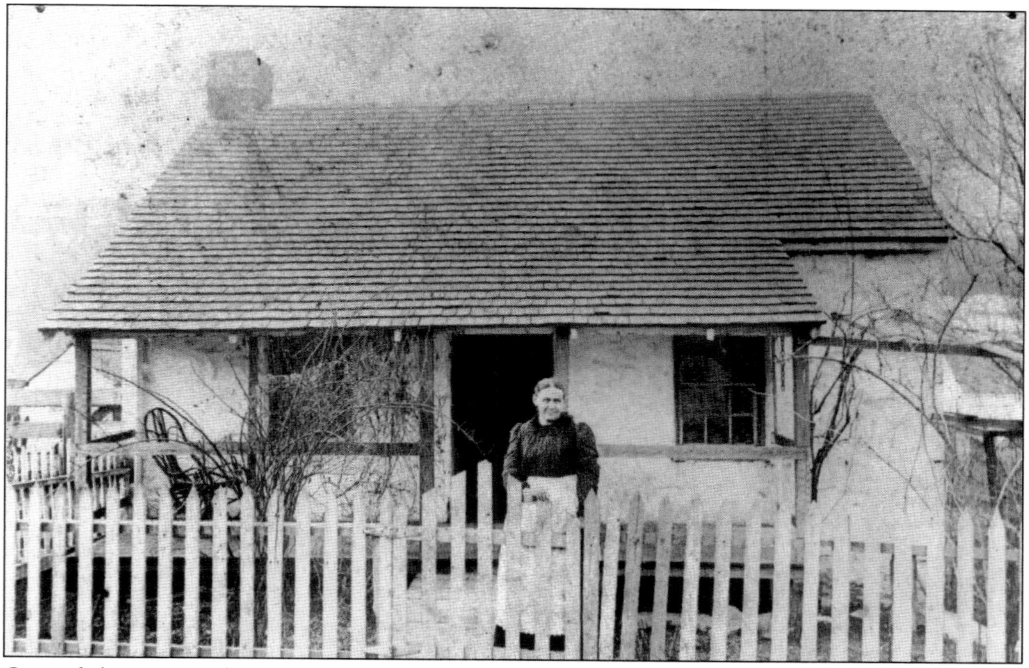

One of the miners' homes is pictured here along the National Road in Eckhart Mines. The whitewashed stone and picket fences of these small, but functional homes made quite a contrast to the stereotype of squalid living conditions found in some other company towns in other coal mining regions.

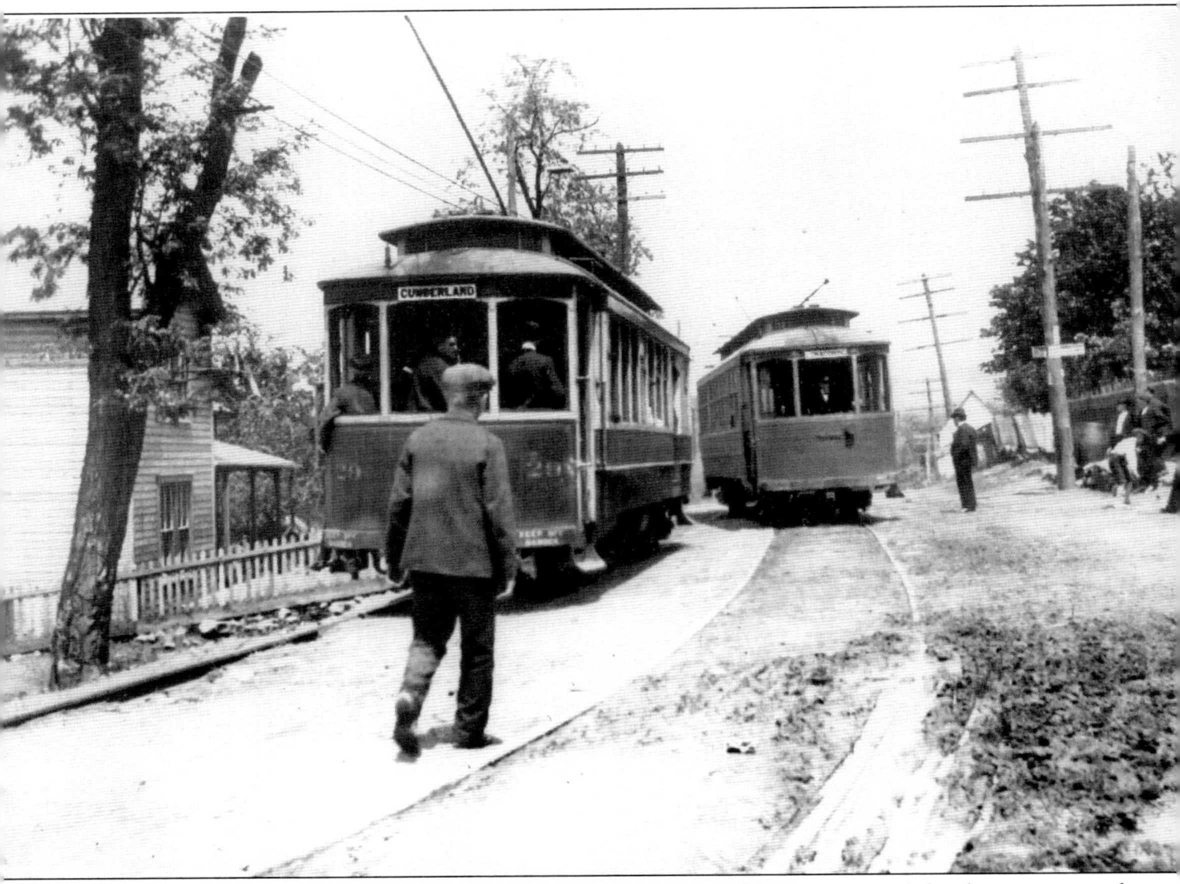

Two trolley cars are passing in front of Byrnes' Store in Eckhart at one of the few sections of dual track on the line. The car on the left is the Cumberland-bound car, while the car on the right is westbound for Lonaconing.

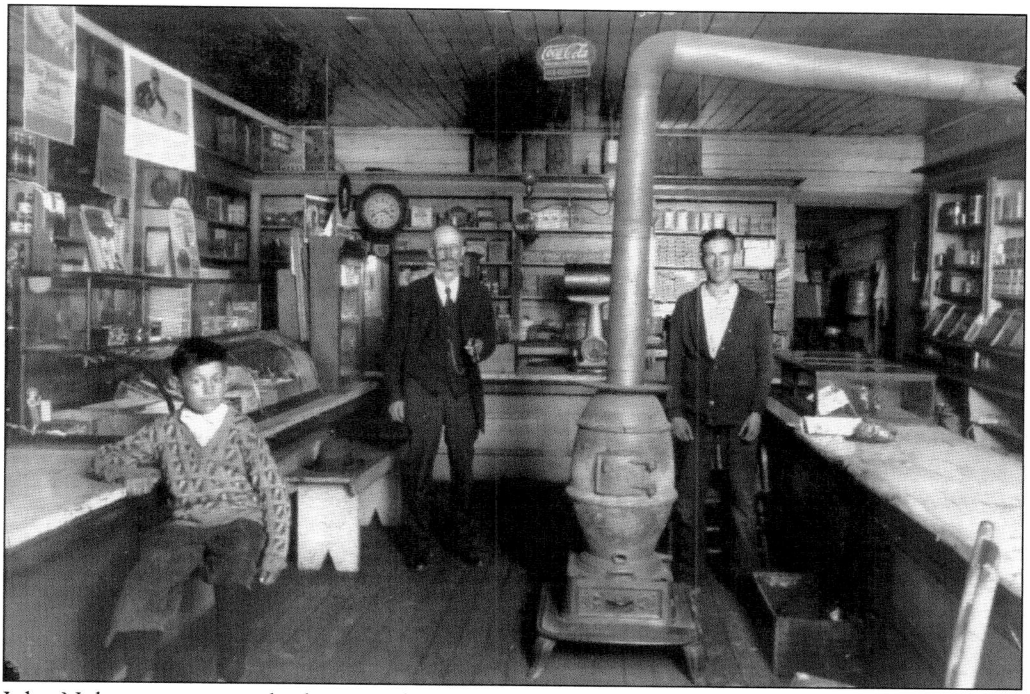

John Nelson, center, with glasses and cigar is photographed in his store in Eckhart Mines. His was one of four general merchandise shops in Eckhart Mines in the early 20th century.

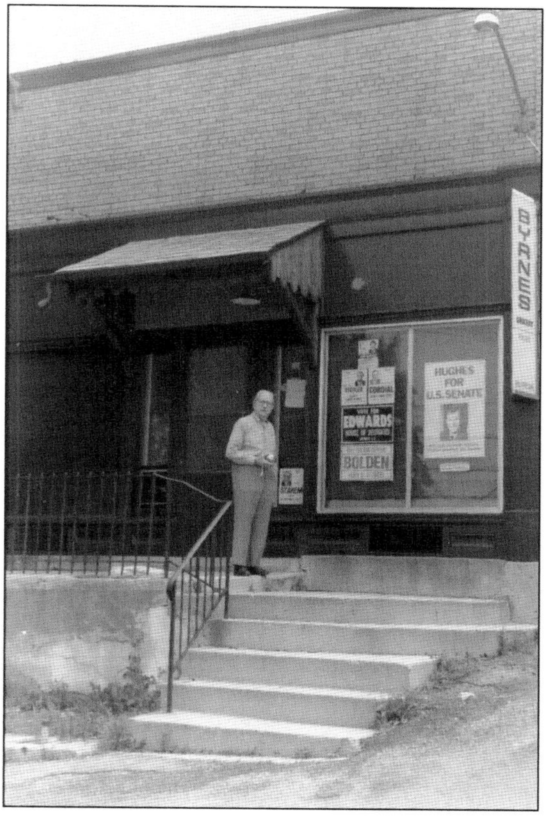

Bill Byrnes was the last proprietor of Byrnes Store, which was a mainstay in Eckhart Mines along the National Road for nearly 100 years. His father, John J. Byrnes, established the store in 1882 and it was run by his sons following his death in 1917. Bill Byrnes was also a prominent local politician, serving in the Maryland House of Delegates for many years.

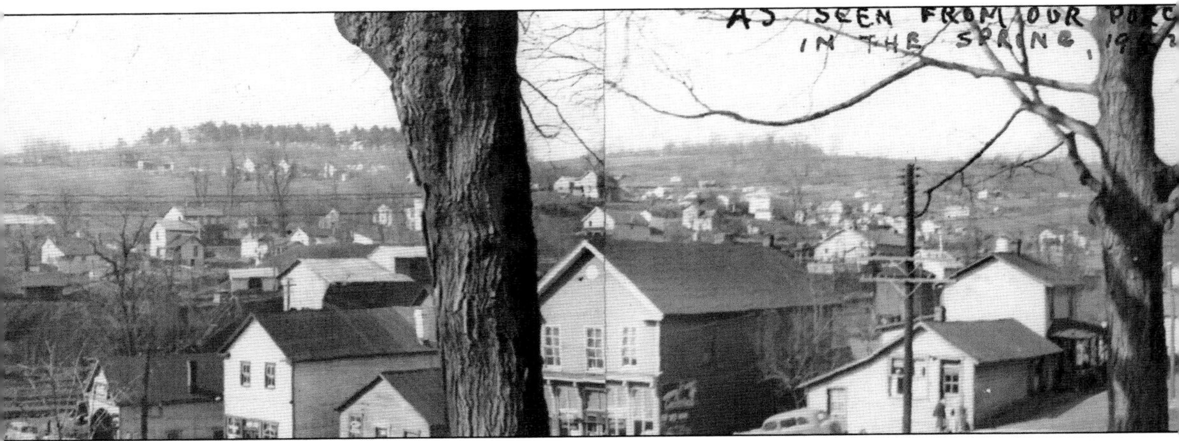

This view of Eckhart Mines looking southwest was taken from in front of the Eckhart Methodist church in 1942. The buildings in the foreground are some of the stores along "store hill" and the tracks of the C&P are in the lower left. The road off to the right passed by several drinking establishments earning the colorful name "beer alley."

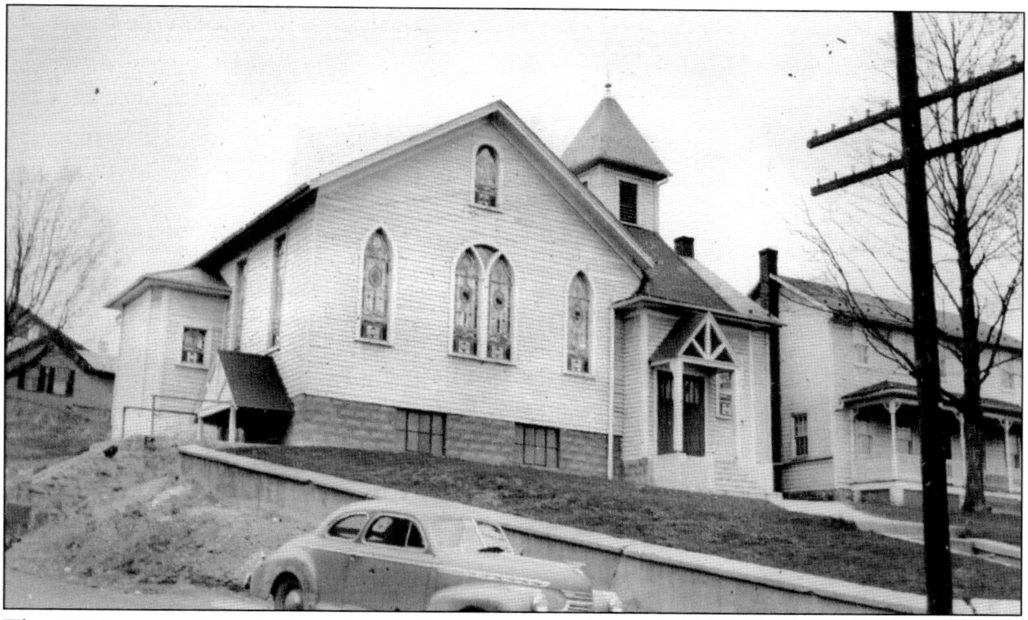

This 1942 view of the Eckhart Methodist Church and parsonage was taken from a scrapbook compiled by Rev. Raymond W. Cooke, the minister at the church in the 1940s.

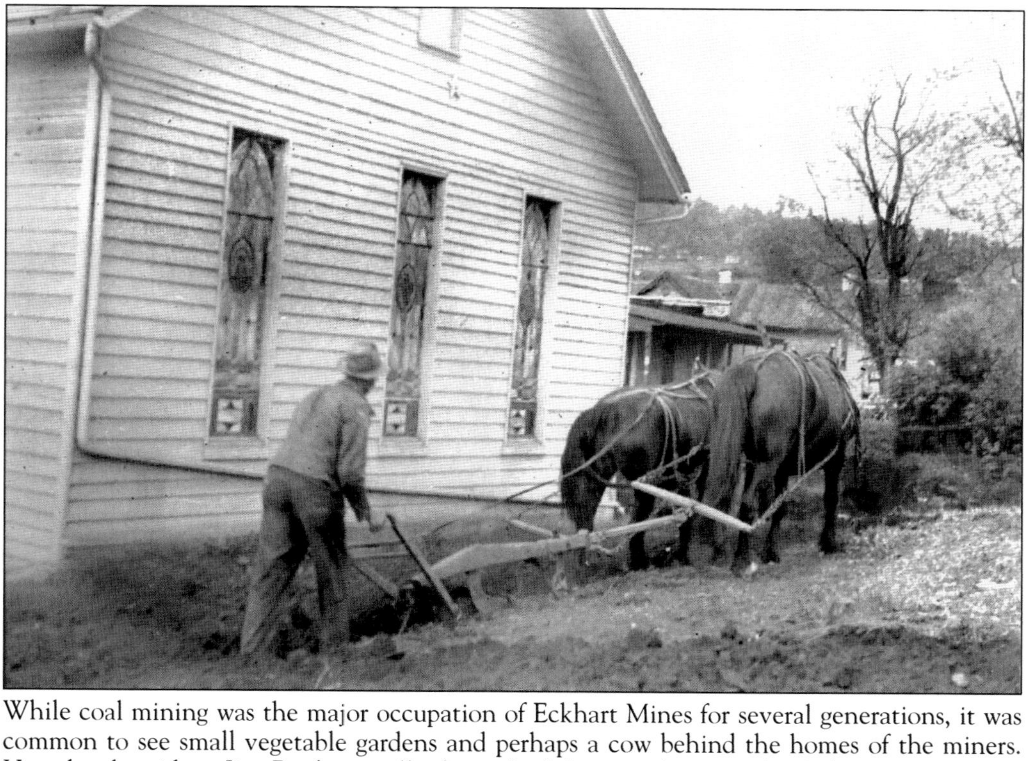

While coal mining was the major occupation of Eckhart Mines for several generations, it was common to see small vegetable gardens and perhaps a cow behind the homes of the miners. Here local resident Jim Rephann tills the soil of the preacher's garden behind the Eckhart Methodist Church.

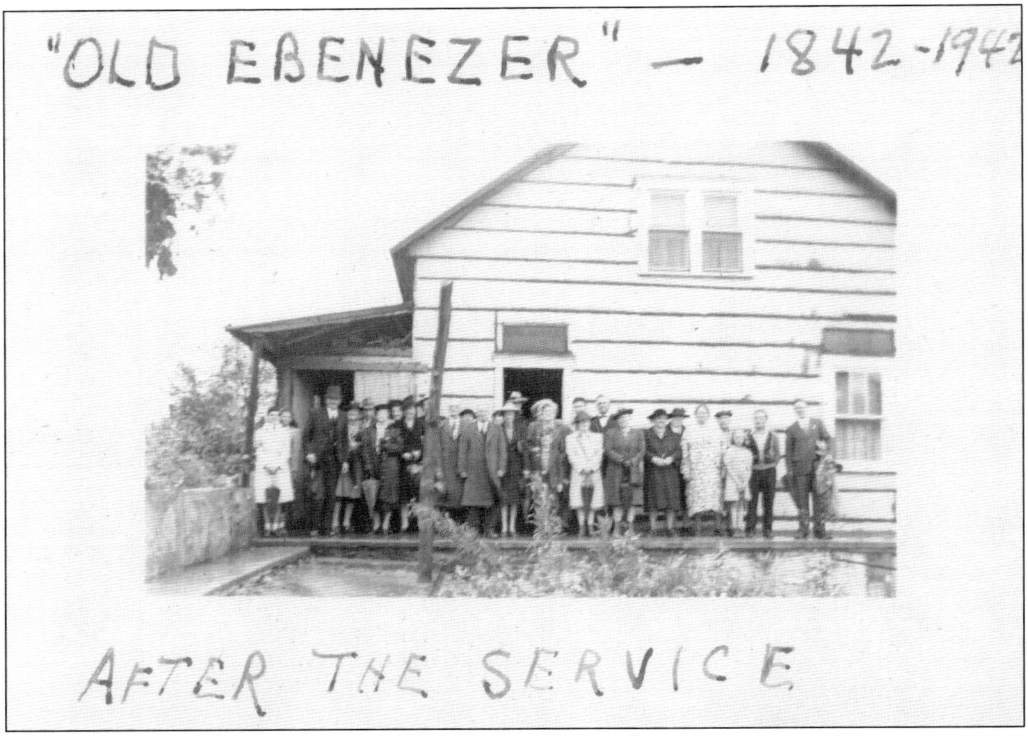

The original Eckhart Methodist Church was known as "Ebenezer" and began services in 1842 and continued there until 1866. In a centennial celebration, parishioners of the church attend service in the old building.

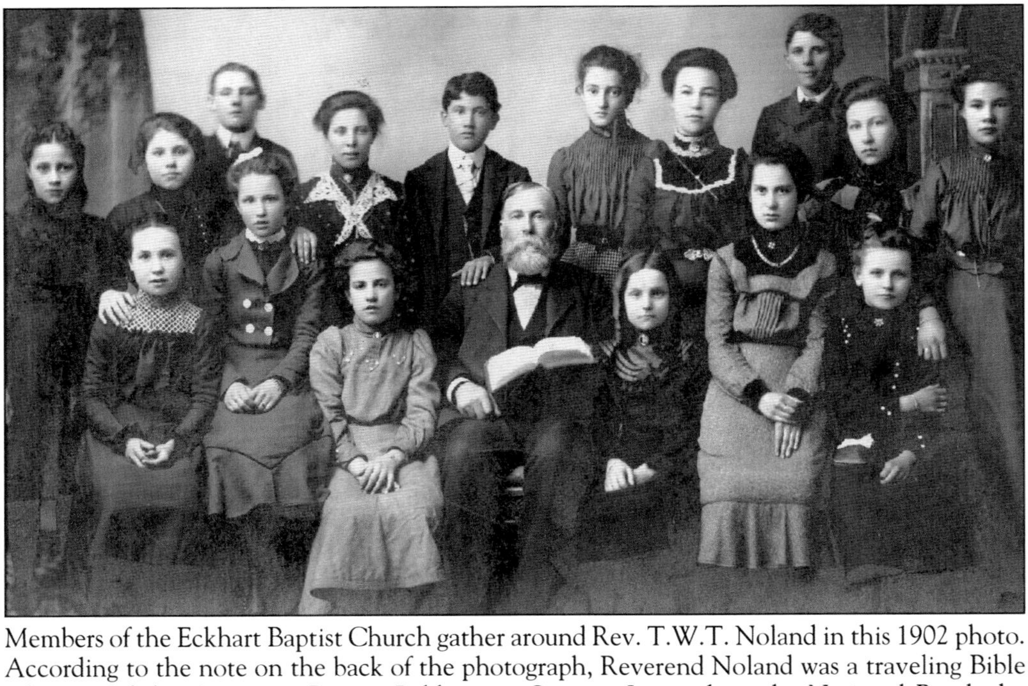

Members of the Eckhart Baptist Church gather around Rev. T.W.T. Noland in this 1902 photo. According to the note on the back of the photograph, Reverend Noland was a traveling Bible salesman of the American Baptist Publication Society. Located on the National Road, the Eckhart Baptist Church was established in the early 19th century.

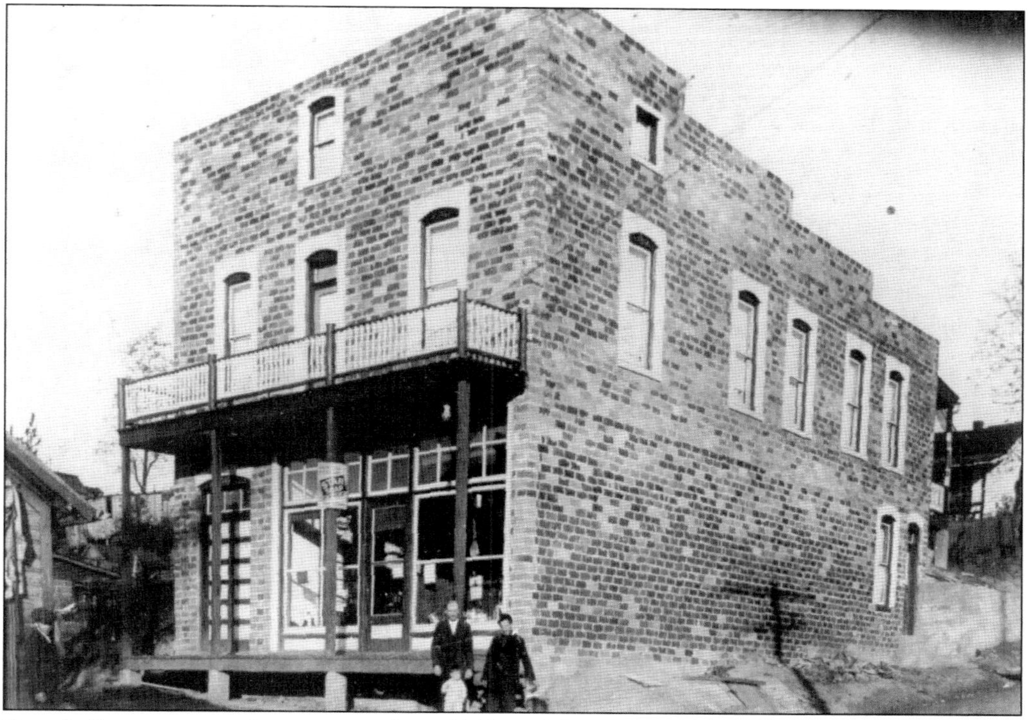

Drum's Store was another mercantile in Eckhart Mines. Located on the hill above the C&P yards and next to the Methodist Church, Drum's store had the enviable address of the corner of Store Hill and Beer Alley (see p. 110), at the center of the village's business district.

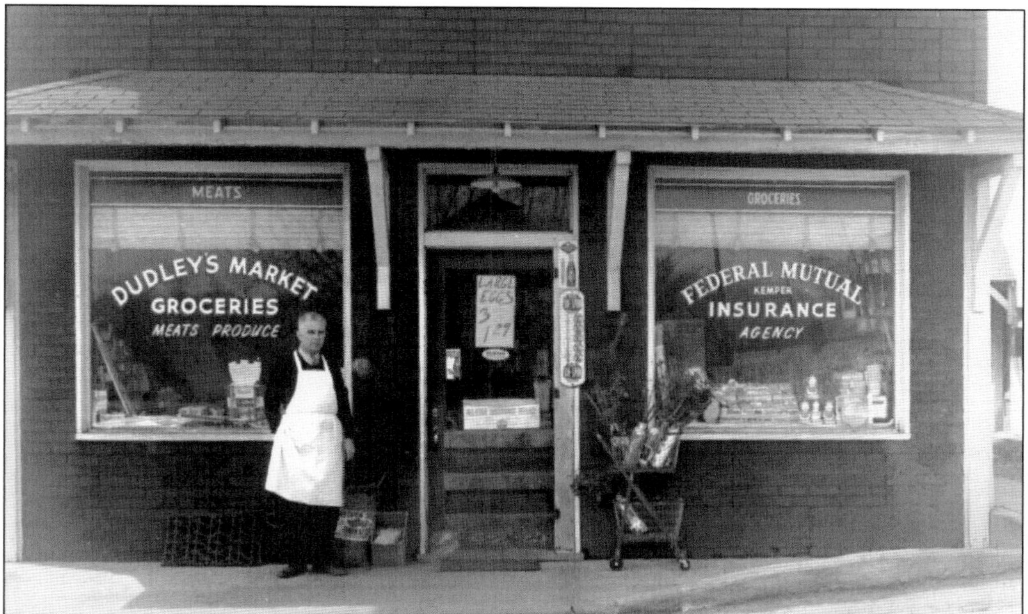

Dudley's Market was another of the stores along store hill up into the 1960s. While many of the buildings still stand, there are no stores along store hill, and one lone drinking establishment still serves patrons on Beer Alley. Few traces of the railroad yards or coal mines are still visible, but the tiny Eckhart Mines, Maryland (21528) Post Office survives.

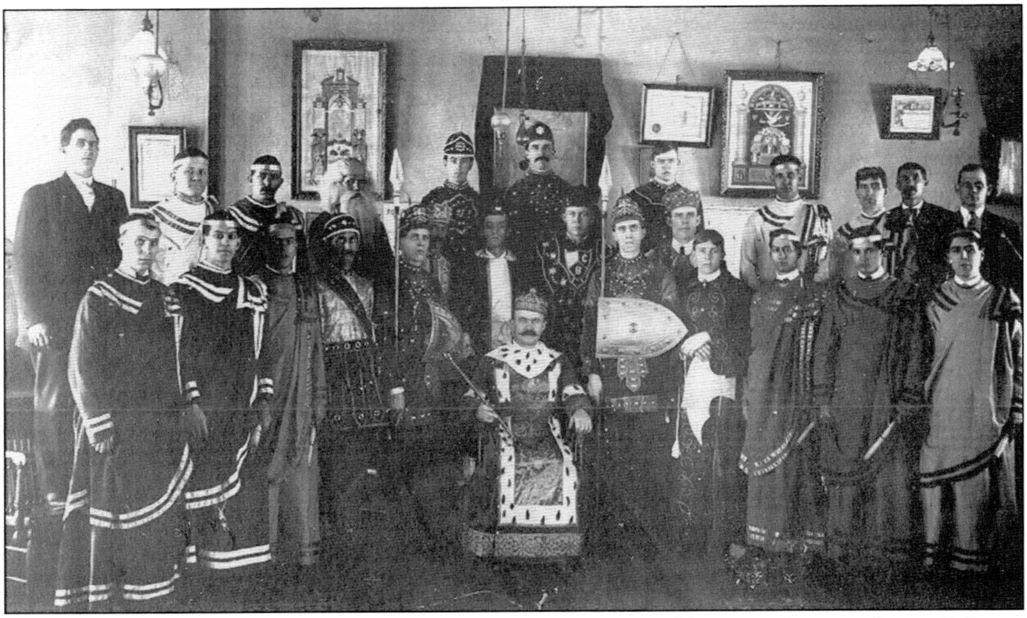

The Junior Order of United American Mechanics are pictured here in their regalia in Eckhart Mines during the late 1880s. The Junior Order was a fraternal organization that was organized in 1853, initially for boys 16 to 21. The age restrictions were removed and the Junior Order accepted any American-born citizen who was white, male, and Protestant and worked for a living and was not engaged in the sale of spirituous liquors! The Eckhart Mines Council (one of 12 in Allegany County) had a lodge hall that was located along the National Road just up from the C&P railroad yards.

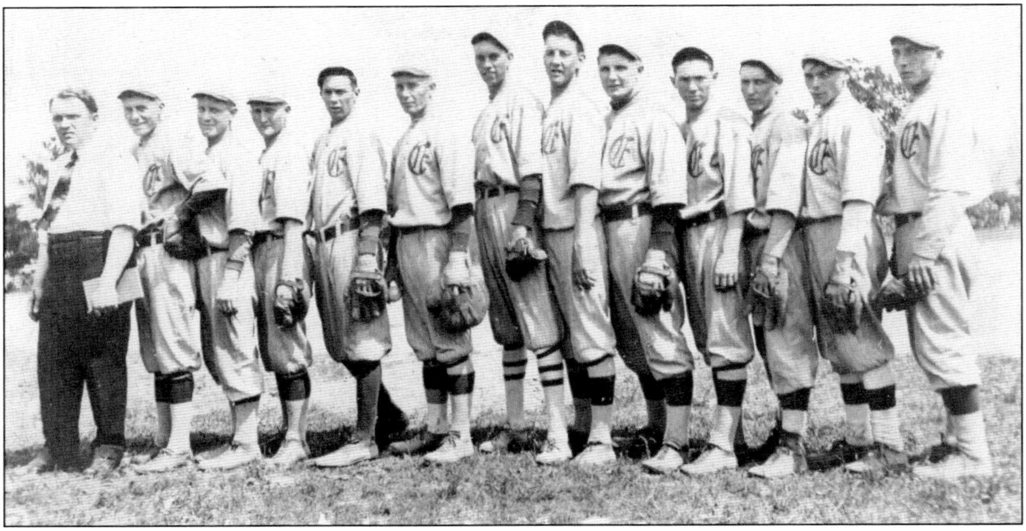

The 1915 Eckhart Mines baseball team included Baseball Club manager Bernard J. Byrnes (far left), Secretary Ray McMillan (fifth from right), and Treasurer Charles Buskey (sixth from right). As in most towns in the area, baseball was very popular in Eckhart Mines. Teams played a variety of opponents. An August 16, 1912 article in the Cumberland newspaper reported, "The Eckhart baseball team will cross bats with a team from Cumberland on Sunday afternoon on the Eckhart grounds. Ty Cobb, who is visiting in Eckhart, will be the umpire. Frank 'Home Run' Baker is also in town."

Seven

Celebration Time

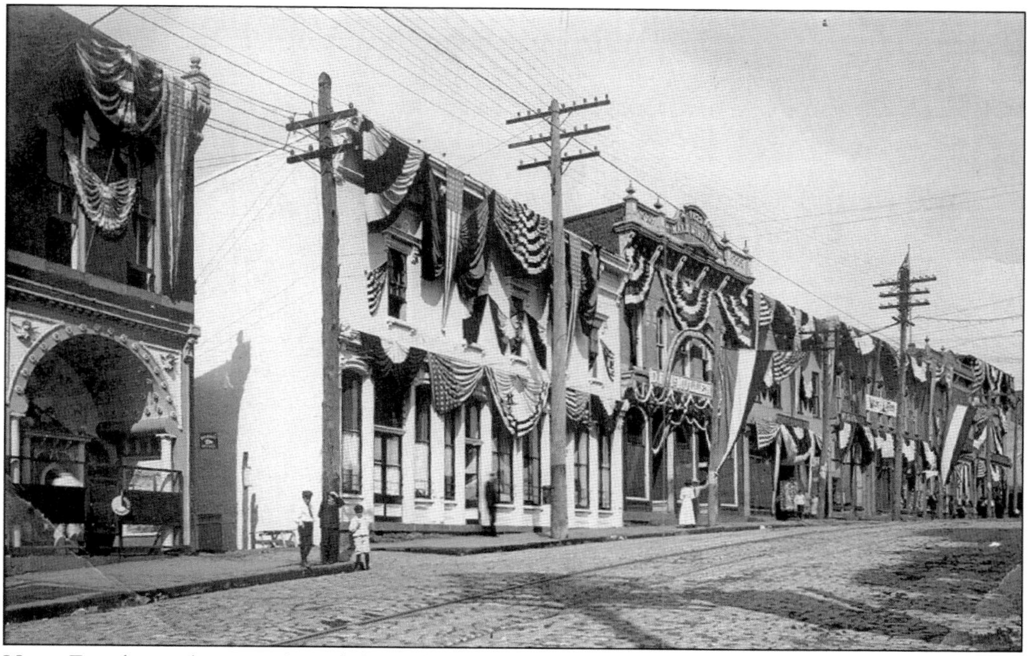

Here Frostburg dons its best bib and tucker for the Fireman's Convention of 1908. The cobblestones of Union Street (later Main Street) and the carnival-like facade of the Dreamland Nickelodeon (soon to become the Palace Theater) are visible.

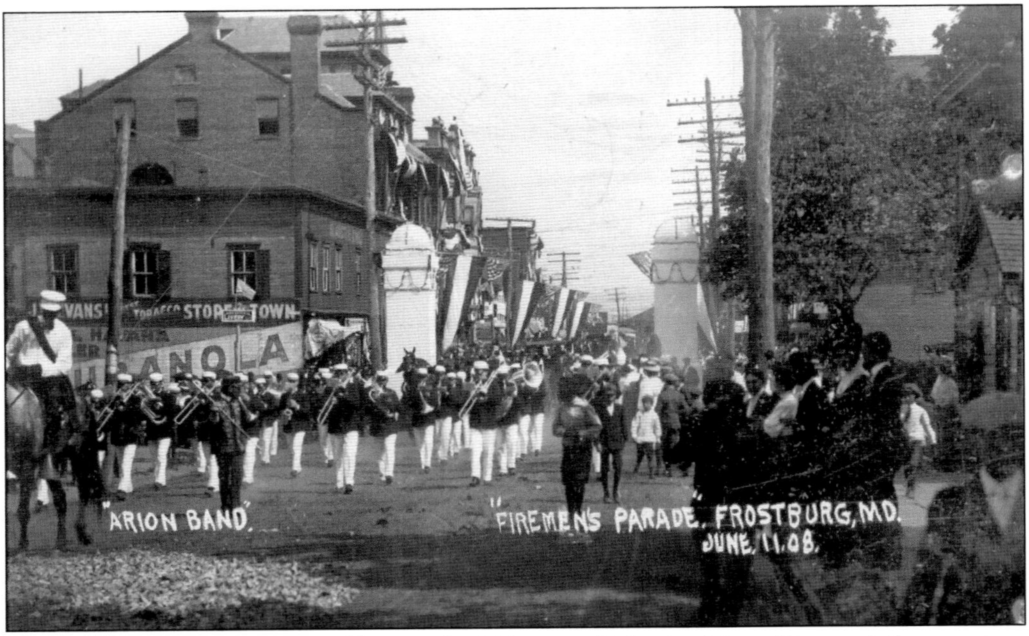

In June of 1908, Frostburg played host to the 16th annual Maryland State Fireman's Convention. Here the Arion band (see page 84) passes Water Street during the parade for the convention that wound up Union (Main) Street.

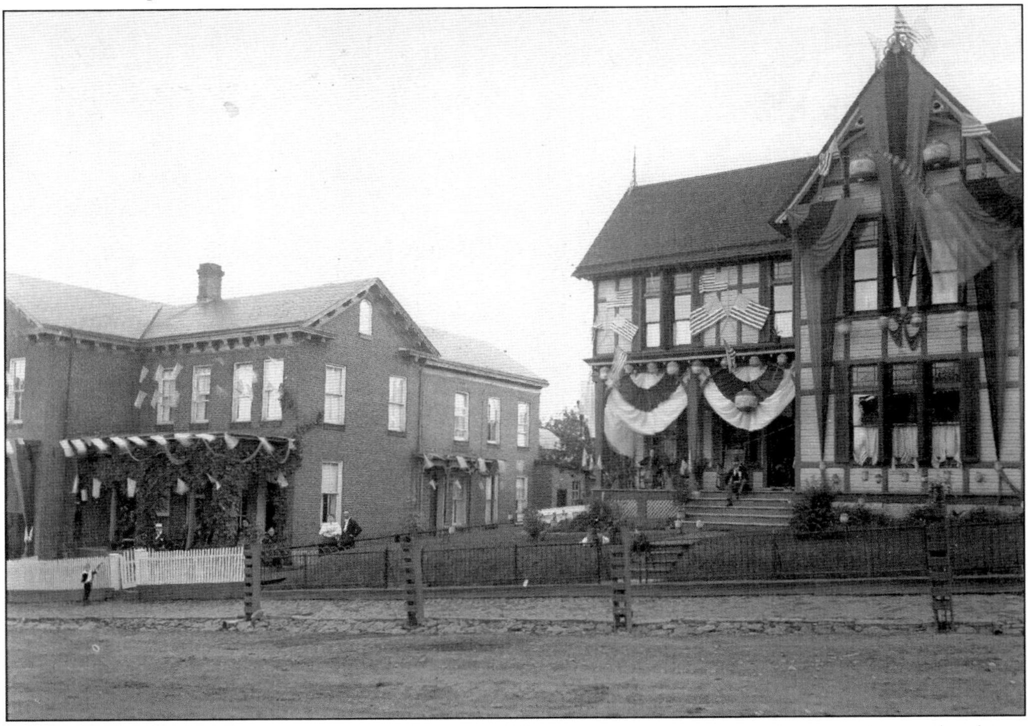

It was reported that just about every house and business in town were decorated in red, white, and blue for the convention. These two west Main Street homes, the Cobey House to the left and the Hitchins house to the right, were the award winners for decorations during the Fireman's Convention of 1908.

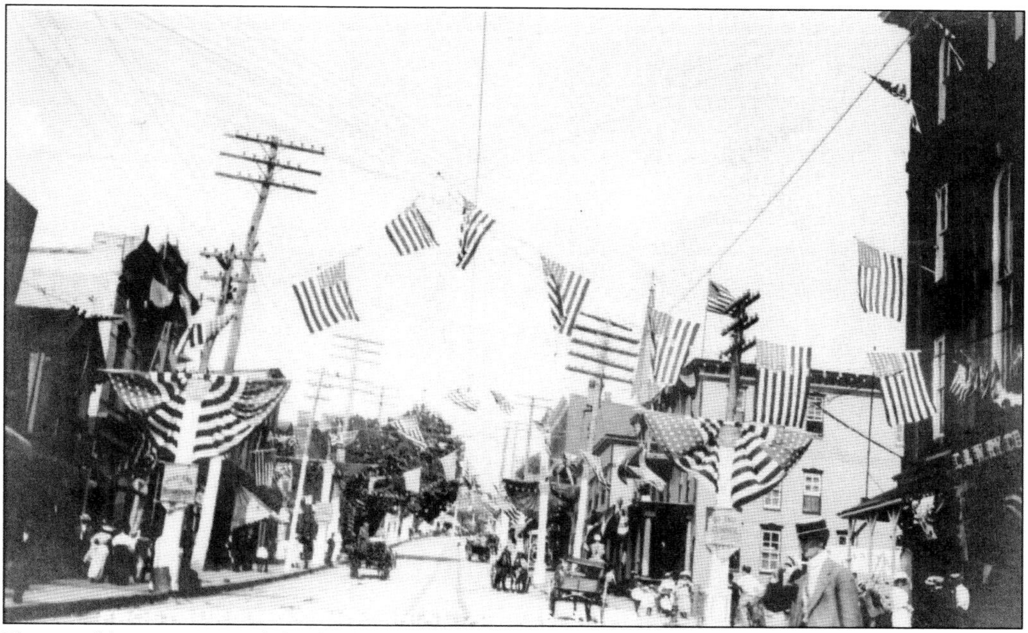

Flags and bunting graced the buildings of Frostburg during the Centennial Celebration of 1912. Here, Main Street is all decked out at the intersection with Depot Road to the right. The building on the immediate right is the opera house, with the St. Cloud Hotel just beyond. The sign on the post at Depot Road reads "To the Tunnel."

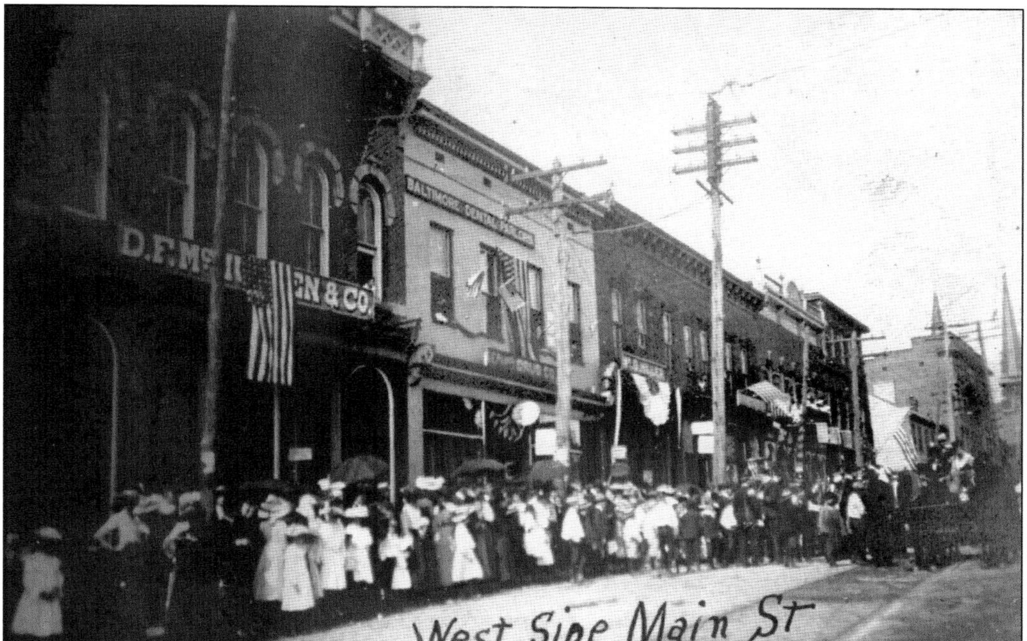

Residents prepare for the Centennial celebrations on Main Street. Held in the summer of 1912 to commemorate the "founding" of Frostburg, the guidebook published for the event admitted that the exact date was not known. It read, "calling this the First Centennial we do so not with the positive assurance that we are absolutely correct as to the exact centennial date, but with the commonly accepted theory and much historical record that it is approximately true."

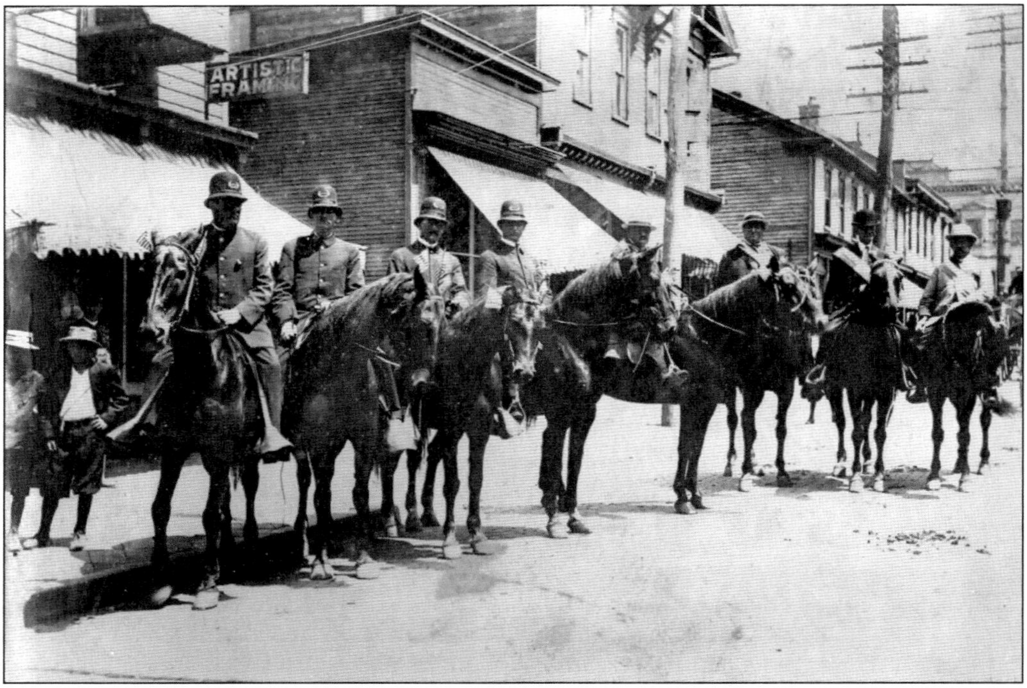

Some of Frostburg's finest gather on Broadway before the Centennial Parade. Originally consisting of just a bailiff (for collecting fines and fees) and a night watchman, local law enforcement grew into the Frostburg Police Department by the early 20th century. It is not certain whether these gentleman performed their daily duties dressed in such uniforms, or if this finery was simply for the Centennial parade.

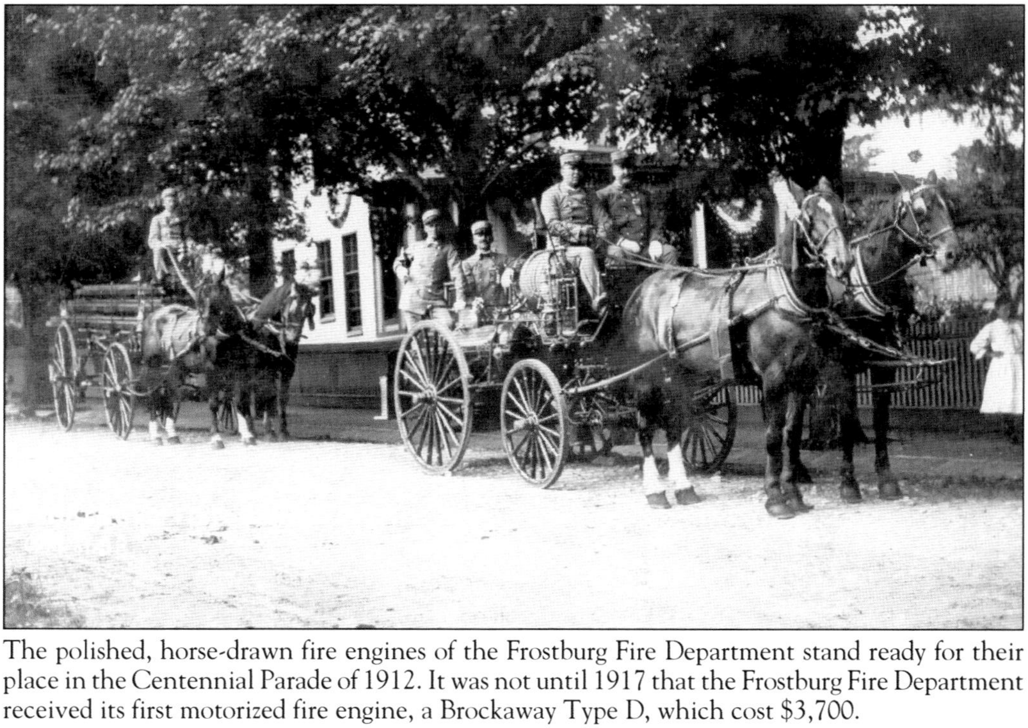

The polished, horse-drawn fire engines of the Frostburg Fire Department stand ready for their place in the Centennial Parade of 1912. It was not until 1917 that the Frostburg Fire Department received its first motorized fire engine, a Brockaway Type D, which cost $3,700.

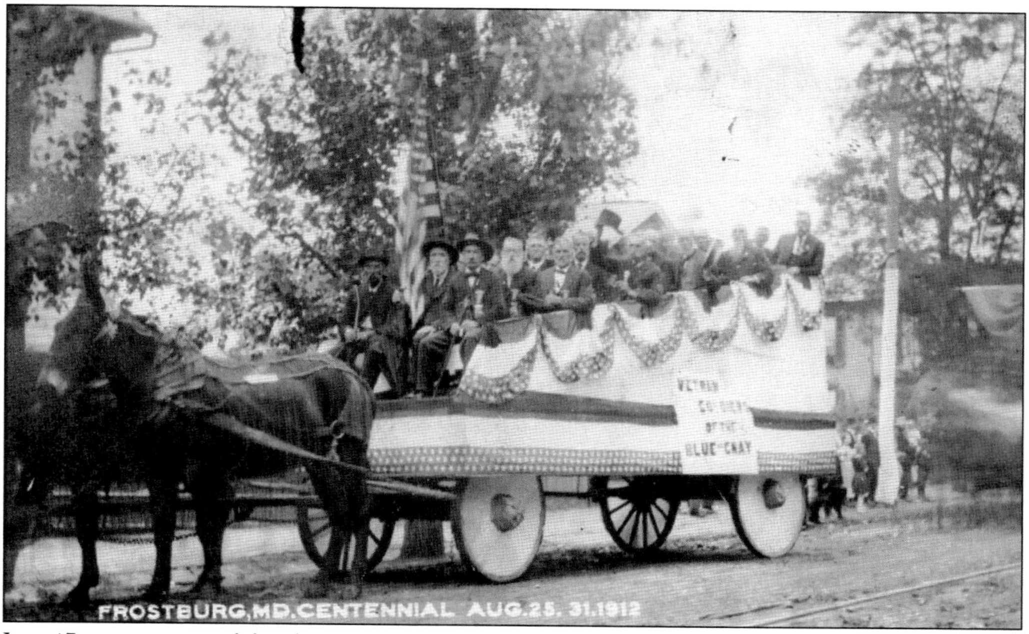

Just 47 years removed for the Civil War, the Centennial Parade included this wagon carrying the Veteran Soldiers of the Blue and the Gray. While Frostburg witnessed no hostilities during the war, groups of soldiers from this area did join forces fighting for both sides in the conflict.

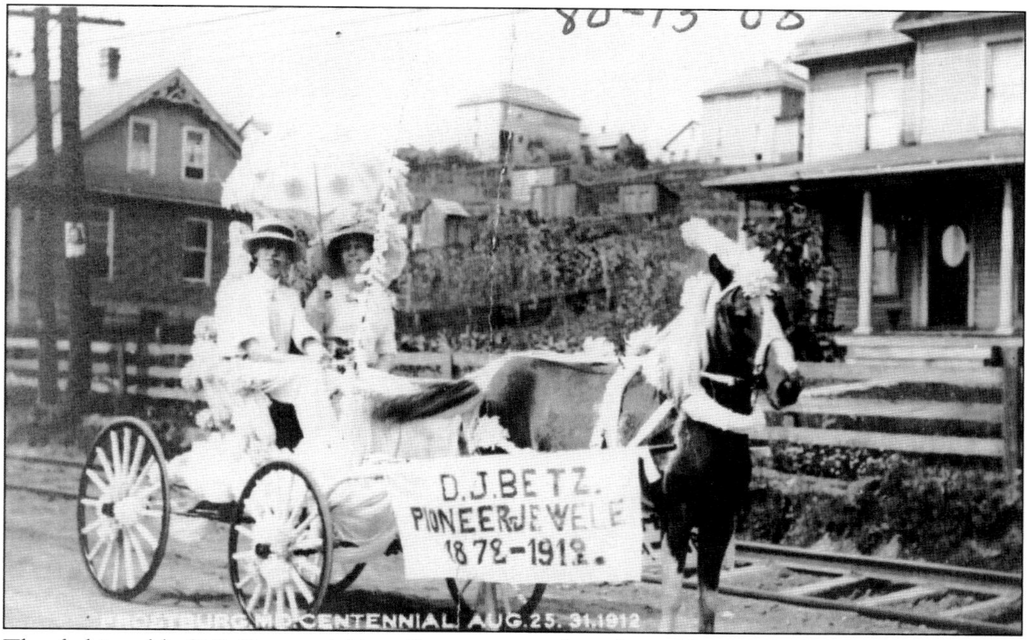

The fashionable D.J. Betz and his wife are pictured on his addition to the parade. The Betz family was involved in the jewelry business trade that was located in the Betz building on Main Street (see page 53).

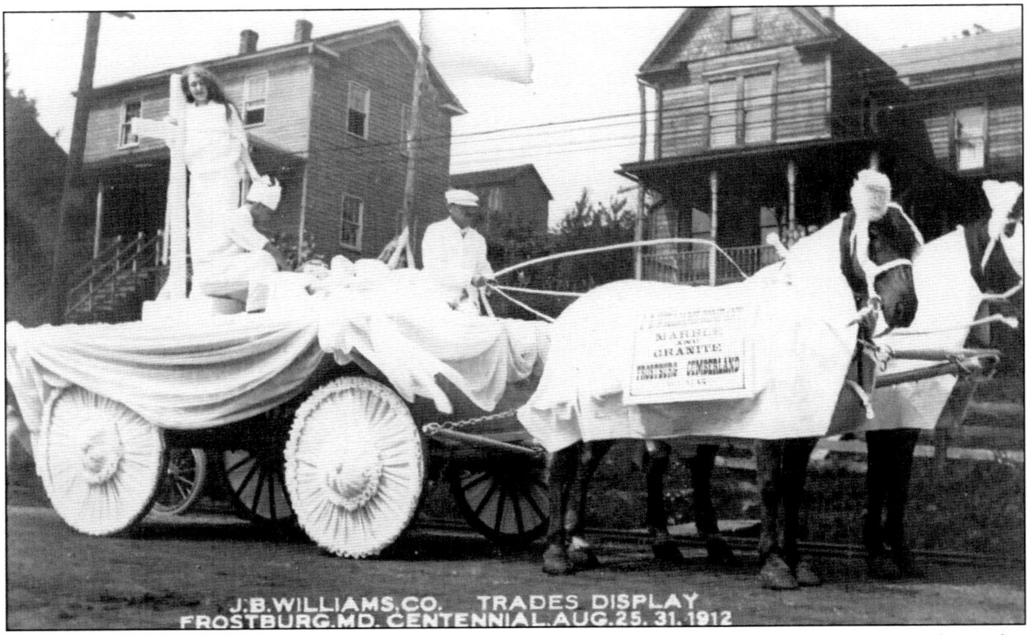

Some of the wagons of the Centennial parade were quite elaborate, such as this entry from the J.B. Williams Company, a masonry firm in town. Using live models, the company advertised their tombstones and other monuments.

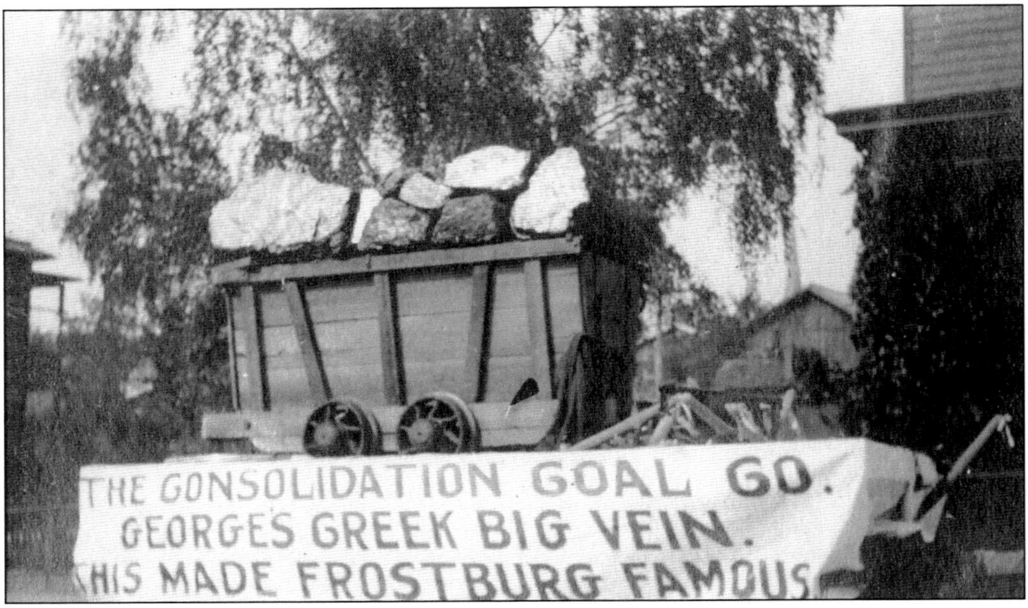

And how could any celebration in the early 20th century be complete without paying homage to the black diamonds that helped the area boom? Here is the Consolidation Coal Company entry to the Centennial Parade showing large chunks of Big Vein coal. This wagon (as seen in the photograph on page 37) was pulled by a large team of 16 mules and horses.

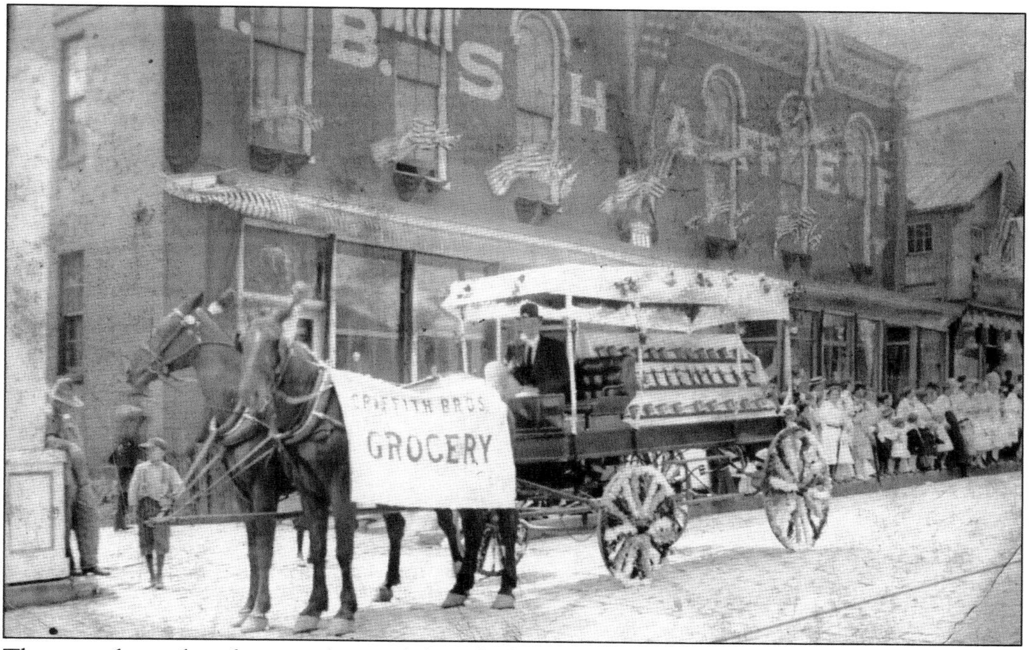

The crowd watches from in front of the Shafer Store near the bottom of the hill on Main Street as a gentleman guides the Griffith Brother Grocery wagon, displaying a variety of wares. The Griffith Brothers, John A. and Richard, ran a grocery at the corner of Water and Union (Main) Streets.

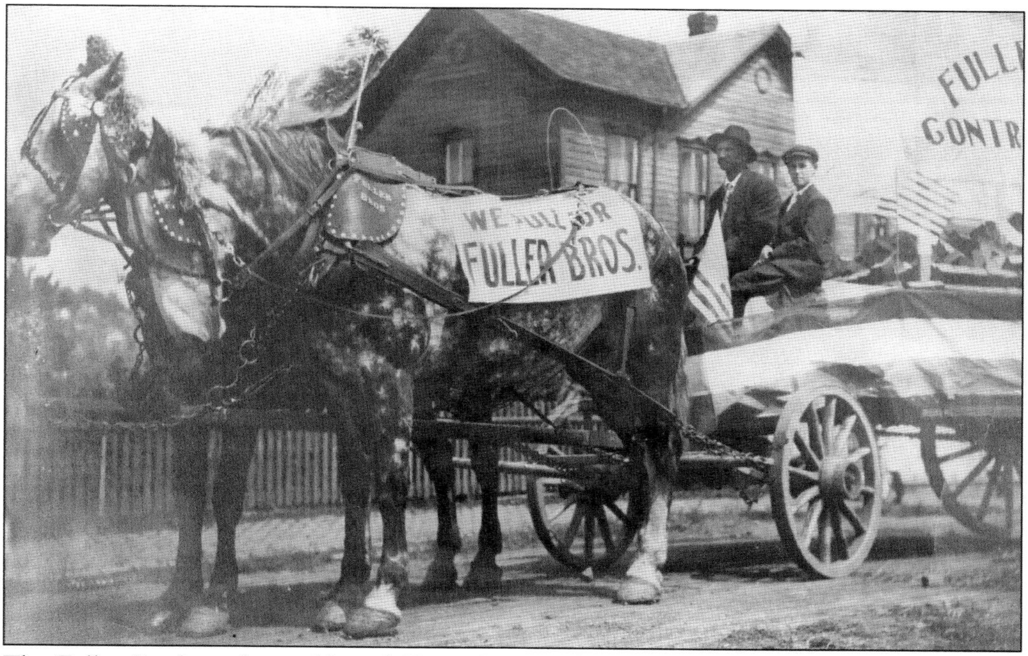

The Fuller Brothers, James H. and Harry S., were brick-laying and masonry contractors in Frostburg, whose work is still recognized today. Many of the town's turn-of-the-century brick buildings were erected by the Fuller Brothers, such as the Gladstone Hotel, Old Main at Frostburg State University, and the post office building. The Fuller Brothers were also involved in paving some of the streets in town with cobblestone. (Courtesy of Thelma Fuller.)

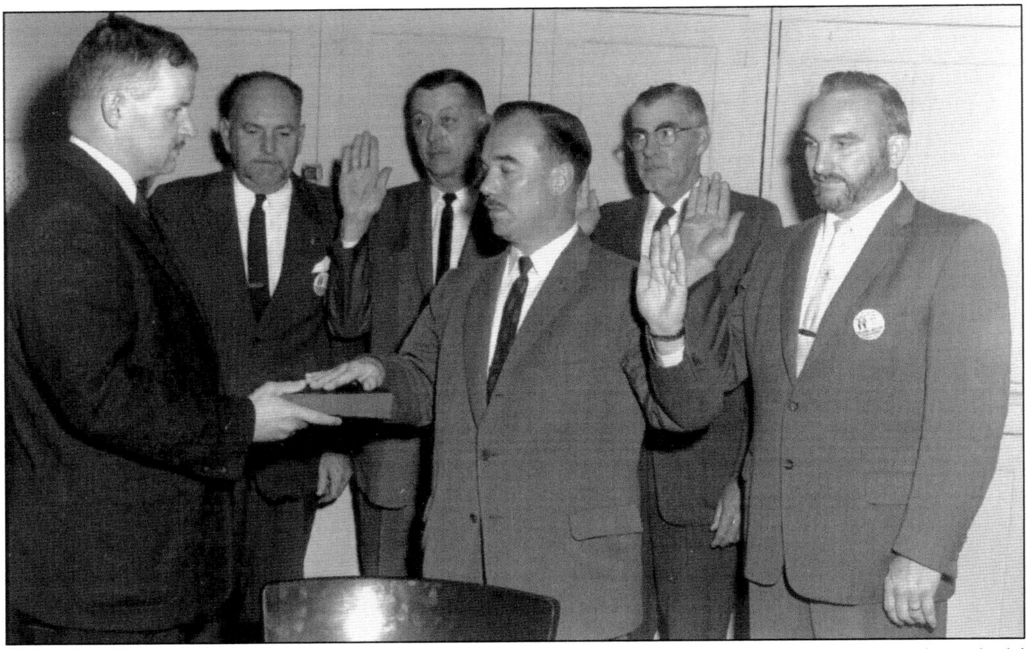

In keeping with the questionable date of 1812 as the founding date of the town, Frostburg held its sesquicentennial celebration in 1962. Here, Mayor Joseph E. James and members of the city council are being sworn into office by Magistrate Edward P. Flanagan. Several commissioners are sporting the whiskers of the "Brothers of the Brush," groups which formed to promote not only growing facial hair, but to celebrate many activities!

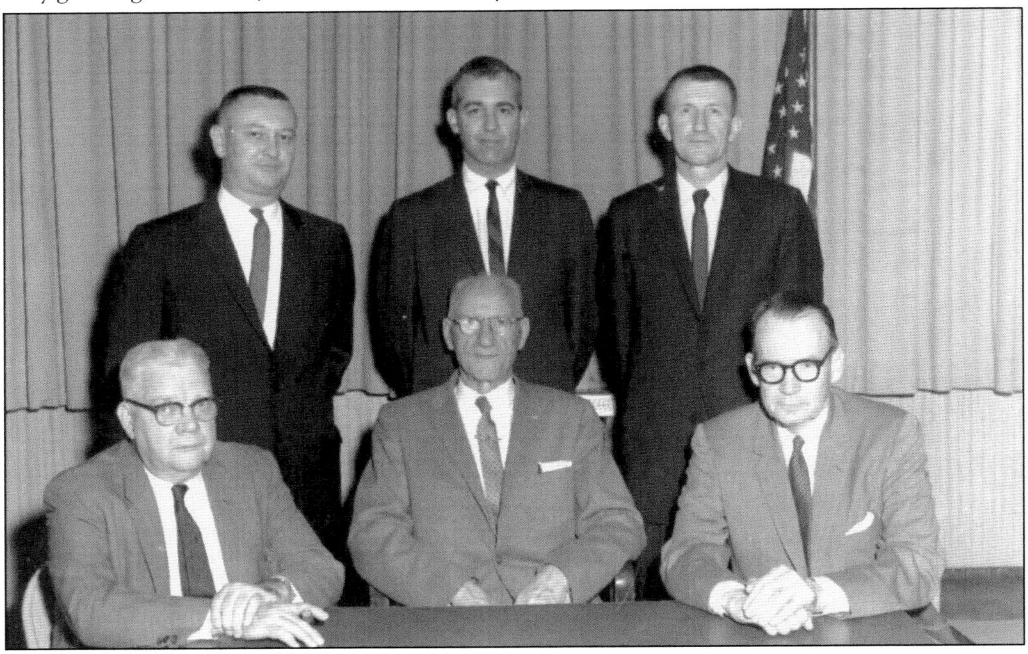

The Directors of the Sesquicentennial Celebration, from left to right, are (seated) Dr. W.O. McLane, William E. Jenkins (president), and W. Earle Cobey; (standing) C. Alvin Kreiling, J. Glenn Beall Jr., and John C. Sullivan. Beall would serve in the United States House of Representatives and the United States Senate, as did his father (see page 102).

Mr. and Mrs. William Jenkins in their sesquicentennial costumes are out for a stroll on Main Street to promote the activities during the Sesquicentennial Celebration. During the event, which lasted from June 29 to July 7, 1962, a variety of activities were available such as pancake breakfasts, fashion shows, games and contests (including the best-dressed dog contest), and "Mountain City Echoes." While short on historical accuracy, "Mountain City Echoes" sought to tell a popular version of the history of the town.

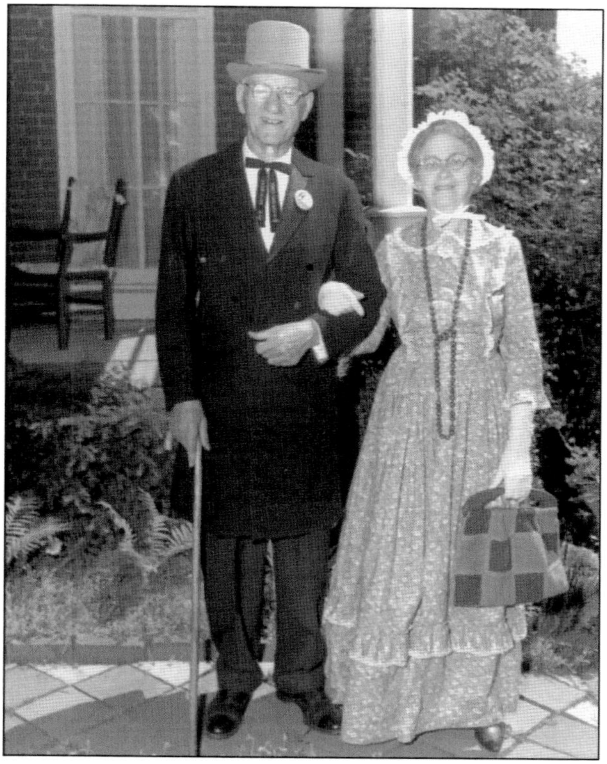

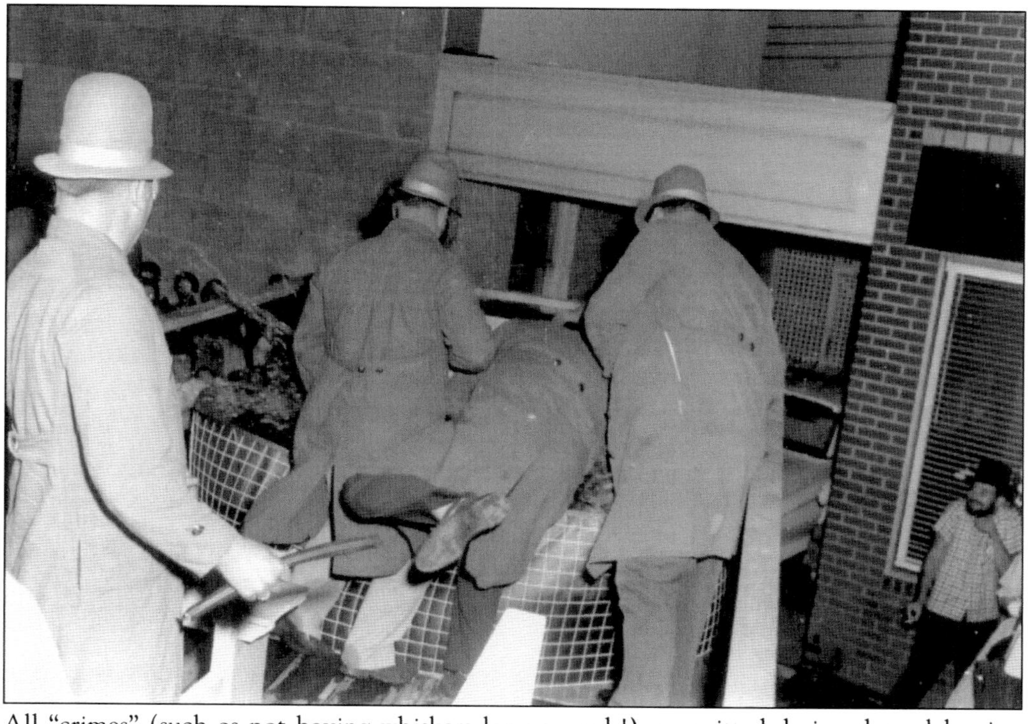

All "crimes" (such as not having whiskers long enough!) committed during the celebration were met with swift justice. A kangaroo court handed out sentences where the punishment could be a plunge in the dunking pool under the auspices of Frostburg's own Keystone Kops.

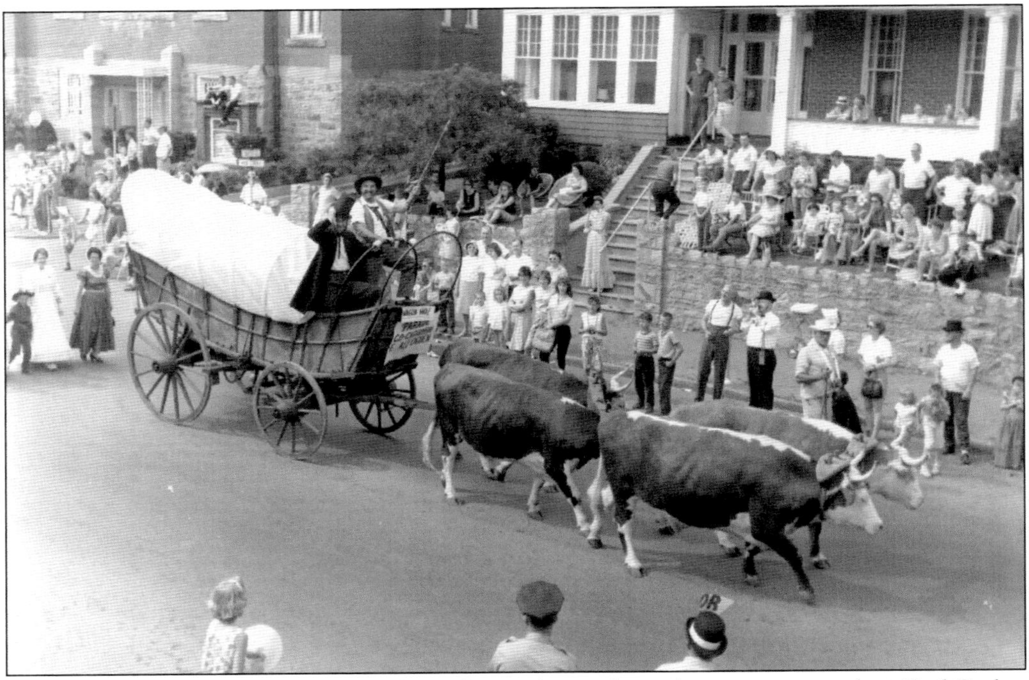

Street commissioner Bill Preston with musket at the ready, and committee co-chair Red Ogden in his Abraham Lincoln stove-pipe hat, are aboard an ox-drawn Conestoga wagon during the sesquicentennial parade held on Saturday, June 30.

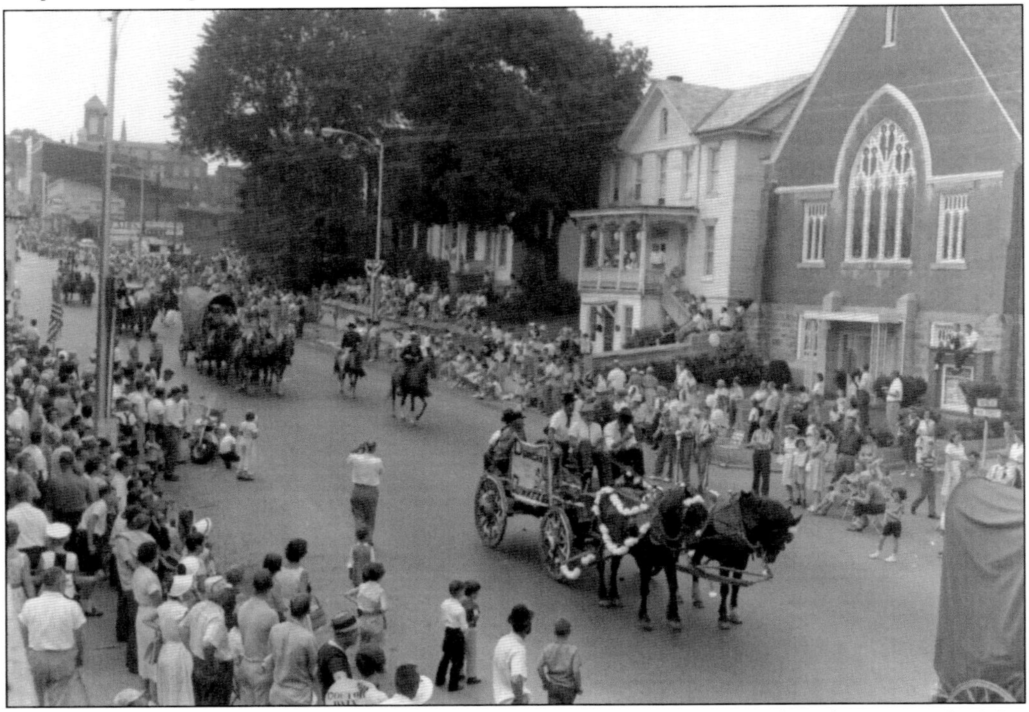

Crowds line Main Street near Bowery Street and the English Baptist Church as several of the horse-drawn wagons, some reminiscent of the centennial celebration, pass during the parade. The parade lasted for two and a half hours, and consisted of ten divisions.

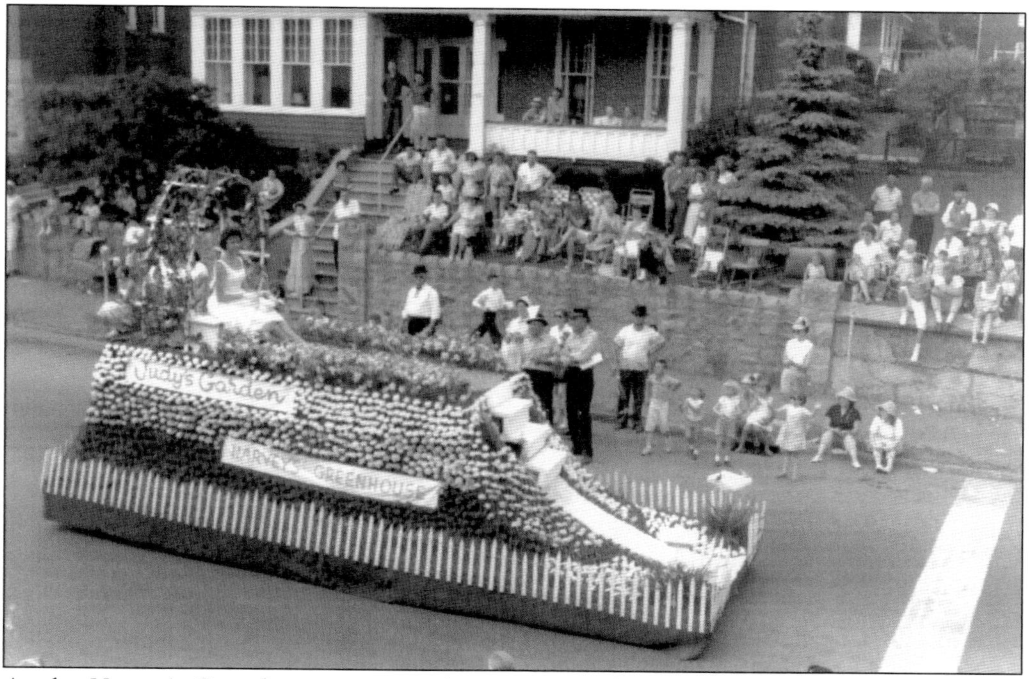

As the Harvey's Greenhouse entry in the sesquicentennial parade passes, children wait for candy and treats. Dozens of bands, fire departments, organizations, and clubs participated in what was reported to be one of the largest parades in the town's history.

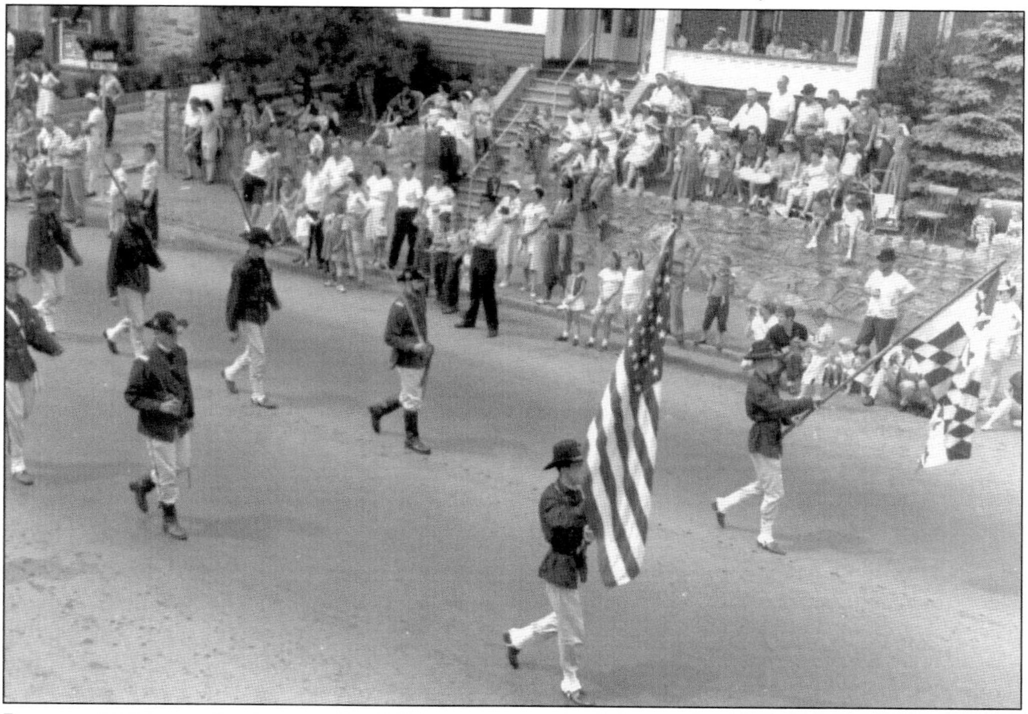

Because 1962 was also host to Civil War centennial celebrations, reenactment groups donned uniforms that resembled Civil War uniform in color only. Here a Union army group marches down Main Street, complete with spats on the color bearers.

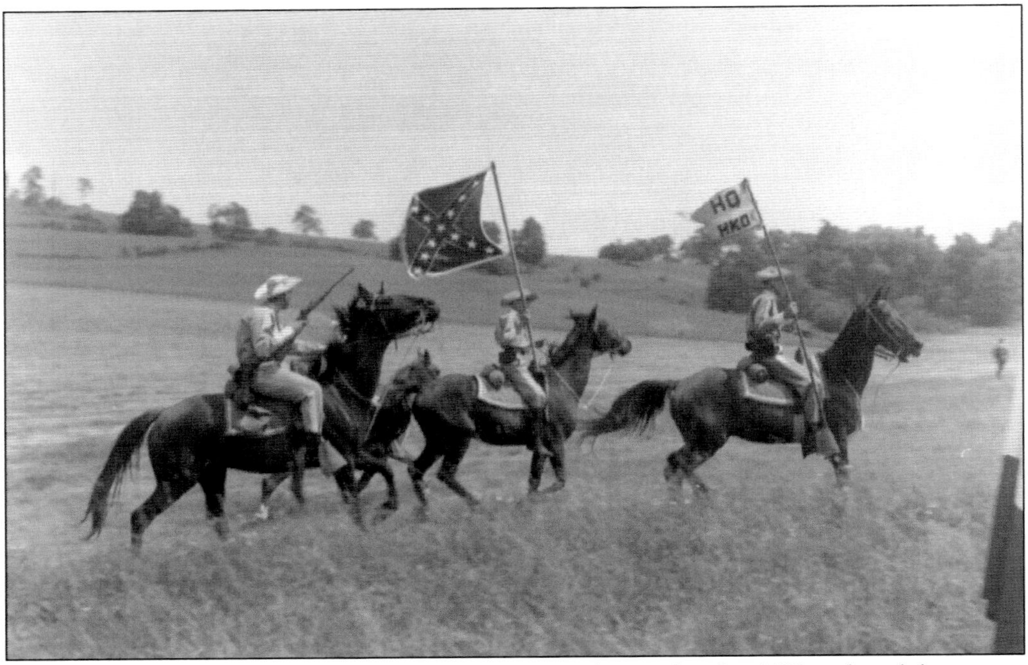

While Frostburg was spared any active participation during the Civil War, that did not stop the Battle of Mt. Pleasant from taking place on Saturday, July 7, during the celebration. Here a troop of rebel cavalry maneuvers for position below Maplehurst Country Club on Layman's Farm. Over 500 re-enactors took part in the mock battle.

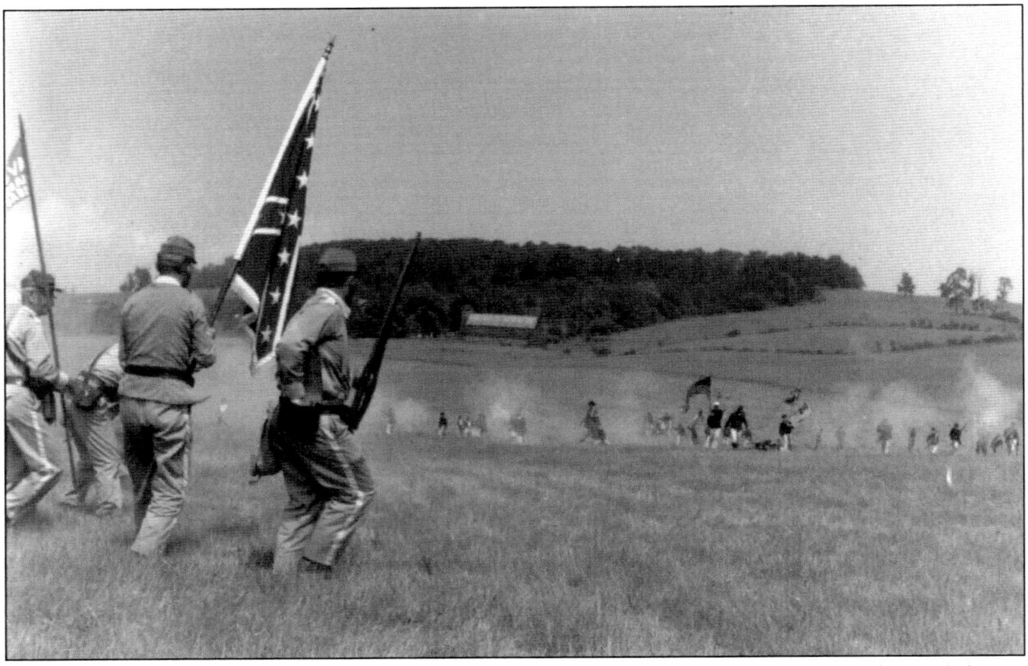

The smoke of gunpowder floats over the field of battle as the mock Union and Confederate troops meet in what was billed as "a typical raid much like the ones made by Confederates on the railroads and the Union troops assigned to this section." The next day newspaper headlines proclaimed, "North Wins Battle of Frostburg."

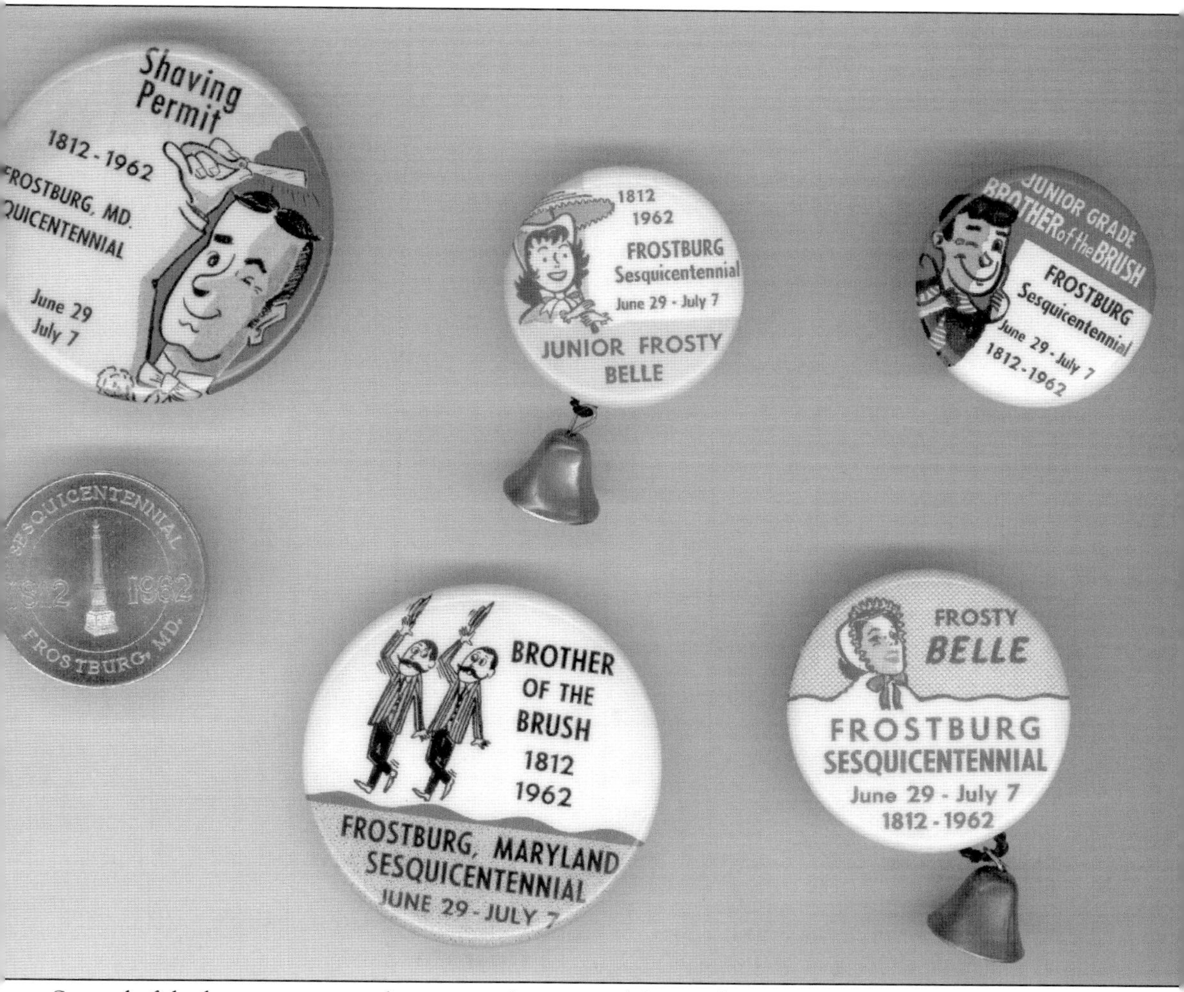

Several of the buttons worn and ceremonial coins used during the Sesquicentennial Celebration of 1962 are shown here. Some of the civic club and organization-sponsored groups included the "Brothers of the Brush" for men and the "Frosty Belles" for women. Young men, or "Lil Shavers," were part of the "Junior Grade," while young women were Junior Frosty Belles. men wishing to remain clean-shaven needed to wear the Shaving Permit button. The coin on the left was worth 50¢ "in trade" during the celebration.

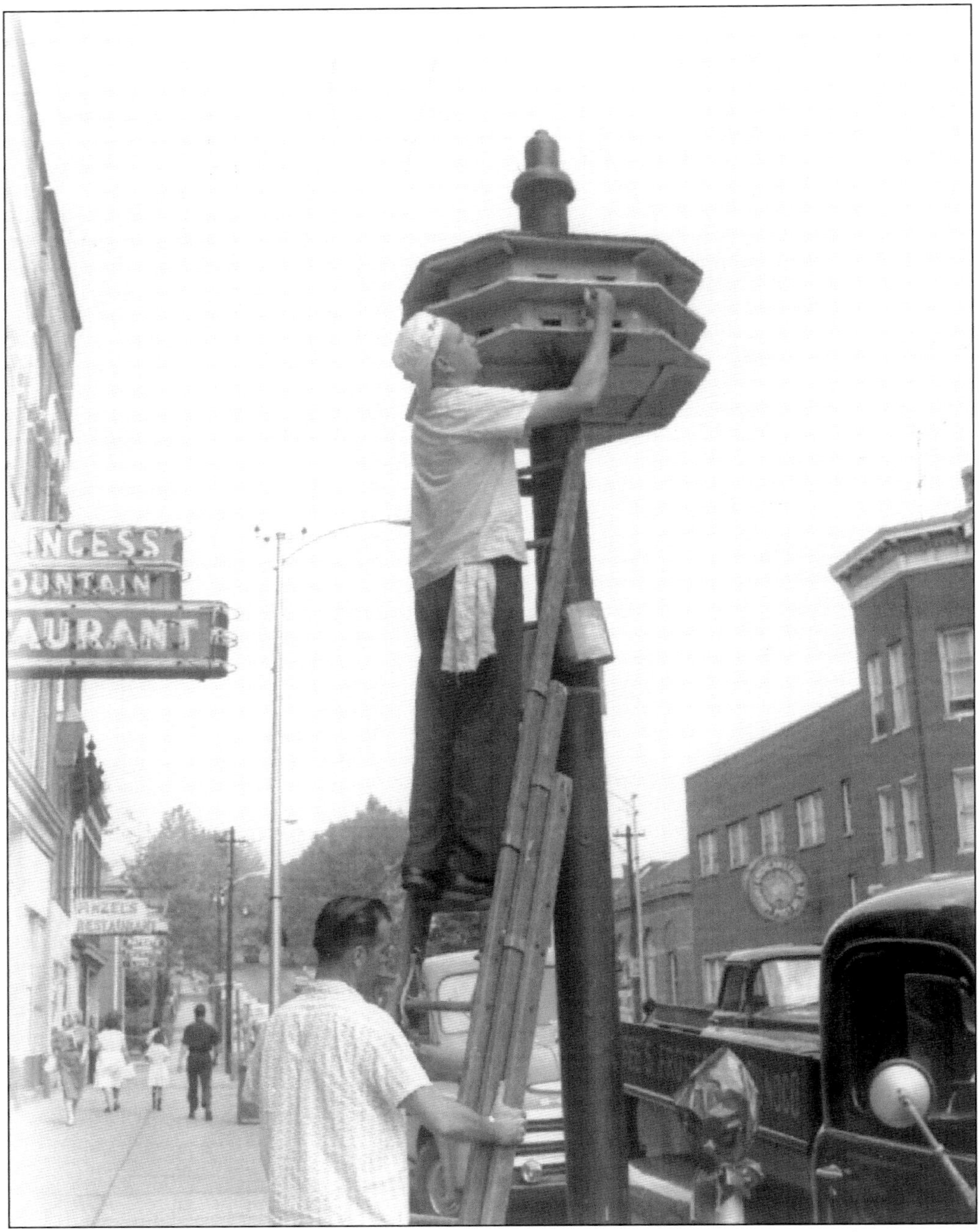

The Purple Martin House, a longtime landmark in front of the bank building at the corner of Broadway and Main Streets, gets fresh coat of paint in the spring of 1962.